Moral Reasoning
for Journalists

Moral Reasoning for Journalists

Cases and Commentary

STEVEN R. KNOWLTON

Westport, Connecticut
London

Library of Congress Cataloging-in-Publication Data

Knowlton, Steven R.
    Moral reasoning for journalists : cases and commentary / Steven R.
Knowlton.
        p.   cm.
    Includes bibliographical references and index.
    ISBN 0–275–94871–4 (alk. paper).—ISBN 0–275–94872–2 (pbk. :
alk. paper)
    1. Journalistic ethics.   I. Title.
PN4756.K687   1997
174′.9097—DC21   96–37734

British Library Cataloguing in Publication Data is available.

Library of Congress Catalog Card Number: 96–37734
ISBN: 0–275–94871–4
        0–275–94872–2 (pbk.)

First published in 1997

Praeger Publishers, 88 Post Road West, Westport, CT 06881
An imprint of Greenwood Publishing Group, Inc.

Printed in the United States of America

The paper used in this book complies with the
Permanent Paper Standard issued by the National
Information Standards Organization (Z39.48–1984).

10 9 8 7 6 5

What is a journalist? Not any business manager or publisher, or even proprietor. A journalist is the lookout on the bridge of the ship of state. He notes the passing sail, the little things of interest that dot the horizon in fine weather. He reports the drifting castaway whom the ship can save. He peers through fog and storm to give warning of dangers ahead. He is not thinking of his wages or of the profits of his owners. He is there to watch over the safety and the welfare of the people who trust him.

—Joseph Pulitzer

Contents

Preface

Anyone whose faith in American journalism is faltering should do what I have done over the last several months—talk to the reporters and editors on the front lines. Although the particulars of their circumstances vary widely, a common thread is found: Journalists are an extraordinarily thoughtful and dedicated lot.

Despite the low starting pay, the lousy hours and the massive abuse heaped upon them by both the self-serving and the justly concerned, journalists remain an inspiring group of people. There is no other industry I can think of where so much time and effort is spent dealing with the ethical dimensions of the product. Factories do not stop at 4:00 P.M. so top management can gather and figure out if the organization should make more widgets the next day, or whether they should be blue or green. Yet the story conference, a staple in newsrooms all over the country, is essentially that—top executives taking 10 or 15 percent of their working day to deal with questions of balance, fairness, decency, and a host of other qualities that go into the notion of news judgment.

The following journalists have graciously contributed to this volume, and I thank them profoundly for their willingness to take time from their busy lives to share their thoughts. Some wrote pieces especially for this volume; others allowed me to reprint pieces prepared for other venues. Bylines in the text reflect these writings. Others were willing to spend time in conversation, often in many conversations, helping me to understand. Normal journalistic attribution, both direct quotes and paraphrases, reflects these interviews. I hope that I have done justice to their positions. Without these working professionals, there would be no book. They are Lisa A. Abraham, reporter, *Warren (Ohio) Tribune-Chronicle*; John Allard, reporter, the *(Columbia, S.C.) State*; Cole C. Campbell, then editor of the *Virginian-Pilot* (now editor of the *St. Louis Post-Dispatch*); Dennis Dillon, assistant professor of English, State University of New York, New Paltz; Sam Donaldson, reporter and anchor, ABC-TV News, Washington, D.C.; Michael R.

Fancher, executive editor, *Seattle Times*; Michael Gartner, editor and co-owner, *(Ames, Iowa) Daily Tribune*; Loren Ghiglione, then editor and publisher, the *(Southbridge, Mass.) News*, now the James M. Cox Jr. Professor of Journalism at Emory University; Marty Gonzalez, reporter, KGO-TV, San Francisco; Mark Hertsgaard, writer, Avery, Calif.; Michael T. Kaufman, former columnist, *New York Times*; Jock Lauterer, associate professor of journalism, Penn State University; Carolyn Lee, assistant managing editor, *New York Times*; Michelle Meyers, then at the *Arlington, (Va.) Journal*, now a reporter in the Northwest; Robert E. Read, then a producer at NBC, now a senior producer, King World Productions; Stephen Klaidman of Washington, D.C., former journalism professor and veteran reporter who is now writing a book on health care in America; Walter V. Robinson, assistant managing editor, *Boston Globe*; Janet Rogers, reporter, WMFJ-TV, Youngstown, Ohio; Michael Schwarz, former senior executive producer, KQED-TV, San Francisco, and now president of Kikim Media, San Carlos, Calif.; Scott Simon, reporter and host, *Weekend Edition*, National Public Radio, Washington, D.C.; Robert E. Sullivan, New York bureau chief, Worldwide Television News; and Amy Zurzola, reporter, *Asbury Park (N.J.) Press*.

There are also many other people who provided kindnesses and information, which were invaluable in the preparation of this book, even though they are not quoted by name in the pages that follow. I thank them, too. Among them are Betsy Hall, departmental secretary, Penn State University; Laurie Harvey, acting director of the Academic Computing Center at Hofstra University; Alex Huppé, director of public information, Harvard University; Ronald Martin, editor, *Atlanta Journal-Constitution*; Dave Modrowski, Assistant Managing Editor, Worldwide Television News, London; Elaine Patterson, departmental secretary at Hofstra University; Professor Jacqueline Sharkey, University of Arizona; Michael J. Stanton, executive news editor, *Seattle Times*.

Thanks also go to Nina Pearlstein, my editor at Praeger, for patience and guidance in the preparation of the manuscript for this book. It was too long in coming (and simply too long, as well) but she bore up well, and both the book and my state of mind are better for her help.

But the most profound and most humble note of thanks must go to my longtime editor and best friend (and, not incidentally, wife), Karen Freeman, as skilled, as talented, and as dedicated a journalist as I have ever known. In a hundred ways, this book is as much hers as it is mine. As anyone familiar with the news business knows, the reporter gets the byline, while the editor does half the work. That's about how it worked out in this case as well, and the book is much stronger, better organized and more useful to both students and instructors for it. More personally, when I falter, which is often, or when my zeal and dedication to the noblest principles of our calling waver, invariably it is she who reminds me, by example as well as by word, that the goals are worth pursuing.

A Note to Instructors

There are several things about this book that make it unlike other casebooks now available for undergraduate and graduate students in journalism.

First, the cases in this book are real—not hypothetical, not composites, and not made up out of whole cloth. In some ways, hypotheticals are easier both to write and to teach from. For instructors, hypotheticals are convenient because they can be constructed to illustrate exactly the points desired without the inevitable clutter that accompanies real life. However, it seems to me that the use of hypotheticals poses a real danger as we try to insist to our students that they be scrupulously accurate. Although I came of age in the 1960s and entered the profession during the heyday of Jimmy Breslin, Tom Wolfe and Hunter Thompson, I have never bought into the idea of a New Journalism that emphasizes revealed Truth sometimes at the expense of accuracy. That sort of practice leads quite directly, and I believe inevitably, to a Janet Cooke, the *Washington Post* writer whose heart-rending story of "Jimmy's World," about the child junkie, had the fatal flaw of being fiction. Thus, I have avoided made-up stories and concentrated on actual events from contemporary journalism.

Second, while it may be used by itself, this book is designed and written to be used in conjunction with *The Journalist's Moral Compass* (Praeger, 1994), an anthology of seminal writings that have an important bearing on the moral dimensions of journalism. I do not claim that a working journalist, writing on deadline, will consult Plato or John Stuart Mill before deciding whether to pipe a quote. But I do maintain that the principles contained in *Moral Compass* are part of the intellectual fabric of the journalistic profession. I am also convinced, from my own thirty years of experience in the news business and from interviews and conversations with literally hundreds of working journalists over three decades, that journalism is a deeply moral profession. There are charlatans and knaves at work in the business, of course, and there are hustlers and cons and folks on the take. There are errors of venality and, far more common, errors of sloth and too much hurry. For all that, however, the great majority of journalists working at newspapers and radio and television stations around the country are highly principled, deeply committed women and men who take the moral imperatives of their work extremely seriously.

While press bashing may be at an all-time high, I am convinced that the profession operates on a nobler plane than it ever has. We have more critics, and many of them have contributed greatly to the improvement of contemporary journalism. But we also have more thoughtful, better trained, more knowledgeable, and more skilled journalists than at any time since the founding of the republic. The documents in *Moral Compass* build the intellectual case for journalism as it should be practiced; the cases in this book provide real-life examples of the inevitable collisions between and among those principles.

Third, while there is not, and cannot be, an instructor's edition of a book such as this with the answers in it, there are questions at the end of each case. These may be used as topics for in-class discussion or for out-of-class written assignments. Anyone—student, professor, or professional—who can take a reasonable stab at all of them will have a serious understanding of what is important in journalism.

For the most part, I have kept my own feelings and beliefs out of this book as much as possible, but doubtless my own take on various issues comes through from time to time. I am unapologetic about that. I care passionately about good journalism and, from a decade of classroom teaching, have become convinced that a fair measure of that passion can be conveyed successfully to students. On the other hand, so can indifference and tolerance of mushy thought and a corner-cutting mentality. Journalism is no place for trimmers.

Finally, this is a book about journalism ethics, not about the ethics of mass media or of all mediated communication. Journalism does reach a mass audience and it is a mediated form of communication, but it is not the same thing as advertising or television serials or feature films. It shares some technical elements with those and other forms of mass communication, but journalism has its own history, its own philosophy, and its own problems to solve.

Part I
Locating Ethical Journalism in the Western Tradition

1
Introduction to Ethical Thinking

Journalism as an American institution has taken quite a beating in public discourse in recent years. In the generation since the go-go years of Watergate, journalists' credibility has fallen precipitously in the minds of the reading and viewing public, showing up in recent polls in the neighborhood of that of used car dealers in the public's estimation.

Media bashing has become almost an industry, with new books every year and new talk-show discussions seemingly every week devoted to decrying the sorry state of the American news business: It's biased; it's shallow. It's boring; it panders. Politicians have always beaten up on the press—and for good reason, given their adversarial relationship. But in recent years, they have been joined in the assault by full- and part-time media critics. Some of these critics are in the legion of academics who make their careers in the university theorizing about why the press is so dreadful. Others are working professionals who sometimes agree with the academics: The press (in its generic sense, including newspaper, magazine and broadcast journalism) is a mess.

Leaving aside the complaints from the targets of vigorous press inquiry, who would naturally prefer to shoot the messenger than discuss the message, the most thoughtful press critics usually cite these reasons for the sorry state of the American news business:

Money. Especially in television, truly staggering sums of money are involved. And now that the old big-three broadcast networks—ABC, CBS, and NBC—no longer dominate television as they once did, competition is keener and the pressures to cut ethical corners are much stronger. Some press watchers argue that the corruption is far more widespread, and that the passion for profits at all costs extends far beyond network television and into newspapers and magazines, both large and small, as well.

Spinmeisters. The image builders for politicians have come of age and are extremely good at what they do: making their employers look good. The result is image over substance, and the American public is by now largely at the mercy of clever public relations experts.

Tabloids, especially those on television. Scurrilous methods and sleaze have been a part of journalism for centuries, but in recent years, the *Daily Mirror* has been replaced by *Hard Copy*, giving the sensational and the tawdry far more visibility and clout than in the bygone days of print domination. More broadly, many critics have seen a blurring of the real and important distinction between news and entertainment, leading to hybrids such as *docudramas* and *infotainment*.

Political bias. Critics within the academy most often assail the press as being hopelessly conservative—as being the tool, witting or not, of the capitalist ruling class. Reporters are rarely called "running-dog imperialists" as they were twenty years ago, but the rest of the litany of the left is intact. Criticism comes from the other side as well. The critics on the talk shows are often political conservatives who see the media are liberals of the deepest dye, forever covering up the sins of their political fellow travelers while maliciously attacking their right-thinking opponents on the right end of the political spectrum.

Perhaps there is a common thread running through these and other complaints about the state of today's journalism. Critics are saying that it has lost its way, that it no longer provides honest information in a form that readers and viewers can use. In the race for numbers—circulation, audience, advertising dollars—perhaps journalism has too often skipped the nutritious main courses of political, economic, and social information and gone straight to the dessert of entertainment, which is tasty in the short run, but, in the end, neither satisfying nor sustaining.

These are important concerns, and there are others, most with some measure of truth to them—although none as universally true as their proponents seem to believe. Although the criticisms vary widely, underlying them all is a presumption, spoken or unspoken, of *should*. The criticisms are that, because of corruption or bias or sloth, journalists are not living up to their moral obligations to report and write certain things and in certain ways. Professional critics and lay readers respond with great vehemence to perceived shortcomings in the press because they see the lapses not just as mistakes but as moral failings. But in the cacophony of press abuse (and, too often, self-righteous self-defense from the papers and stations) little constructive action is taken. Notions and accusations become certainties and convictions as informed debate on legitimate subjects of concern degenerates into mere shouting matches. Thought becomes noise.

Journalists and journalists-to-be need to be able to respond to the criticism and to join in thoughtful discussion concerning what newspeople do and why, and what they *should* do and why. American journalists enjoy astonishing constitutional protections and wield awesome amounts of power. The abuse of that power can have disastrous consequences for our government, our society and its major institutions, including the press itself.

First, we will look at ethics itself, then at the historical roots of the American concepts of the responsibilities of a free press. Finally, we will consider case studies involving questions of applied ethics, looking at what real journalists have done and *should* do with real information and real sources. The intention is not to provide clear-cut answers to vexing questions in contemporary journalistic practice (although the cosmos is not without its spots of firmament), but to provide enough background and context to enable those interested in the problems to take a reasonable stab at solving them. But before looking at the *should* of journalism, we need to look at the broader question: Is there a *should* at all? Do the very notions of right and wrong have any real meaning outside the walls of religious institutions? What follows is an introduction to the branch of philosophy called ethics, or moral reasoning.

A BRIEF HISTORY OF ETHICAL THINKING

To deal with first things first: What is ethics? According to the Greeks, who provided the foundation for most philosophical thought in the West, ethics was one of the fundamental branches of philosophy. Aesthetics was the study of beauty, epistemology was the study of knowledge, and ethics was the study of the good. The intention in all three areas was to get past the purely emotional, the subjective, and the intuitive, and to arrive at a reasoned understanding, a thoughtful analysis. The aim was to avoid making statements that began "I just think . . ." or "It seems to me . . ." moving toward statements such as "I conclude that . . ." or "The weight of the evidence indicates . . . ."

You should note that while the Greeks and their dedication to reason have had and continue to have a great influence on Western thought, their rationalism has by no means been universally accepted or gone unchallenged. The Romantics of the early nineteenth century, for example, were generally antirationalist and explicitly rejected the power of reason in favor of presumptions about "natural" folk wisdom, intuition, and so on. Much that falls under the broad New Age umbrella is a latter-day incarnation of this Romantic movement.

Ethics asks such questions as What is good? Is it the same for each of us? Is good synonymous with pleasure, as the hedonists believed, or, perhaps, with excellence, as Aristotle argued? Is it immutable, or does it change from time to time, from place to place, and from person to person? In a world that is leery of declaring that value *a* is better than value *b*, ethicists try to find a firm footing of right and wrong—not necessarily eternal verities in a religious sense, but principles grounded in *something* beyond expediency and impulse.

At this point, it is important to make the distinction between ethics and prudence. To be prudent means to be careful or circumspect, not rash or foolhardy. Both ethics and prudence suggest rational, thoughtful behavior, and a great many choices we make are both. But the terms are not synonymous because prudence does not require a moral ranking of the available alternatives as ethics clearly does.

There is nothing wrong with being prudent—nothing necessarily immoral or unethical. Most of us make a great many decisions every day on the basis of prudence, but it should not be confused with morality. Consider the question of whether to obey a speed limit, for example. Most motorists drive within a few miles per hour of the posted limit. If you ask why, the most common answer would be: To avoid getting a speeding ticket. That is a good reason; that is, it is a considered and careful one. But it is not an ethical reason.

The ethical argument for obeying a speed limit would be quite different and could go something like this: Statistics show that driving faster than the posted speed limit increases the chance of an accident and increases the chance that an accident would result in serious injury or even death for myself or someone else. I have adopted as an ethical principle that I should cause no harm to myself or to other human beings without due cause. Speeding, or even the good of getting to my destination a few minutes sooner, is not sufficient reason to risk causing harm or death, so I will obey the speed limit.

But what if you note that it is a clear day, that your car is in excellent mechanical condition and that you are alert and attentive? Should you still be bound by a speed limit that was designed for average or even poor drivers, for all vehicles under all highway and weather conditions? Or you may even recall that some speed limits used to be higher, that they were lowered mostly to save fuel during the 1970s' oil shortage and that they were not raised again in some areas when the shortage was over because of political reasons. In short, you might decide that the law setting speed limits is a bad law. Are you not free, on ethical grounds at least, to violate a bad law? Perhaps. Many noble figures, including Mohandas Gandhi and the Reverend Dr. Martin Luther King Jr., to name but two, have deliberately broken bad laws when the grounds were good enough.

But there is a case to be made for obeying bad laws, even unjust laws. It could go like this: Our society, with its remarkable amount of personal freedom, exists primarily because the great preponderance of its citizens obey the great bulk of its laws voluntarily, not because the authorities compel them to. If people stopped obeying the laws, the result would be anarchy or a level of police-state compulsion that American citizens would find intolerable. Thus, for American citizens, in order to preserve the kind of society most of them; prefer to live in, are obliged to obey its laws, even if they encounter from time to time a law they find inconvenient or even injust.

That argument may seem far-fetched, but it is a variation on one of the most famous arguments for obeying even bad laws that has ever been made: Socrates' argument for not escaping from prison when he had the chance. According to Plato's account in "The Crito," part of *The Republic*, Socrates, who had been unjustly imprisoned and was facing execution, argued that the state was more important than any of its individual citizens and that obeying its laws was essential, even if the law was being unjustly applied, as it was in his case. Thus, to escape would contribute to general lawlessness and a destruction of the social order. Almost nobody today, it would seem, has the reverence either for the state or for the law that Socrates had, but the point is still valid: Widespread breaking of laws would almost certainly lead to social chaos and a society in which we would not care to live. There may well be grounds for breaking a law, but to do so requires a clearly stated appeal to principles that, in a given instance, seem to outweigh the dangers of promoting lawlessness.

To the Greeks, as in the example of Socrates above, the key was in the *telos,* the outcome. For any ethical question, the way to determine the best choice from those available was to consider what would happen, or was most likely to happen, in each case, then take the choice that would produce the most good. In *The Responsible Self,* a modern examination of this ancient problem, the philosopher H. Richard Niebuhr describes one model of the moral being as "man-the-maker." This figure is goal directed and strives toward an end, much as a cobbler makes boots and a carpenter builds houses. Cutting leather and pounding nails are neither good nor bad, nor even important, in and of themselves; the value those activities have is in their outcomes. Niebuhr notes that "Aristotle begins his *Ethics*—the most influential book in the West in this field—with the statement: 'Every art and every inquiry and similarly every action and pursuit, is thought to aim at some good.'" Throughout the classical Hellenic period, this outcome-based moral philosophy, called *teleology*, was dominant.

But with the emergence of the Roman Catholic Church as a powerful institution in the early Middle Ages, a new way of determining right and wrong came to hold sway. The church, the institution most involved in moral questions, determined morality through a series of rules, the "thou shalts" and the "thou shalt nots" of religious orthodoxy. This rule-based ethical theory is called *deontology*, although deontology does not necessarily have to be based on religious rules.

The deontologists argue that behavior has moral weight in and of itself. Certain things are right and other things, usually the negatives of the right things, are wrong. For example: Killing is wrong, stealing is wrong, and kindness and compassion are good. For a millennium and more, religious deontologists in the West were virtually unchallenged in the ethics business. The church provided both the rules and the keys to their interpretation and understanding. This model is what Niebuhr calls "man-the-citizen," as opposed to his teleological notion of "man-the-maker." The citizen metaphor suggests that the world in which we live has laws that we are bound to obey. We might like to think of ourselves as wholly free agents to build whatever world we might like—to obey whatever principles we like—but, in truth, we are not.

With the Reformation and the Renaissance, people's minds began to turn from the hereafter to the here and now. One of the bedrock principles of the Reformation was a belief in the power and worth of the human mind, which was a monumental change in the way people saw their world and saw themselves in it. The human mind, people increasingly came to believe, could actually figure things out. It was, Renaissance thinkers argued, capable of rational thought. From the sixteenth century on, more analytical ways of thinking, with their origins in classical antiquity, increasingly challenged the spiritualism and mysticism of the church.

It is not at all coincidental that one of the most profoundly important advancements of the Renaissance was the development of the printing press and, with it, moveable type. All across Europe, the explosion in the availability of printed materials following Gutenberg's developments in the mid-1400s fundamentally challenged the *ancien régime* and its heretofore unrivaled power. By making the printed word available on a scale unimaginable in the era of hand copying, the printing press showed people firsthand that their own minds were, indeed, capable of reason and rational thought. Teach people how to read and put books in their hands and, voilà! You have a whole new level of rational discourse. What people believed came to be vastly more important than mere physical prowess.

That return to rationalism reached its zenith during the Enlightenment of the mid- and late eighteenth century, an era in which the rational mind was thought to be capable of solving all problems, working out all mysteries. To some, the human mind came to replace the omnipotence and mystery of an older god. To others, the realization of the astounding power of reason was proof anew of God's presence. But however people saw God's role in this new scheme of things, the historical record is clear that many of the most advanced minds of the West were increasingly convinced that humankind could eventually approach perfection through the exercise of the human intellect. There was less and less room in this world for intellectual confidence in rules-as-rules, for people blindly and willingly accepting the dictates of their ancestors or their landlords or their bishops and devoting their best energies to trying to live by others' rules. Not that these rationalists discarded ethics. On the contrary, the can-do attitude led to the assumption that the intellect could fix moral problems and solve injustice just as effectively as it could turn steam power into textile factories and, a little later, iron ore into railroads.

In the field of ethics, such confidence, fueled in part by an emerging faith in science, prompted a return to the Greek notion of teleology, which many took as a challenge to the church's rules. What is morally right and wrong, this thinking went, is not blind obedience to a set of rules; instead, it is based on rational predictions of the consequences of certain acts. The greatest champions of this new way of thinking were Jeremy Bentham and his godson, John Stuart Mill. The name they used for this new outcome-based ethical system was *utilitarianism*.

The name *utilitarianism* is somewhat unfortunate for the term seems to contain, at least to modern ears, a sense of mere practicality or usefulness, like consumer ratings on a brand of toaster or the recommendation to inflate one's automobile tires to 32 psi. True, Bentham and Mill were very much intellectuals of this world and were concerned with the real-world application of their thought, but utilitarianism is a good deal more than a philosophy of what works. Instead, the term *utilitarianism* means the philosophy of determining, as well as one is able, the most likely outcome of the various choices under consideration and then acting on the choice that will produce the greatest possible amount of good for the greatest number of people, which Mill called the "greatest happiness principle." As a philosophy, utilitarianism is very consistent with populism and democracy, for it insists that each person is as important as any other and that all are entitled to their fair share of the good.

The most common complaint about Mill's "greatest happiness principle" is that it specifically denies any sense of right or wrong that is independent of outcome. Many of Mill's critics see this as a serious flaw, arguing that pure utilitarianism would allow a government to condemn an innocent person if the execution would calm an outraged populace and prevent a murderous riot. Mill does not deal specifically with this question in his classic book on the topic, *Utilitarianism*, but a close reading of the book makes this complaint seem specious. For Mill did stress the importance of impartiality and of providing people with their just deserts, rewards as well as punishments. Mill was, in fact, quite troubled by this sense of justice that he believed was both real and universal but for which he could find no completely rational explanation. It certainly seems to be a violation of this sense of justice that the state, acting in our name, would condemn an innocent person in the name of social order. And if we factor in the respect for law embodied in "The Crito," it seems reasonable to conclude that Mill would have seen a blatant injustice like a show trial and unjust execution as a serious tear in the social fabric, one that would produce, in the long run, far more harm than good.

Regardless of the path taken, many philosophers have maintained that all people have a moral sense of some sort, something that would find repugnant, for example, someone who enjoyed maiming children, wholly independent of whether good or ill resulted. Recently, James Q. Wilson, a criminologist, took a stab at defining and then finding this moral core in his book *The Moral Sense.* Wilson combs the social science literature, especially work in sociology and anthropology, looking for a Darwinian explanation of human morality. The studies he cites are consistent with such an evolutionary sense of morality, but, in all candor, they do not prove its existence. It is probably unprovable.

If the existence of morality cannot be proved, why bother with it at all? Is the question of morality, perhaps, outdated nonsense or a pleasant diversion for the idle rich? Aren't ethics just too, well, nice, for the rough-and-tumble world in which we live? Was George Bernard Shaw right in *Pygmalion* when he had Colonel Pickering react with dismay when Eliza Doolittle's father asked to be paid for Higgins's borrowing of his daughter in Higgins's famous test of his ability to teach proper diction to anyone, even a Cockney like 'Liza?

"Have you no morals, man," Pickering thundered.
"Can't afford them, guv'nor," the senior Doolittle answered. "Neither could you, if you was as poor as me."

There are two answers to these questions. Neither may be fully compelling, but between them they cover most of the necessary ground. There is an explanation grounded in theology, which may be satisfying for those who are themselves religious and those who acknowledge theological influences on their lives. While the world's great religions differ in rites and in details, all contain a core principle of concern and kindness for one's fellow human beings; the version of this found in Christianity is the Golden Rule. Across the centuries, many philosophers have echoed the sentiments of Sir Francis Bacon, the great English philosopher, when he wrote at the beginning of the seventeenth century, "All good moral philosophy is but an handmaid to religion."

For those who deny not only all religion but also the moral worth of all religious teaching, there is a societal reason to behave ethically. For people to live in societies—and all of us do—those societies have to function. And a society functions, not merely smoothly but at all, only if most members of that society obey its rules voluntarily. Take, for example, the very common societal dictum that people should tell the truth. It is not just that telling the truth is nice or pleasant or even enlightening. More profoundly, it allows society to function.

Here's why: One of the key features that distinguishes a genuine society from a mere aggregate of isolated individuals is the level of sophistication in our communication with each other. But that level of communication presupposes that the information being transmitted, from the trivial to the crucial, is true. At the trivial end, if someone on the street asks you for the time or directions, both sides expect you to respond honestly. At the other end of the importance scale, what is at the root of the national malaise concerning elected officials? The conviction that many of them do not tell the truth. What is at the heart of all contract law? The insistence that all sides do what they say they will do.

The same is true in the animal world. Animal behaviorists bring us fresh data all the time to suggest that many species have far more sophisticated forms of communication than scientists had earlier thought. The same principles governing individuals in human society are true there as well. If a honeybee "dances" in the midst of the hive to give directions to the other bees through a complex set of vibrations to help them find a good field of clover, that information is valuable only to the extent that it is true. If the dancing bee were to transmit false information to the other bees and thus send the others off in the wrong direction, the whole hive would suffer.

This argument gets into social contract theory, which we need not deal with in detail here, but which is worth a brief explanation. At its most fundamental, social contract theory, espoused initially in 1651 by Thomas Hobbes in *The Leviathan,* argues that there was a time, before society, when people were born with the unlimited natural right to do just as they pleased, including the right to kill one another to take one another's food and possessions. But this world of one-against-all proved unsatisfactory to everyone, for, as Hobbes noted, people are similar enough in both brains and brawn that no one is safe from attack—if not from an individual, then from a small gang assembled for the purpose. The upshot, in Hobbes's most famous phrase, is that life under such conditions is "solitary, poor, nasty, brutish and short." The solution to this intolerable situation, he argued, was for people to surrender voluntarily many of their natural rights, including their right to predation, in return for the collective security of not being preyed upon. This theory of how human societies evolved was refined and elaborated upon for the next century and beyond by John Locke, Jean-Jacques Rousseau, and many others, but the essential principle remained intact: People are not wholly autonomous agents, just so many separate atoms whirling across the cosmos. Rather, they are, by necessity, part of a larger unit called society, the survival of which is crucial to the survival of its individual members.

We are primarily interested, however, in how an individual comes up with an ethical philosophy, even as we recognize the inevitable overlap between any individual's sense of morality and the moral code into which that person was born and socialized. There has been a good deal of discussion among philosophers and students of ethics over the centuries about the role of the self in ethical thinking. If I am a teleologist and therefore decide that I will act on that choice designed to produce the greatest ratio of good over evil, I have to decide whose good I am interested in, or most interested in. Some philosophers have argued that all of us are, eventually, concerned only with our own well-being, and properly so. This way of thinking is called *ethical egoism*. If you are an ethical egoist, you are declaring: I will act upon that choice that will produce the greatest good for me.

One ethical egoist was Friedrich Nietzsche, an important German philosopher of the late nineteenth century. Nietzsche is most well known for two observations: first, that "God is dead," by which it is thought he meant that the era of Christian morality and theology was over; and second, that the world was properly destined to be ruled by a tiny group of Overmen, or Supermen, who were not bound by the "slave morality" of the "herd" of the rest of humanity. Nietzsche saw himself as the prime example of this new breed of Overmen. If Nietzsche was correct, then it is, morally speaking, perfectly acceptable for people to declare themselves bound by one set of rules and everyone else bound by another.

The problem with such thinking is that, by definition, ethical reasoning must be concerned with the notion of self-in-society, not merely with self. That is what Niebuhr called "man-the-answerer," as he stressed that moral behavior must be seen in the context of how our behavior affects others, the complex web of actions and interactions that make up human society. Even thinkers like Thomas Hobbes, who was convinced that people truly cared only for themselves, realized that it was in each individual's interest that the larger society continue to function. It must be noted, however, that Hobbes's views of people as wholly self-centered has received a good deal of support in the twentieth century from psychologists and sociobiologists who believe that we are, in a sense, hardwired for selfishness. But even if there are innate tendencies in this direction—something that is open for debate—one can still contend that people can learn to overcome these selfish tendencies through intellect and force of will, just as all social conventions, manners, and mores are learned. In hot weather, there is no physiological need to wear clothes at all, but most people beyond the toddler stage do anyway.

A person who is a teleologist but not an ethical egoist tries to take those actions that will result in the greatest amount of good over evil for everyone, the self included. "Good" in this sense does not need to have a moral connotation; the good to be sought could be to provide food or shelter or some other nonmoral good. It is difficult in many situations to predict the balance of good over evil with any accuracy, although Bentham, the founder of utilitarianism, was convinced that it could be done. He established an elaborate morals matrix involving intensity, duration, proximity, and many other dimensions that he thought made it possible to determine total "good" with great precision. How would such a teleologist choose between an action that would bring a moderate amount of good for many people and an action that would bring much good for a very few people? A strict teleologist would have to go with the one that would bring the most good, period. However, teleology can be molded by combining it with deontological principles. For example, a principle of justice could be brought into the equation, making it necessary to consider the fairness of the distribution of good as well as the absolute amount of good. It is easy to see that an individual's ethical principles, teleological or deontological or both, could sometimes come in conflict with each other. When that happens, the individual must establish a hierarchy, deciding which principles should take precedence.

If ethics exists, and if it is important, what are the most important guiding principles that good journalists should follow and why? What conflicts can arise? For answers, it seems reasonable to examine the same intellectual history that is the core of our collective sense of moral propriety and look for the special ethical obligations incumbent upon journalists. This is because the same intellectual forces that created the nation granted the press enormous freedom under the First Amendment to the Constitution.

Many books on journalism ethics contain a discussion of whether journalism is a profession or a craft. A case can be made for using each term. Those who argue that journalism is a profession note its similarities to other professions—especially medicine and law—that it resembles to a greater or lesser degree. Journalism, medicine, and law all have important public service roles, their own national organizations, and their own codes of standards of behavior, including ethics codes. Those who argue that journalism is a craft and not a profession note that, unlike medicine and law, journalism does not require any special training or license and that, while journalists do have their own codes of ethical behavior, there is no governing body for journalists that has the power to prevent transgressors from practicing or to drum out miscreants. Therefore, they say, journalism is more like a traditional craft, albeit one with somewhat more individual autonomy than some other crafts. Academics often like to discuss such differences (as do lawyers—the difference between craft and profession has important legal ramifications, such as individual autonomy and its resulting implications for responsibility and liability). But many working journalists consider what they do to be more like a calling; they think of themselves as both the bulwark of democracy and as the last, best defense of individual rights. This sense of ethical responsibility and duty, as we shall see, can be best understood in the context of the philosophical and political underpinnings of American journalism.

2

The Political Case
for Moral Reasoning in Journalism

For at least two broad reasons, the journalist's primary obligation is to tell the truth. The first reason is political, the second philosophical.

To make the political case that journalists *should*, that is, are morally bound to, get at the truth as well as they are able, requires a review of the core political principle of the United States, that of democratic self-government, or popular sovereignty.

As already noted, in the seventeenth century, and increasingly in the eighteenth, the leading intellects of Europe, particularly in England and France, came to believe in the power and value of the human mind. They came to appreciate, really for the first time since the Greeks, that human intellect was a powerful force and that human reason could be brought to bear successfully on solving life's greatest challenges. The reasons for this development are complex and tightly woven into the fabric of history. It was closely connected to the great explosion of Newtonian science and in other ways was a direct outgrowth of the Renaissance and the Protestant Reformation.

The upshot for political theory was the growing belief that people were capable, under the right circumstances, of running their own lives. The belief in the possibility of self-governance was a frontal assault on what had been the dominant theory of government for a thousand years, the so-called divine right of kings. In brief, this theory held that kings were selected by God to run their countries for the greater glory of God. The belief in self-governance did not by any means deny the existence of God or diminish God's power and authority—although those ideas would come later for some—but it did hold that human life was well worth living and that human society was worth improving for its own sake as well as for the greater glory of God. Such political thinking mirrors the shift in ethical thought from deontology to teleology, a shift noted earlier.

The new line of thinking came to be called the Enlightenment. It held that kings and princes did not have divine appointments to their thrones. What gave a king the right and the ability to govern other people was knowledge, not godly intervention. Further, Enlightenment thinkers believed that if ordinary citizens could only know enough, they could govern themselves. At first, the task of governance would be assumed by each individual; as societies grew, that task would be taken up by representatives serving at the people's pleasure.

The most significant assault on the old theory of the divine right of kings came from Thomas Hobbes, who developed the natural-rights theory about the origins of government, which was mentioned in the last chapter. In Hobbes's view, as laid out in *The Leviathan,* each person in the community or state started out with absolute rights, including the right to harm other people to better oneself. However, in Hobbesian theory, people voluntarily surrendered those rights to a government that was established to protect people from themselves. Hobbes had a bleak view of human nature and thought that without a very strong central government— indeed, an absolutist one—individuals or groups would overthrow the government and society would revert to its natural state of war, in which each individual was pitted against all the others.

A generation later, another English political philosopher, John Locke, revisited the world of Hobbes's Leviathan and came away with a view of government that is similar to Hobbes's in many ways, but that also has profoundly important differences. In 1691, Locke published his own theory of the foundation of government and the proper role of the state in managing the affairs of its citizens. This document, *On Civil Government: The Second Treatise*, begins with natural rights, as Hobbes did, which leads to the idea of a government created to provide services, including protection, to the citizens. But there was a crucial difference. Whereas Hobbes saw people as depraved, always and inevitably looking out for only their own interests, Locke saw people as capable of great good and possessing a broad concern for the well-being of their fellow citizens.

It is impossible to know for certain why the two men differed on their views of humanity, but there is little doubt that a major factor was their religious views. Hobbes was not a religious man by the standards of his day. (He was not, however, an atheist in the modern sense of the word. His detractors accused him of atheism, which has led to some misunderstanding, but in the seventeenth century, the term did not carry with it the modern meaning of a direct denial of the existence of a deity. Hobbes did believe in God.) Locke, on the other hand, was a deeply religious man and had studied for the Anglican priesthood. He left before ordination, he said, because he feared that he would be only a middling priest. People with proper religious training in morals, Locke argued, could be trusted to have a stable society with more personal freedom, and far less governmental coercion, than in the absolute state that Hobbes had envisioned.

The notion of where ultimate political power should lie is the single most important difference in the worldviews of Hobbes and Locke. In Hobbes's world, people initially held power through natural rights, but they surrendered it permanently and irrevocably to the government; they could not be trusted any other way. But for Locke, ultimate political power—that is, political sovereignty—remained with the people. In Locke's view, government worked for the people, not the other way around.

The people hired legislators and tax collectors and diplomats to do the people's will, and if those hired functionaries did not do their jobs to the satisfaction of the sovereign people, then the people were entitled to get rid of them, Locke said. If the governors would not leave office when told to do so by their masters, the people could, as a last resort, throw them out by violent means. Thus, within the concept of the people retaining ultimate power—that is, popular sovereignty—Locke provided a philosophical justification for armed revolution. That justification would be cited again and again by revolutionaries for centuries to come, including the revolutionary generation that led the armed breakaway of the American colonies in 1776.

At the time when Hobbes was exploring the nature of political power, another Englishman was exploring the notion of free speech, although from quite a different starting point. That was John Milton, the most important poet of his era and one of England's leading intellectuals. In Milton's day—the middle of the seventeenth century—everything printed had to be published by the small monopoly of government-sanctioned printers or had to get approval from them before publication. The government monopoly on printing, called the Stationers' Company, was a holdover from the days of Henry VIII, who saw the first printing press come into England in the generation after Gutenberg and who immediately saw the potential power it contained. Trying to harness that awesome power, Henry clamped tight controls on printing. The controls were continued under the reign of Henry's daughter, Elizabeth I, and were still in place at the time of the Stuart succession in the early 1600s.

Milton got involved in the free-speech question because he wrote a pamphlet advocating more liberal divorce laws, a political hot-button issue of his day. Milton was interested in liberalizing divorce laws because he wanted to divorce a young country woman whom he had married and then separated from. When strict divorce laws kept him from ending his marriage, Milton, in exasperation, wrote a scathing pamphlet essentially demanding that he, the mighty Milton, should be allowed a divorce if he wanted one. In the ensuing debate over the divorce pamphlet, some of Milton's critics noted that Milton, either in his rage or his arrogance, had not secured the required stamp of prepublication approval from the government censors, causing the debate to shift from divorce to prepublication censorship. Milton responded to this new criticism with a thundering denunciation of the censorship statute and a request—or demand—that the British House of Commons repeal it. He made his appeal in the form of a speech to the Commons, and it was subsequently published as a pamphlet entitled *Aeropagitica*. In towering prose, full of classical allusions and ringing phrases, Milton made the case for abolishing prepublication censorship.

Although many of Milton's phrases were memorable enough to be adopted centuries later as newspaper mottoes, what is frequently forgotten is that Milton made his argument primarily on religious grounds, not political ones. In Milton's day, the leading indicator of political affiliation and loyalty was religious affiliation, whether one was Church of England or Anglican (the church in the United States is called Episcopalian) or Roman Catholic. For more than one hundred years, since Henry VIII's famous break with Rome in 1534, religion had dominated English politics and had largely determined political loyalty. To the Protestants, a group that included Milton and every member of the House of Commons he addressed, the Roman Catholic Church was seen as narrow minded, dogmatic, intolerant, and anti-intellectual. The church, also, was held responsible for the infamous Inquisition and the Index of Forbidden Books. Protestants, by contrast, saw themselves as broad minded, tolerant, and intellectually curious. *Their* religion could withstand rigorous inquiry, whereas, as they saw it, the Catholic religion could not. So Milton's ringing argument for free speech is an argument made by an Anglican to a room full of Anglicans, asking for a distinctly Anglican decision. The same speech that demanded, "Let her [Truth] and falsehood grapple; who ever knew Truth to be put to the worst, in a free and open encounter," also went on to say, "I mean not tolerated Popery," that is, Roman Catholicism. To Milton, Roman Catholics were so intolerant, so opposed to free inquiry, that they should be banned and their books prohibited.

So while it is true that Milton demanded "the liberty to know, to utter, and to argue freely according to consciences, above all other liberties," it is a misreading of history to make him a champion of free speech in anything like the political sense that we use the term today. That argument did not begin until after Locke's work on civil government and the origins of political power. Among the earliest and best of those who worked through the free-speech implications of Lockean popular sovereignty were a pair of eighteenth-century political journalists who wrote under the pseudonym of "Cato."

Cato, the name of a Roman statesman noted for his honesty and integrity, was the pen name of John Trenchard and Thomas Gordon, who began a weekly column in 1720 for a number of liberal London newspapers. The column ran for four years and covered a wide range of political topics, including government corruption and foreign policy. The columns were extremely popular with the liberal political faction called the Radical Whigs. The pieces were frequently republished in popular anthologies and widely sold among progressive political thinkers, both in Britain and in the American colonies. It was Cato who first explored the implications for journalism of the notion of popular sovereignty, which Locke had espoused a generation before and which had caught on like wildfire. This argument, made in *Essay No. 15*, was the clearest statement yet of the *political* need for free speech. At its most basic, it says that if the people are sovereign, that is, they retain ultimate political authority over their hired governors and functionaries, then the people have to know how well or how poorly their employees are doing their jobs. Cato went further, arguing that even though other principles might be violated, popular sovereignty was, in effect, trumps. It was more important to keep the sovereign people informed than it was to keep people thinking highly of their governors. Nothing less than human liberty was at stake.

In a subsequent column, *Essay No. 32,* Cato took the notion of free inquiry even further, challenging the centuries-old notion of libel in English common law. Since the founding of the modern state, toward the end of the Middle Ages, one of the most serious concerns of any government had been law and order, mostly order. No monarch anywhere felt truly secure on the throne, probably with good reason. There was always danger about, usually in the form of a potential usurper trying to stir up discontent that could lead to revolution. Most broadly speaking, libel entailed saying (in modern usage, it means writing) something derogatory about someone else, either a private citizen or the government. In either case, according to the British common law, the government was entitled to prosecute. A person who was libeled had a right to sue, but the government also had a right to prosecute because the person who had been libeled might react violently against the assailant. The point of libel law was to keep the king's peace far more than it was to prohibit derogatory words, so truth was not a defense for libel—in fact, it exacerbated it. If the defamation were untrue, the reasoning went, the defamed person could probably mount a successful verbal defense against the libel. But if the accusation were true, the person being libeled was considered less likely to rely on mere words for a defense and more likely to resort to physical violence, thus violating the king's peace. Hence the popular aphorism: "The greater the truth, the greater the libel."

That concept was firmly entrenched in English law long before John Locke came up with the notion of a sovereign citizenry. Here was a direct clash of legal principles. Speaking ill of government officials was clearly libelous, but the press had to be free to do just that if Lockean democracy had a chance of surviving. Cato was clear: The libel laws had to go. "Truth," Cato wrote, "can never be a libel." It was another seventy-five years before that principle became law in either England or in what had by then become the United States, but it has been a bedrock principle of journalism ever since.

The Enlightenment was in full swing by the second half of the eighteenth century and was responsible, in large measure, for massive political upheaval in the two nations where Enlightenment thinking had taken root most successfully. In France, the storming of the Bastille prison by a Paris mob in 1789 led to the overthrow of the monarchy. During the very height of the revolution, the radical Jacobin Maximilien Robespierre made an impassioned defense of liberty of the press, borrowing Cato's phrase about a free press being the "bulwark of liberty" and arguing that a free flow of information was essential, especially in times of tumult. "The liberty of the press is the only effectual check of arbitrary power," Robespierre told the National Assembly. The revolution in France sent tremors of fear throughout Britain and the Continent because the French monarchy was the very embodiment of the old order, the *ancien régime*.

But France's revolution was the second of the great Enlightenment revolutions. In Britain thirteen years earlier, the revolution happened not in England proper, but in England's richest and most important colonies in the New World. The intellectual leadership of the Colonial rebellion was determined to put into practice the Enlightenment theories that so stressed the power of the intellect. The founding generation went to great lengths to curb the power of the government they were building, borrowing heavily from English and French intellectuals the notions of checks and balances, divisions of authority and protections against what they saw as the inevitable desire of those in power to try to gather more power for themselves, at the expense of the citizenry. The founders were determined to create, for the first time in human history on a massive scale, a country built on the Lockean notions of popular sovereignty. The citizens, not the politicians, would hold ultimate political power.

Of all the things the founding generation did to try to ensure that political power would continue to rest with the people, nothing was more important than the guarantee of a free press, of a free flow of information that the governors themselves could not control. Knowledge alone did not guarantee that the grand experiment in popular self-government would work—even the most devoted Enlightenment thinkers never made that claim—but a free flow of information made it possible. That is the thinking behind the famous words of the First Amendment, "Congress shall make no law abridging . . . freedom of speech, or of the press. . . ."

The first fragile years of the new nation saw a furious political debate over whether the high-sounding principles of the Enlightenment could truly be implemented successfully. American politics broke along a European fault line, the more conservative forces allying themselves with the Britain they had just broken from and the more daring seeing great virtue in the revolution then going on in France. Those split allegiances led to the formation of two political parties: the Federalists, led by John Adams, and the Democratic-Republicans, led by Thomas Jefferson and James Madison.

As the arguments raged back and forth, supporters on both sides tried to find the balance point between individual liberty and the civil state. Among the best of the Jeffersonian writers was a New York lawyer named Tunis Wortman. Wortman contributed very little that was truly original, but his 1801 book, *A Treatise Concerning Political Enquiry and the Liberty of the Press*, provided an outstanding summation of the Democratic-Republican position. There is little truly new in Wortman's book, but it is one of the most eloquent summations of free-speech thought ever written.

About the same time, another Jeffersonian, one John Thomson, wrote *The Uncontroulable Nature of the Human Mind*, a remarkable book, which evokes Milton's "truth will out" argument and neatly sums up the popular sovereignty arguments for a free press. Thomson also foreshadowed much of John Stuart Mill's argument in *On Liberty*, written half a century later. But Thomson's main point, suggested by the title of his book, is that human beings start out as blank slates—shades of Mill's tabula rasa!—and that they respond to external stimuli and learn, layer by layer, from experience. He argues that people thus have no control over their thought processes and that expression, written or oral, is merely a manifestation of thought. To Thomson, it is both wicked and foolhardy for a government, which is, as he points out, made up only of people, to try to control the minds and expressions of others when they cannot, in truth, control their own.

Mill, who contributed the concept of utilitarianism to ethical thinking, also argued for freedom of expression. By the middle of the nineteenth century, when he wrote *On Liberty*, he thought it safe to assume that there was a widespread understanding of and belief in the free press—popular sovereignty arguments of Cato and Wortman. He endorsed those principles in a paragraph, then went on to argue, as Thomson did, that free inquiry led inevitably to greater truth. If an argument is right, Mill argued, it should be expressed for all to hear it. If an argument is wrong, Mill said, it can be and must be successfully refuted by better thinking—thinking that will be sharper and more acute for the exercise. And if an argument is partly right and partly wrong, as Mill believed most were, both of the preceding principles would come into play.

There is another dimension to Mill's argument about the importance of refuting a bad argument. That is the notion of the *dialectic*, often called the Hegelian dialectic for one of its chief developers, the early-nineteenth-century German philosopher Georg Wilhelm Friedrich Hegel. In the Hegelian dialectic, progress is always achieved by an idea, the *thesis*, coming into collision with its opposite, the *antithesis*. The result is a new entity that Hegel called the *synthesis*. The synthesis becomes the new thesis; it is, in turn, opposed by a new antithesis, leading to a new synthesis.

Mill also made a valuable point that is sometimes lost upon Americans because of their belief in majority rule. Mill argued vehemently for minority rights within majority rule. In a famous passage, Mill argued, "If all mankind minus one were of one opinion, mankind would be no more justified in silencing that one person than he, if he had the power, would be justified in silencing mankind." Mill was so committed to the notion that the individual be fully free that he argued that human behavior should be limited only if it would cause direct harm to others. People engaging in intemperate, foolish or even self-destructive action could be argued with or cajoled, Mill said, but they should never be coerced unless their behavior would be harmful to others.

The United States has long struggled with the idea of protecting minority rights. In the early nineteenth century, John C. Calhoun argued that legislation should be passed according to the principle of "concurrent majority," which would mean that the people affected by the legislation would have to concur with its passage, even if they were in the minority. In the late twentieth century, efforts to address the question of minority rights have led to the gerrymandering of some voting districts to ensure political representation for minorities and to the idea of cumulative voting, espoused by the legal scholar Lani Guinier, to give minority candidates a better chance of winning elections. A free flow of information is also important for minority rights; even without political clout, the right of minorities to express and disseminate ideas is a powerful tool, perhaps their most powerful one.

However, journalism can bring people harm as well as benefits. One of the harms that most seems to bother readers and viewers concerns the invasion of privacy. During periods of intense media attention to spectacular events, such as the O. J. Simpson murder trial in 1995 or the Nancy Kerrigan-Tonya Harding "Morality on Ice" show in 1994, two seemingly contradictory things almost always happen. First, the news media—from the staid *New York Times* to the gaudy tabloid TV shows like *Hard Copy*—focus massive attention on the events and on the backgrounds and personalities of the people involved. Second, thousands of media critics—a relative handful of professionals and many thousands of readers and viewers—complain that the press is invading the privacy of some or all of the people involved. The complaint is almost always some variation of "how dare they?"

The notion of privacy seems almost intuitively to be part and parcel of what it means to be a free citizen in our society, but the notion is relatively new in the legal system. For more than a century after the Revolution, there was little attention paid to privacy as a legal concept. It was not until two technological developments of the late 1800s—high-speed newspaper presses and the halftone process, which allowed photographs to be run in newspapers—that privacy became a serious issue. It was a heyday of what we now call the paparazzi, the photographers who make a living shooting and selling photographs of the rich and famous without their consent.

In the 1890s, in the midst of a great outcry against this practice, two young Boston lawyers, Samuel Warren and Louis Brandeis, who would later become famous as a Supreme Court justice, developed the modern notion of the right to privacy. In a famous 1890 article in the *Harvard Law Review,* Warren and Brandeis went back to first principles and said they had discovered a fundamental right to be left alone. The argument builds its case on the familiar and cherished Lockean guarantees of life, liberty, and the pursuit of property. Over time, the young lawyers argued, the definition of property has expanded from the concrete to the abstract, just as assault, which is the threat of violence, was added to the crime of battery, which is actual physical contact. In the same way that the notion of property was expanded to include intellectual property, they argued, the idea of the right to one's person and estate should be expanded in law to include the right to enjoy those things away from public scrutiny.

Just as Cato made a nod to privacy with the observation that some trivial things, even about public figures, were not worth knowing, even if true, so

Brandeis and Warren acknowledged that their notion of the right to privacy was far from absolute. In good Lockean tradition, they contended that matters and people of "public and general interest" were the legitimate targets of press scrutiny.

How does a journalist determine whether a given piece of information is rightly of public concern or is what Cato called "truths not fit to be told"? That is one of the hardest problems in journalism. One of the difficulties is that the argument for publishing and the argument for not publishing have their intellectual roots in the same Lockean political theory, the theory that is so dominant in American politics and culture. It is impossible to write hard-and-fast rules, and it is getting harder all the time, because of changing public values and the emergence of the public relations professionals and their political counterparts, the spinmeisters.

To achieve an understanding of modern image crafters and how they have made journalists' jobs much more complex requires an exploration of the second major thread of journalistic thought, the philosophical problem of determining what the truth is. If we are to consider how spinmeisters distort the truth to serve their own ends, we need to know what is meant by the word "*truth.*" Is the truth merely a jumbled array of pieces of information, each of them technically accurate, or is it something broader, more ephemeral? As the demands grow for greater complexity and context in stories, and as politicians and other public figures rely ever more heavily on their image crafters, the journalist's job gets tougher and tougher. What follows is intended to be enough of a foundation that new journalists will be able to cope with the multiplicity of demands on them without getting hopelessly lost in the thicket of appearances, half-truths and outright lies.

3

The Philosophical Case
for Moral Reasoning in Journalism

The most straightforward reason that journalists are morally obliged to tell the truth is that the search for truth is one of humanity's most powerful intellectual drives. In this regard, journalists are among the most important of a broad array of communicators, voices of the citizenry who try, to put it most simply, to help us understand us. The record of human thought is filled with efforts to know and to discern truth from illusion or falsehood.

A brilliant early example is Plato's "Allegory of the Cave" from *The Republic*, written in the fourth century B.C. In the parable, Plato describes a row of people who spend their lives chained within a cave, their heads bound so that they can look only straight ahead. He further imagines that a fire is burning behind the prisoners and that puppeteers are positioned behind them as well, but in front of the light source, so that their puppets will cast shadows on the wall in front of the prisoners. Plato then suggests that one of the prisoners gets loose. He leaves the cave and discovers the real world beyond the shadows on the wall of the cave. Plato then discusses the difficulty the freed prisoner would have in returning to the darkness of the cave and trying to persuade the prisoners to believe his tale of what he had seen and heard in the world above.

The parable is a complex piece of philosophic thought, and readers over the centuries have found much in it to debate. For journalists, it provides a good lesson in how longstanding is the human search for truth and a caution against relying too heavily on surface appearances. Some print journalists, somewhat waggishly, have seen the puppeteers as an obvious metaphor for television producers and have seen their shadow images on the wall as the images on our television sets. The analogy is not entirely without merit, but the parable has far broader and more profound implications as well.

It is worth noting the context of the statement from Plato about the existence, and the comprehensibility, of reality. Plato is clearly arguing that a reality exists but that many of us are so blinded by our own circumstances that we neither see reality nor are aware that we do not. In this, Plato was arguing against the position held by a group of Greek thinkers called sophists, who were by no means convinced that there was such a thing as reality. The sophists were willing to argue any side of any question, contending that, in the absence of reality, it did not matter much which side one argued. The debate in early Greece over the existence of reality is strikingly familiar to the debate among intellectuals in recent years over a twist in cultural relativism: the question of whether there are enduring values—ideas and principles that are valid and valuable across time and space—or whether everything is relative, in which case no values would be better than any others, and none would be more true than any others, just different.

In Plato's cave, those who have been chained together inside the cave are clearly not at fault, in the sense of being morally liable for some failing or shortcoming. But Plato is quite clear that they are mistaken in believing that the two-dimensional shadows on the wall are reality.

If Plato's fight with the sophists seems to have a familiar ring, so should the arguments for clearheaded thinking and objective analysis advanced in the early seventeenth century by the English philosopher Francis Bacon. Bacon, one of the earliest champions of the scientific method, agreed with Plato that truth was attainable but hard to find. In his great work, the *Novum Organum*, he sought nothing less than a wholesale rethinking and codification of human thought. In a famous passage of the book, he listed four barriers—idols, he called them—to true understanding. The barriers were the various traps of faulty reasoning and comprehension, beginning with the individual's propensity toward misunderstanding, which he called the Idol of the Cave in obvious reference to Plato's cave. But humankind in general also tends to get things mixed up, Bacon argued, calling this trap the Idol of the Tribe. Next, he noted that when people talk to one another, the information transfer is far from perfect, a situation, which he called the Idol of the Marketplace, not in the sense of a marketplace where things are bought and sold, but in the sense of a place where people gather to talk and exchange information. Finally, Bacon described what he called the Idol of the Theater, his dismissive description of virtually all philosophic thought that preceded his own. He called it the Idol of the Theatre because, he said, those systems of thought were "so many stage-plays, representing worlds of their own creation," rather than accurate and honest representations of reality. The solution, Bacon said, was to turn to empirical observations, even though there are daunting possibilities for error in that realm, and to pay strict attention to what later came to be called the scientific method.

Much has happened in the world of intellectual thought in the nearly four centuries since Bacon published his *Novum Organum* in 1620. Modern political theory was developed in those years, and democracy as we know it was not merely dreamed of, but implemented, however imperfectly, in many nation-states in the West. In the early days of this century, mercantilism had largely been replaced by capitalism, but the Industrial Revolution and the horrors of the factory system, pointed out by Charles Dickens among many others, cast serious doubt on its long-term survival. Yet Marx and other major critics of capitalism seemed able to fashion nothing better. The Enlightenment, with its cool reason, and a successor movement, the richly emotional Romantic period, had come and gone. Freud had shattered, probably forever, the widespread optimism that progress was inevitable, or even likely. War of unfathomable atrocity had bled the West into exhaustion, with an entire generation of the best and the brightest perishing at Verdun, the Sommes, Gallipoli, Ypres.

In the years just after the horrors of the war, perhaps the most prescient mind in American journalism was that of Walter Lippmann. He noted the massive complexity of then-modern life, at one point likening the contemporary citizen to a deaf spectator at a stage play—able to see and to understand a little, but painfully aware that much was going by without comprehension. Lippmann's solution was, essentially, Bacon's—recognize the pitfalls of the idols, challenge received information and bench-test ideas. Apply as much mental rigor to news copy as to any other intellectual endeavor.

What Lippmann was advocating was essentially the often confused and still more often maligned notion of objectivity. While it seems true today that whole industries have sprung up to denounce the dreaded *O* word, the concept is quite simple. The job of the journalist is to provide citizens in a democracy with the information they can use to make rational decisions about how best to govern their own lives. It is not to govern for them, nor to decide for them, but to provide the tools that people can use in making their own decisions. At the same time, Lippmann recognized that a mere collection of unsorted information was virtually useless; factoids, as CNN calls them, are amusing, even interesting, but hardly the serious stuff with which to build an informed citizenry. Information is all but useless without context, shape, color, and background.

It is important to note that the goals of objectivity and context often work against each other; the more one tries to achieve one of those goals, the more the other is jeopardized. In a given situation, it is fairly easy to arrive at a set of facts on which most reasonable people can agree. As a hypothetical example, imagine a simple article on an automobile accident. At the time of the accident, car A was going 30 miles per hour in its own lane, while car B was going 75 in the wrong lane. Most people would agree that those two facts are germane to the story, and nearly all journalists would include them in the account of the accident. How about the details that the driver of car A was sober and that the driver of car B was legally drunk? These, too, would be considered germane. How about the facts that the driver of car A was a woman and the driver of car B a man? Almost certainly not. Or a Christian and a Jew? Probably not. How about the fact that the malefactor (the driver of car B) had been in five earlier accidents? Yes. How about the fact that the apparently innocent driver, the woman in car A, had been in five earlier accidents, two of them fatal? That is less clear. How about the fact that she had just come from a funeral and was extremely distraught, suggesting that her reaction time was slowed by inattention? How about road conditions, weather conditions, and the mechanical conditions of the two cars? Clearly, if one were to include *everything* one could find out about the accident, the story would be hopelessly complex and loaded with irrelevant details. On the other hand, it is very difficult to say with great certainty which details are illuminating and which are gratuitous. But agreeing on the pertinent details of an automobile accident looks easy when compared with doing the same in a sexual assault case. How much of the suspect's background is pertinent then and how much of the victim's? Keep in mind that both of these examples are relatively straightforward police stories. Political stories can be vastly more complicated.

Lippmann also provided an important reminder that journalism is not designed to supply, and is probably not capable of supplying, all the information citizens need. In his most famous book, *Public Opinion,* he suggested that journalism is much like a searchlight, moving here and there in the night sky, illuminating one small section and then another, but never providing the broad, even light needed to conduct the public's business. The last generation has witnessed many demands on journalism—that it provide more trends and lifestyles articles, that it do a better job with traditionally underrepresented groups, that it explain art and economics and a host of other subjects better than it did in the past. And, in truth, during the last generation or so, journalism has made enormous strides toward providing these things. Doubters should read newspapers, listen to radio tapes and watch television broadcasts from the 1950s and even the 1960s. Overall, news material from a generation ago is almost farcical in its triviality and superficiality when compared with the best of today's print and broadcast journalism.

Still, it is valuable to recall Lippmann's disclaimer that newspapers (and, now, radio and television news as well) cannot convey all of the necessary or important information to a passively receptive public. Full participation in the democratic process takes considerably more than twenty-two minutes of the evening news or even a conscientious daily hour with the *New York Times*. A truly informed citizen needs to read books and magazines, attend lecture series, engage in discussions with friends and colleagues, and, perhaps above all in Lippmann's mind, have access to public policy institutions that aim to make themselves intelligible to those they serve. The journalist can help, and the journalist may in fact be a critical element in all this, but, Lippmann said, news and truth are not the same thing. News, at bottom, is an honest and comprehensible report of current events; truth is vastly more complex than any single article or series of articles can possibly convey, however artfully and honestly crafted.

One of the most serious problems that Lippmann noted in the journalist's quest for understanding was the rise of contrived events—the "news events" and, worse, "photo ops" that are the products of public relations, a fledgling profession in Lippmann's day. The impact of such information manipulation was explored in great detail by Daniel Boorstin in a classic book, *The Image.* Boorstin, a former Librarian of Congress and the author of a number of important popular histories, devoted a considerable portion of his book to the rise of what he called the "pseudo-event" and the relationship of such events to news gathering.

The pseudo-event, as Boorstin defined it, is anything that does not happen spontaneously but rather is deliberately staged for the purpose of generating news coverage. At its most extreme, a pseudo-event may be a political photo op—shorthand for photographic opportunity—typically, a political figure appears to be doing something while photographers and camera operators capture the event on film or tape. It could be a president or secretary of state sitting in a formal office talking with a foreign dignitary, suggesting the importance of that foreign country in American policy, or a candidate walking through a flag factory, suggesting that the candidate is both deeply patriotic and is concerned about factory workers.

Typically, these photo ops are staged for still photographers and, more important, television camera crews. Reporters are usually allowed to watch the "event" of cameras taking their empty pictures, but they are usually not allowed to ask any questions on the grounds that questions might divert attention from the visual image that has been painstakingly contrived by the politician's media handlers.

Pseudo-events include far more than just picture-taking sessions, however. Other staged events are press conferences, most political rallies, civil rights and other popular demonstrations, and a host of other events that are put on primarily or exclusively for the benefit of the journalists who may cover them. They range from Ronald Reagan having his picture taken in a working-class tavern in Boston to show his "sympathy for the working stiff"—as Reagan's media handler extraordinaire, Michael Deaver, put it—to the political radical Abbie Hoffman staging massive protest rallies during the 1968 Democratic National Convention in Chicago.

Boorstin does not blame the image makers entirely for the phenomenal growth of the staged event. He blames journalists for swallowing such events whole, then demanding more. Publishers have known for more than 150 years that they stand to make a great deal of money out of selling information, provided it is lively enough and interesting enough for the consuming public. As a result, Boorstin argues, news outlets are set up to handle massive amounts of news, the "great yawning maw" of the news hole, as some reporters term it. If there are not enough real events to fill up the paper or the broadcast in a given news cycle, stations and papers are extremely vulnerable to the lure of covering the staged event. Staged events are much easier to cover than real ones, because little or nothing is left to chance. A contrived happening will be staged at a time and place convenient for reporters to get to, often with a coffee urn nearby. Anyone who has ever wandered through Disney World has doubtless noticed the little yellow signs recommending where to take the most scenic pictures. Pseudo-events have their own versions of the little yellow signs, less obtrusive but just as manipulative. The production will be painstakingly set up, and the places for still and television cameras will be selected with care so the photographers will get what they want—compelling pictures—and the event's arranger will get the desired image across to the viewers.

The pseudo-event presents at least two serious problems for journalists, especially journalists who depend upon pictures to tell their stories. One problem is that the pseudo-event may not be news; paradoxically, the other problem is that the staged event may have real news value. A candidate's trip through a flag factory can be dismissed as a blatant attempt at news management, although stations will find it very difficult to turn down pictures of such a colorful event, particularly in markets with keen competition, which descrubes most of them. But the pseudo-event that produces real news is more troubling for the thoughtful journalist. Deaver, President Reagan's chief image maker, raised the pseudo-event to high art, acknowledging freely to reporters that the event was staged and phony but knowing that the reporters would cover it nonetheless because it fit their definitions of news. In journalists' understandable effort to provide readers and viewers with as much information about their elected officials as possible, they have, in the last generation, considered newsworthy virtually anything that the president does. Lower-ranking government officials are generally less newsworthy. Knowing this, Deaver and his successors were happy to provide opportunities for television cameras to photograph the chief executive doing things that the image makers wanted him to be perceived as doing, knowing that journalists would be largely unable to resist.

4

The Economic Case
for Moral Reasoning in Journalism

T he problem of being unable to resist compelling videotape brings up the next broad category of concern in the world of journalism: money. However one argues that journalism is a craft or a profession or even a calling, it is undeniable that it is also a business, and it exists in the world of contemporary American capitalism. Therefore, a brief review of the world's most powerful economic model is in order.

The basic text of capitalism's most fundamental features is *An Inquiry into the Nature and Causes of the Wealth of Nations,* written by Adam Smith and published in 1776 as an answer to the then-dominant economic model called mercantilism. At its most basic, mercantilism argued that nations should set economic policy designed to increase the amount of gold and silver residing in one nation at the expense of the amount of gold and silver in another. Mercantilism, which was popular in the sixteenth, seventeenth, and eighteenth centuries, was an early version of what in contemporary parlance is often called a zero-sum game. It argued that there was a fixed amount of wealth and that governments should erect tariff boundaries to keep out imports, offer bounties to increase exports, and otherwise try to control the flow of money into the country.

But Smith argued that economics is a win-win phenomenon, if we can again borrow terminology from modern game theory. All nations could increase their wealth, Smith contended, if only governments would get out of the way and let natural forces take over. The term most often associated with Smith's economic policy is the French term *laissez-faire*, meaning "let it be" or "leave it alone." Smith said governmental tinkering with economic matters only gets in the way of what he called the "invisible hand." That metaphorical hand, Smith argued, sets the natural price of goods and services. Two cobblers, for example, will compete with each other for customers by trying to make better boots and by selling them at a cheaper price. The result will be the highest possible quality of boots and the lowest possible price, consistent with the bootmaker making a comfortable profit for the labor expended. If, because of better climate or cheaper raw materials, a French bootmaker can make and sell high-quality boots in England cheaper than an English bootmaker can, everyone would benefit by having the English artisans seek a different trade in which to prosper. Smith argued that unrestricted competition would inevitably produce the best possible combination of price and quality for all goods and services. Any governmental interference simply adds inefficiency to a natural system, he said, and interferes with the natural principles of supply and demand. All people should be allowed to follow their own best interests, and the "invisible hand" will guarantee that the result will be the best possible system, Smith said.

Wealth of Nations was published in the same year as the American Declaration of Independence. That is in some ways an unfortunate coincidence because it tends to link the principles of laissez-faire capitalism with the founding of the United States, giving free-market economics an even stronger position in American lore than it deserves. In fact, United States economic policy was interventionist from the very beginning because the founding generation freely used fiscal tools to try to shape the type of society they wanted.

As one example among many possible, consider the government's economic policy toward the news business. As noted above, the founding generation believed that a free flow of information was absolutely critical to the survival of the popular democracy they were trying to build. On the legal front, they protected the free flow of information with the First Amendment. On the economic front, the government granted important favors to journalists. Foremost among them was cheap postage—essentially a major government subsidy—which newspapers still enjoy and many rely upon more than two centuries later. Government bestowed other financial favors on journalists as well: for example, building many roads and post offices that were very beneficial to newspapers but were otherwise not necessary. But the proximity in time of the publication of the Declaration of Independence and that of *Wealth of Nations* has contributed to the notion, popular among many in business, that American-style liberty means nearly absolute economic as well as political freedom.

For the news business to succeed economically, all that was needed was a buying public large enough to create a huge market for news and a technology able to feed that market. Those two elements came into being in the 1830s with the birth of what is known, in historians' shorthand, as the "penny press." The growth of major Eastern cities and the arrival of new printing technology enabled journalism to enter a powerful new phase. No one better represents that new world than James Gordon Bennett, who began the *New York Herald* in 1835. Bennett soon realized that journalism could not only enlighten its readers, but could also enrich its publishers.

More than anyone who had gone before, Bennett realized that people would pay for information if it was fresh and entertaining. Bennett confirmed on a new scale what had been learned much earlier, going all the way back to Benjamin

Franklin a century before: Advertisers will happily pay for access to a newspaper's readers. So what Bennett contributed was not the realization that advertising pays, but the idea that news itself pays, that information can itself become a commodity. Thus, with Bennett, the most enduring dichotomy of American journalism truly began. Someone approaching journalism purely from its political, popular-sovereignty dimension is clearly interested in putting important information in the hands of as many people as possible because democracy depends upon broad participation. At the same time, providing interesting information, whether useful or not, can make its provider, that is, the publisher, wealthy. From Bennett's day onward, it has been difficult to separate the political and philosophical motives of journalism from the economic ones, especially since the freedom to make money—Smith's free-market capitalism—is as deeply ingrained in the American psyche as is the political freedom to say what one chooses and the philosophical freedom to follow truth wherever it leads.

In Europe, where the Industrial Revolution came earlier than it did to the United States, Karl Marx, Charles Dickens, and other critics of the factory system pointed out that Smith's argument for free-market capitalism belonged to an era of individual artisans, with cobblers making their own boots. With the onset of the factory system, owners did less and less of the actual work of manufacturing; instead, they hired wage laborers by the hundreds and then by the thousands to run the machinery of the Industrial Age. The cost of that labor quickly became the most significant part of a capitalist's cost of doing business, so when Smith's invisible hand set to work controlling the price of goods, the first drop in costs came inevitably from the lowering of wages. As early as 1800, such critics as David Ricardo and Thomas Malthus were arguing that in the new industrial world, free-enterprise capitalism guaranteed massive human misery because the "iron law of wages," as Ricardo put it, would keep workers at no more than subsistence pay.

While Marx had his supporters in America, it was not until nearly a generation after the American Civil War that the first serious voices of protest were raised against the unrestrained accumulation of capital. For journalists, one of the most interesting of such voices was that of Joseph Pulitzer, who in the late 1870s anticipated that which, a generation later, would come to be known as the muckraking tradition. Money brings with it power, Pulitzer observed, and money can and does corrupt the political system. Pulitzer's warning concerned a specific U.S. Senate campaign in which wealthy industrialists were trying to buy their way into office (shades of the 1990s!), but his point is well taken on a broader level as well. The First Amendment guarantee of a free press was established, at considerable social cost, to enable democracy to work. If money corrupted that democracy, despite the free flow of information, then the political influence of that money needed to be curtailed. What the muckrakers were saying—and what Pulitzer really was foreshadowing—was the idea that however well the press guardians defended the city on the hill from frontal assaults by the political barbarians, the city was still in danger from the monied interests coming in through a back gate.

The muckraking era proper got under way a few years later, about 1900. Although Pulitzer's *New York World* undertook many serious stories about corruption of the political system, especially by wealthy interests, most muckraking was done for magazines, which had more space and time to devote to the long, complex stories that muckraking often entails. In a sense, it is unfortunate that Pulitzer was a muckraker at all, for the fact that he championed good causes adds to the confusion over the differences between muckraking and its ill-mannered cousin sensationalism, also called yellow journalism, which is also associated with Pulitzer, especially during his great circulation war of the 1890s with William Randolph Hearst's *New York Journal*.[1] Yellow journalism has come to stand for irresponsible pandering and focusing on salacious details of sex, violence, and wrongdoing.

There are several reasons that people often confuse the two genres: They were both at their height around the turn of the century; they had some overlapping memberships; and, less obvious but just as important, they were often deliberately misidentified by the people who were the objects of the muckrakers' attention. Then, as now, muckraking exposés of malfeasance had elements that were personally embarrassing to their targets, and those targets often fought back by labeling the attacks yellow journalism. The answer from a responsible journalist, then as now, would be that the public interest served by publication overrode any concern about private discomfort. However much journalists dislike causing personal pain or embarrassment—and the good ones dislike it acutely—providing the information that citizens need to have in order to govern their own lives is paramount. The problem, of course, is that some information is embarrassing and important, while other information is merely titillating, and people of good will and bad may differ over which is which. Since Bennett's day, when pandering became extremely profitable, unscrupulous publishers have been willing and eager to confuse the two. The test of what belongs in the public arena may not have changed since Cato's day, but the financial stakes have gone up considerably.

By the 1920s, some of the best muckrakers turned their attention to the news industry itself. Upton Sinclair, a dedicated socialist, concluded sadly that the watchdogs had caught the disease they were trying to keep at bay. In *The Brass Check*, Sinclair argued compellingly that news organizations had themselves become big business and were no more honest and no more concerned with the real welfare of the working classes than were the big steel and big oil industries.

---

[1] The term began when major New York publishers began experimenting with spot color in their pages, starting with a cartoon character called "The Yellow Kid." Both Hearst's *Journal* and Pulitzer's *World* had such comic strips, and as these two papers were the biggest and boldest of the sensationalist papers, the term "yellow journalism" was applied first to Hearst and Pulitzer and then to their many imitators.

A generation later, the press critic A. J. Liebling made much the same argument from a less extreme political perspective. Liebling noted the decline of genuine competition among news outlets and saw in that decline a loss of interest in ferreting out important stories. In the current generation, Ben Bagdikian, a veteran journalist and journalism educator, has chronicled the trend toward having a handful of huge corporations controlling more and more of the nation's and the world's information providers, print and broadcast. His argument is eloquent evidence supporting an argument Marx made more than a century ago, that capital tends to accumulate in fewer and fewer hands. With each new edition of Bagdikian's important book, *Media Monopolies*, the author notes the dwindling number of corporations controlling the world's mass media.

Turning a profit and providing a democratic citizenry with the information it needs are both measures of freedom, but of different kinds of freedom. They may well work in tandem. As the highly respected journalism educator Philip Meyer has noted, there is an economic dimension to providing a credible news product. At one end of the credibility spectrum lie supermarket tabloids, newspapers filled with space aliens, Elvis sightings, and other nonsense. What these papers are *not* filled with is advertisements; the ads they do carry tend to be for diet pills that claim to work while you sleep and similar foolishness. Meyer points out that the range of advertisements is limited to products that only the most gullible of readers would consider purchasing. At the other end of the credibility spectrum lies the *New York Times*, full of long, richly detailed, and meticulously edited articles of local and world affairs. It is also full of extremely expensive advertisements for luxury real estate, designer clothing, fabulous jewelry, and other goods and services befitting the *Times*'s upscale market. The paper is a perfect example of doing well by doing good.

But that does not always happen. In 1947, a commission of academics and professionals—usually known as the Hutchins Commission for its chair, Robert M. Hutchins, then chancellor of the University of Chicago—studied contemporary news media. The upshot of this commission's work was a new sense of *should* for journalists that has come to be called the "social responsibility" theory of a free press. The commission did not really break much new ground; most of what it recommended comes out of the moral arguments made earlier in this essay. The Hutchins Commission argued that readers— viewers came later—needed and were entitled to an honest and accurate account of the day's events in a context that gave those events meaning and that journalists had a moral obligation to provide that information. This idea became what we now call "the people's right to know."

The social responsibility model runs counter to what has come to be called the libertarian model of press behavior. The libertarian model denies that the press is obliged by government, obliged by readers, or obliged by morality to do anything. This concept of a free press says there is no such thing as the "people's right to know" principle; its adherents say that if there is a right to have information, there must be a concomitant obligation to provide it, an obligation that they do not recognize. The libertarians argue that the First Amendment guarantee of "no law . . . abridging freedom of speech, or the press" means exactly what it says. Government cannot control what journalists write, according to the libertarian argument, but neither can the readers demand coverage of, say, a city council meeting instead of a feature story about a new ice cream parlor.

How are we to resolve this dilemma? Any effort to curtail press freedom is dangerous, yet surely Madison and the rest of the founding generation had more in mind when they invented this government than simply encouraging press barons to get filthy rich with unlimited pandering. This much is clear. The First Amendment was written, not as an end in itself, but with a purpose. Free speech may lead toward pleasure or individual self-fulfillment or any number of other good things, but in a political context, free speech has a clear and identifiable purpose: that of allowing democratic self-government a chance to work. Speech that fosters democratic self-government deserves greater protection than speech that does not.

However, there are enormous dangers in trying to insist that journalists be responsible—that they be fair, that they be accurate, that they be unbiased, and that they be complete. However laudable these goals, this question immediately arises: Who is going to do the insisting? Insisting connotes some power of coercion, and the only institutions in this country with coercive power are part of federal, state, or local governments. But the First Amendment exists expressly to prevent the government from controlling the press because the founding generation was sure that any such control would become corrupt with time.

One answer to the question of who should be insisting on high journalistic standards is that the push should come from the members, critics, and scholars of the profession. Should journalists police themselves individually or collectively? In *Existential Journalism*, John C. Merrill has argued that even though the Hutchins Commission came up with a laudable and reasonable concept of social responsibility, journalism must, in law at least, remain much closer to the pure libertarian model. The burden of responsibility must rest with the individual journalist, Merrill insists, because there is no one else with whom to entrust the awesome power of regulating what the press says and does.

However, there is a great deal of evidence that many print and broadcast journalists, left to their own devices, will do all sorts of irresponsible things—invade others' privacy for no good reason, pander to their readers' and viewers' baser instincts with gratuitous violence and titillating sex, sound the public alarm when there is no fire, and a host of other sins. What should be done about this? Surely the members of the founding generation did not have all of this irresponsibility in mind when they were protecting the press—or did they? In fact, the press in the late eighteenth century was far more scurrilous than almost anything on the market today. Gentility in public commentary is a relatively new development, and the abuse that Jefferson and Madison had to put up with was far more hateful and vituperative than anything Bill Clinton has had to endure. It simply is not true that public discourse has deteriorated since the founders decided to stake the fate of their grand experiment upon the world's freest press. Yet, even if the abuse of public figures and the public trust, is no worse than it was two centuries years ago, the question remains: Is the greater good served by such irresponsibility?

One response would be to turn the question on its head: Would the public be better served by reining in the press? Presumably, some panel or board would be established to distinguish responsible from irresponsible journalism. In fact, such boards or panels have been tried from time to time with similar results. The most recent, the National News Council, was established in 1973 under a grant from the Twentieth Century Fund, as a way for journalists to monitor themselves. But it lacked the cooperation of many major news outlets, who said they feared that any institution designed to critique the profession could one day lead to an infringement of journalistic freedom. With such tepid support, the National News Council went out of business in a little more than ten years. However, one can see another potential threat to the news media's freedom in the reluctance of journalists to hold their colleagues to professional standards. Could not the reluctance of journalists to take on this task lead someday to a push by government to take on that job? Some newspapers have attempted to become more accountable in the past couple of decades by creating the post of ombudsman, or reader's advocate. These ombudsmen have often done a good job of investigating readers' complaints and taking staff members to task for failing to meet high standards. But their credibility has always been weakened by the fact that they are employed by the newspapers they critique.

Could an independent panel be set up in such a way as to make journalists more accountable to each other and the public without jeopardizing their freedom under the First Amendment? One could envision a council run by journalists, for journalists, that would not only praise the good and criticize the bad but would also play a role in helping the public understand how journalism works and why it does what it does. Unless journalists could be assured, however, that the opinions of such a council could not be used against them in court by plaintiffs in libel or privacy lawsuits, the council could well exert a chilling effect on hard-hitting journalism, and that would be a price too high to pay. The best cautionary note may have been sounded by the late Alan Barth, a longtime editorial writer for the *Washington Post*. "If you want a watchdog to warn you of intruders, you must put up with a certain amount of mistaken barking," Barth once wrote. "If you muzzle him and teach him to be decorous, you will find that he doesn't do the job for which you got him in the first place. Some extraneous barking is the price you must pay for service as a watchdog."

5

Objectivity: Is It Possible? Should We Still Try?

One of the most important concepts in journalism—and probably the least understood—is the notion of objectivity. The notion has honestly bewildered many and has been deliberately misunderstood and made into a straw man by many more. As part of the culture wars and the postmodern critiques sweeping America's college campuses in the last decade, many of journalism's critics have defined objectivity as something that approaches perfect truth and then dismissed the term so defined as an absurd idea. Because of the misunderstanding, many of objectivity's defenders have grown fainter in their praise. The 1987 iteration of the Code of Ethics of the Society of Professional Journalists considered objectivity a fine goal, but the tepid wording of the praise suggests language worked out by a committee. The new version of the code, adopted in 1996, does not mention the word at all. So in trying to explain what the term does and does not mean today to working reporters and editors, a little history of the term may help to turn down the heat and turn up the light.

The term *objectivity* and the notion of objective journalism came into common use in journalistic circles only in the 1920s. True, the notion of neutral reporting goes back another three generations to the early days of both the telegraph and press associations created by newspaper publishers looking to share the costs of distant correspondents. The modern ideas of neutral reporting, hard-news ledes[1] and inverted pyramid writing style did indeed get their start in the 1850s: When publishers had to pay for each transmitted word, flowery prose went out of vogue. When newspapers of very different political persuasions shared the cost of a

---

[1] In keeping with universal journalistic convention, I have used newsroom spelling of the term for the beginning paragraph of a story in order to distinguish it from *lead*, pronounced with a short *e*, which is the soft metal formerly used to put space between lines of type, and now, by extension, refers to that spacing.

correspondent covering distant events, for example, the Mexican War, a down-the-middle report had enormous advantages. And when telegraph transmission problems could interrupt a story at any point, putting the most important information at the beginning of the story was a prudent idea. But nobody called that objective journalism, even though, in today's parlance, objectivity certainly connotes neutrality and impartiality.

The term came into being just after World War I as a possible cure for the problems then besetting journalism. Briefly, three of those problems were rooted in society at large and a fourth within the news business itself. First, as the nation hurtled into the modern age, life, and especially government, were becoming bewilderingly complex. The period was called the Roaring Twenties or the Jazz Age, and it had a frenzied quality more familiar to the MTV generation than to those who grew up on *The Brady Bunch* and *Leave It To Beaver*. Governing by town meeting and firsthand knowledge of events was long gone, but increasingly, secondhand knowledge was inadequate, too. Major cities had a dozen papers with a cacophony of voices, and radio, the new miracle, exploded into the air and into America's ears seemingly overnight. In 1925, Walter Lippmann opened his new book, *The Phantom Public*, this way: "The private citizen today has come to feel rather like a deaf spectator in the back row, who ought to keep his mind on the mystery off there, but cannot quite manage to keep awake."

Second, growing mostly out of U.S. propaganda efforts of World War I, came a new profession, that of the public relations professional. Though press agentry dates at least to the 1870s and circus master Phineas T. Barnum, it was not until the 1920s that the profession came of age. Its leading light was Edward L. Bernays, who spent the war years in the Committee on Public Information doing propaganda and then emerged into civilian life to legitimize the willful manipulation of public opinion. Yes, Bernays noted, the United States was run with the consent of the governed, but that consent could be engineered or manufactured.

And third, Sigmund Freud and his successors in psychiatry had finally convinced the world that human beings were not nearly as rational as had been believed in an earlier age. The Enlightenment, the intellectual era in which the American system of government—and, with it, the American system of a free press—was born, had been eclipsed. The Freudians argued that the human psyche was buffeted by dark forces, unseen and unknowable, making it hard to trust any longer the vaunted American common sense. That which seemed reasonable might not be.

The combination of these three factors put at risk the most fundamental premise of American journalism and the American system of government: that well-informed people were capable of self-government. If the world was becoming, as Wordsworth had it, "too much with us; late and soon," and if public relations people were causing us to see things as their employers wanted them seen, not as they were, and if the mind was not so reasonable as had once been thought, how could journalists do their job?

As Professor Richard Streckfuss put it, "Objectivity was founded not on a naive idea that humans could be objective, but on a realization that they could NOT. To compensate for this innate weakness, advocates in the 1920s proposed a journalistic system that subjected itself to the rigors of the scientific method."[2]

The fourth problem, one that lay within the journalistic profession itself, was the sensationalism and emotionalism of the turn of the century, the period called "yellow journalism." It was the chicanery of the newspaper circulation wars, after all, that largely got the United States into the Spanish-American War. Then, as now, serious journalists looked at their day's version of *Hard Copy* and saw serious troubles ahead for the sovereign republic.

The answer Lippmann and others found was to borrow from the hard sciences. Many disciplines in the social sciences—political science, economics, sociology—were adopting the scientific method, so why not adapt the same approach for journalism as well? The entire philosophy that is embodied in the term *scientific method* cannot be compressed adequately into just a few words, but some of the most fundamental ideas can be. It relies on evidence, not conjecture; on testing, rather than guessing; and on concluding, rather than imagining. Under this system, metaphysical explanations may lead to faith, but scientific ones lead to understanding. This notion became literally carved in stone, in this case over the doorway to the University of Chicago's social science building, dedicated in 1929: "When you cannot measure your knowledge is meager and unsatisfactory."

As early as 1920, Lippmann wrote in his first major book, *Liberty and the News*, that the "basic problem of democracy" was trying to ensure accuracy and reason in the formation of public opinion. "Everything else depends upon it," he wrote. "Without protection against propaganda, without standards of evidence, without criteria of emphasis, the living substance of all popular decision is exposed to every prejudice and to infinite exploitation."[3] As the tabloids of the 1920s got more and more lurid, the serious papers became more and more wedded to the principles of objectivity, of relying first and foremost on verifiable fact.

The notion of objectivity in journalism survived into the 1950s, with Lippmann's vision becoming the standard orthodoxy. But then, two things happened that so profoundly shook the stolid principles of objectivity that forty years later there is still no consensus as to exactly what objectivity means and how hard journalists should strive for it. The first was Joe McCarthy, the junior senator from Wisconsin, who for five years terrorized the nation with claims of Communist infiltration in government and in the arts, in education and in journalism, in every facet of American life. McCarthy destroyed thousands of careers and lives as he

---

[2] Richard Streckfuss, "Objectivity in Journalism: A Search and Reassessment," *Journalism Quarterly* 67:973-83 (1990).
[3] Walter Lippmann, *Liberty and the News* (New York: Harcourt, Brace and Howe, 1920) p. 62, quoted in Streckfuss, op. cit. p. 978.

sought to expose Communists and their sympathizers and drive them out from hiding and into ruin. He never found a single Communist, but in the aftermath of the manic witch hunt that still bears his name, journalists realized that McCarthy had done terrible things and that under the rules of objectivity as they were then practiced, the reporters had been largely powerless to do anything but help McCarthy along. It had begun with McCarthy's famous speech in Wheeling, W.Va., in February 1950, in which he told a Republican fund-raising dinner, "While I cannot take the time to name all of the men in the State Department who have been named as members of the Communist Party and members of a spy ring, I have here in my hand a list of 205 that were known to the Secretary of State as being members of the Communist Party and who nevertheless are still working and shaping the policy of the State Department."

It was not true. McCarthy did not hold any such list because there was no such list. But under the rules of objective reporting, whatever a duly elected U. S. Senator said in a public place about matters of public importance was news. It met all the criteria. So what he said got reported. Some journalists tried harder than others not to assist McCarthy in his vicious smear campaign, but McCarthy was, by and large, enormously successful in getting all the publicity he wanted because most journalists felt they could not refuse to cover him without forfeiting their objectivity. Eventually, McCarthy fell, in part because the Republicans came to power and McCarthy became an embarrassment, in part because broadcasting's most influential journalist, Edward R. Murrow, finally attacked him on the air, and in part because television was emerging as a powerful medium and McCarthy looked positively demonic on television. But in the aftermath of McCarthy's wild five-year ride on America's news wires, journalists worried about whether the old rules of objectivity should still apply, and, if not, what should replace them.

The reporters had barely had gone beyond agreeing that it might be a good idea to demand evidence from speakers when there arose an even greater challenge to their notion of fairness and objectivity in journalism. The challenge was the beginning, in the mid-1950s, of the civil rights movement, which ushered in a generation of protests, street theater, and a host of other activities that made neutral reporting harder than ever before.

The biggest problem for journalists trying to cover the civil rights movement was the question of evidence. As it had evolved, the safest, and therefore most objective, information was that which was most fully verifiable. Typically, that meant written records, and written records are usually kept by people in power—legislators, police, and officials of all sorts. The heart of the complaints by those in the civil rights and later protests was that those in power were unfairly abusing that power. On one side was nearly all of officialdom, with all its records and all the trappings of power. On the other were people whose very complaint was that they were without those elements of power and legitimacy. Yet they maintained that they, too, were legitimate and that the rules were wrong.

Journalists responded to this challenge from outside the normal channels of power only fitfully. Made painfully aware of how badly they had been used by McCarthy on the right, they were wary of being similarly used by those on the left. Yet out of the civil rights and antiwar movements of the 1960s, most responsible journalists eventually came to believe that the old definitions of news, essentially unchanged for half a century, were inadequate. There *were* people, ideas, whole schools of thought that almost never crossed the threshold of newsworthiness. Out of this reexamination, the definition of news itself gradually expanded to include a much broader tableau than ever before.

Journalism has come a long way since the 1950s' brand of objective journalism, which was tantamount to coverage of the written record and the official word. That reliance of specific, narrow kinds of evidence had the advantage of accuracy, but it heavily skewed the journalists' depiction of the world toward those who wrote the records, who held the offices, and who had (or hired) the media savvy needed to deal effectively with reporters. Today, virtually every paper and station in the country devotes a great deal of time and space to topics that a generation ago were not considered legitimate subjects of news, to the have-nots along with the haves.

But once the notion of what constituted a legitimate subject for news inquiry was broadened, the notion of objectivity had to be redefined. Relying on the written record was still important, but it was no longer enough. Truth is still journalism's most important goal, but many now regard as naive the idea that truth in human affairs can ever be nailed down as solidly as it can be in the hard sciences.

Most journalists today do not believe that there is such a thing as perfectly objective Truth. Carolyn Lee, the former picture editor and now assistant managing editor at the *New York Times*, represents much responsible mainstream thought in saying, "You are never going to get a purely objective look at anything." Reality, she said, "is always in the eye of the beholder." Two reporters "can take the same set of facts and write two very different stories." Similarly, she said, two photographers will approach an assignment "with different eyes" amd will come back with quite different pictures.

Still, it is important to add quickly that this clearly does not mean that journalists quit trying to find that elusive ultimate truth. "Of course, we try to," Lee said, while still recognizing that it is impossible. That is where judgment is involved, she said, from both the reporter and the editor. The reporter makes choices, deciding which facts to include in the story and in what order to put them. The assigning editor also makes choices, not only about which stories to cover and which to ignore, but which reporters to send to which assignments. In making such decisions, Lee said, the journalist has to think: "Do I see this story as a feature or do I see it as hard news?" The selection of the writer assigned to a story will have a great deal to do with the eventual story that gets into the paper. "You're not going to tell me I am *wrong* if I see it as something humorous that needs a certain kind of writing," Lee said.

The reason to strive for total objectivity, even while recognizing that it may sometimes be impossible to attain, is that those who try to achieve objectivity will get closer than those who do not. Closer is better.

One of the greatest misunderstandings about objectivity is that it is bloodless, or mechanically balanced. Objectivity does not demand that reporters treat all sides of a story equally. On the contrary, it requires that they exercise their best and most honest judgment and then report stories from there, not from the dead center. Eric Severeid, a longtime reporter for CBS, first on radio and then on television, spoke during a retrospective on his late boss and mentor, Murrow, by saying, "Murrow always tried to be objective, but he could not always be neutral. There is a difference. To some stories," Severeid said, "there were not two sides, only a side and a half or a side and a quarter." Murrow, he said, "reacted accordingly, especially if the story concerned human justice."

Scott Simon, the host of National Public Radio's *Weekend Edition* and one of the nation's most highly regarded reporters by fellow journalists, essentially agreed with Severeid. "I have been outspoken about the terrible crimes that have been occurring in Bosnia. I don't think that it would give us any satisfaction to look back on it years from now and think that we were evenhanded about that," Simon said. "I think the real truth of the story is not evenhanded." Being objective "doesn't mean that you don't ask tough questions and that you don't report the other side," Simon said. But he added, "It is ridiculous to pretend that all sides of that question are morally similar. Is there another side to a massacre in Srebenica?"

Finding artificial balance—an opponent to every view, a naysayer for every advocate—is both easy and bad journalism, Simon said. In journalism, he said, "Too often we just get the tub-thumpers because they're the easiest to bump up against each other. The fact is, that's not really engaging the issue." He said it was "much more fair and rewarding to the audience to find moderates than extremists."

As Simon prepares a story, he said, "I like to look for people who have the strength of their doubts as well as of their convictions." Such people, he said, have things to say that the audience "can connect with and begin to run around in their own minds," which is much more rewarding than simply finding people "on opposite sides of the tub, thumping."

Objectivity does not mean indifference. Simon said, "I like reporters who care about things. I don't think you want a lot of people in this business who don't care about things or have no personal feelings for what they are doing." Professional training and practice will allow a reporter to account for personal feelings in the crafting of a story, Simon said, adding that "it is possible to be pretty open about my feelings and recognize that they are my feelings" and still report fairly and accurately the story at hand.

Simon's devotion to "journalism that comes from someplace and stands for something" does not mean abandoning reporting for advocacy. Indeed, it is in becoming advocates, or coming under the sway of advocates, that journalists wind up losing a great deal of their power and influence. The famous case of the NBC

Dateline story involving the exploding GM pickup truck (see Chapter 24 for a detailed examination of the issue) is a classic example, according to Michael Gartner, who was president of NBC News at the time, of a show that got too close to a source.

This by no means suggests that journalists are not interested in exposing corruption or uncovering injustice. "I'll rake the muck and revel in it, take great pleasure in doing it," Gartner said. "But after I've raked it up, then somebody else takes over. Maybe it's the editorial page, maybe it's the citizens. Maybe it's the sheriff." And he said, "Maybe it's nobody. Maybe the citizens say, 'That's OK.'" So that is also OK with Gartner; he is an editor, he pointed out, "not a king."

Part of the running debate on objectivity deals with the journalist's role in the community. Up until the turn of the twentieth century, major newspapers were deeply and often passionately involved with the cities and towns in which they were published. William Randolph Hearst's *New York Journal* and Joseph Pulitzer's *New York World* were prime examples of news organs dedicated to improving the lives of their home cities. But after World War I, when the new notion of objectivity became dominant, such conscious involvement began to be suspect in the eyes and minds of most thoughtful journalists. It began to be seen as boosterism, as something that threatened to turn reporting into cheerleading. Journalists began to keep their distance, and then greater distance still, in an effort to find a neutral vantage point from which to report the matters of interest and importance to a paper's readers.

By the late 1980s, there was something of a backlash as some editors began saying that news outlets had gone too far in distancing themselves from the cities and towns they served. Editors, including many in the Knight-Ridder chain, began to argue that objectivity had become confused with indifference and that journalists had not only a right but a duty to take a much more active role in their communities, including ferreting out social issues and helping to solve them. The journalism industry seemed to approve of this trend toward civic journalism, awarding a Pulitzer Prize in 1994 to the *Akron (Ohio) Beacon-Journal* (a Knight-Ridder paper), for organizing a series of forums on improving race relations in that city.

Some historians noted that this sort of civic involvement had a long history—the base on which the Statue of Liberty rests, for example, was built with nickels and dimes sent in by readers of Pulitzer's *New York World*. But while many editors were busy reinventing their connection with their readers' world, some editors of small dailies and weeklies saw something amusingly familiar: Many a metro daily was doing (or coming back to doing) what the editors of the smaller papers had never quit doing. In the essay that follows, Professor Jock Lauterer, a veteran editor and publisher of successful community newspapers and now associate professor of journalism at Penn State University, draws parallels between what the big-city newspapers are doing and what people like him have been doing all along.

WHO'S ON FIRST: A COMMUNITY JOURNALISM PERSPECTIVE ON THE CIVIC JOURNALISM DEBATE*

There is a growing consensus among news media professionals and journalism educators that civic journalism—like it or not—is the most thought-provoking to occur to the media in years. Indeed, civic journalism (sometimes called public journalism) may be new and exciting to the people working at big-city papers. But what about the rest of the industry, the 97 percent of papers in the United States with circulations of fifty thousand and under—the small newspapers of this country? Many small-town publishers, editors, and reporters are wondering what civic journalism means for community journalism, the distinct "local first" style of journalism practiced at thousands of newspapers in towns most people have never heard of.

Perhaps the most constructive dialogue focuses on the relationship between community and civic journalism. How are the two practices alike? How are they different? And, in the tradition of the green-eyeshade-city-editor litmus test: So what? And who cares?

First, what constitutes "community?" What is community journalism? And what is civic journalism?

Geographically, a community can usually be defined as a small contiguous population center where individuals feel cherished as individuals, share core values and social mores, and possess a highly defined sense of place and a strong civic identity.[4] Philosophically, community can also be said to exist, regardless of geography, when people share an intellectual or professional orientation, ethnic background, religious persuasion, or even sexual preference. Thus, affinity groups (the Polish-American community, the academic community, the gay-lesbian-bisexual community) can be called communities.

People crave acceptance and inclusiveness; they want to be part of a real community, a place with a strong civic identity. They want to be recognized, valued, heard, and affirmed in the context of their hometowns. According to community development consultant Danielle Withrow, American citizens of the '90s have come to insist that home must be more than Exit 45.

Although it is difficult to define a community newspaper by circulation numbers alone, a useful yardstick has been provided. The American Society of Newspaper Editors draws the line in the sand between large and small newspapers at the 50,000 circulation mark. According to the *1996 Editor & Publisher Yearbook*, 84 percent of the nation's 1,533 daily newspapers are classified as "small newspapers" by ASNE. Of those 1,287 papers, 82 percent (1,061 papers) have circulations under 25,000. In addition, there are 7,437 weeklies with an

---

* Written for this volume by Jock Lauterer
[4] Beittel, K. *Zen and the Art of Pottery.* (New York: Weatherhill, 1992), p. 27.

average circulation of 7,600. So community newspapers are reaching 56.7 million readers—an all-time high.[5]

In terms of numbers, small newspapers dominate the industry. The overwhelming majority of them can be considered community newspapers by virtue of their fundamentally reciprocal, and at times synergistic, relationships with their host communities. Community newspapers throw much of their news and editorial weight behind providing local coverage and bringing the news home by finding the significant local angles in national and international stories. They also embrace their civic role by recognizing their public mandate to promote the general welfare of the community. The finest community newspapers recognize and accept this veritable covenant with their towns: that they are key stakeholders and players in the forces that help build and celebrate their communities.[6]

Writing for the ASNE spring 1996 convention in Washington, D.C., Rick Thames, the public life editor of the *Charlotte Observer* says, "Public journalism (or civic journalism) essentially means equipping readers with what they need to be responsible citizens." Therefore citizens become the primary stakeholders in the newspaper's news judgment. Citizens ("ordinary people," i.e., nonexperts) are invited to become involved with the story content of the paper through focus groups and community conversations. The focus of the reporting on any given issue becomes nonconfrontational and positive as the paper seeks to become part of the solution, or at least to keep the dialogue open until the problem is solved. Civic journalism is often issue driven and involves partnerships between media outlets. An example can be found in Seattle: Dissatisfied with the adversarial, horse-race-style news coverage typical of the early '80s elections, the *Seattle Times* teamed up with National Public Radio stations KPLU-FM and KUOW-FM and television station KCTV to tackle a 1994 election project called "The Front Porch Forum." Civic journalism, often called "the journalism of inclusion," is most often practiced under that name by large newspapers, those with circulations above fifty thousand.

Civic and community journalism are alike in that both share a perception or even a vision of their NDM (newspaper-designated market) not as a market or a city—but rather as a Community in the spiritual, intellectual, and philosophical sense. For most big-city newsrooms, that amounts to a paradigm shift; for most community newspapers, that's the way it's always been.

"We're all in this together," the managing editor of the *Binghamton (N.Y.) Press*, Martha Steffens, said to a gathering of civic journalists and journalism professors at the 1996 Association for Education in Journalism and Mass

---

[5] *Facts About Newspapers*. (Reston, Va.: Newspaper Association of America, 1994), p. 21.

[6] Lauterer, J. *Community Journalism: The Personal Approach*. (Ames, Iowa: Iowa State University Press, 1995), p.5.

Communication's annual convention. Though she was speaking of her newspaper's civic journalism project dedicated to solving the Binghamton area's economic crisis, Steffens could have been addressing the entire newspaper industry.

The *Charlotte Observer*, a Knight-Ridder newspaper with a circulation of roughly 240,000 in a city of 340,000 people, is not a community newspaper by this author's standards, yet with the 1994 landmark public journalism project "Taking Back Our Neighborhoods," the *Observer* shed its detached perspective, got out of the newsroom and into the community, and became involved with residents in a way very familiar to community journalists. Thames wonders about public journalists "treading the slippery slope" of becoming too involved.[7] Quality community journalists, too, spend much of their time negotiating that slope, constantly gauging the proper balance.

At smaller community newspapers, this dance along the edge is made even more treacherous because of economic considerations. Even as far back as 1948, Frank E. Gannett recognized this ethical conundrum, saying, "The independent community newspaper has two incentives: to promote the general welfare and to make money. Like the physician, it [the newspaper] must be more concerned with the good that it does."[8]

Community journalists, by virtue of their natural proximity to their communities, do not have the luxury of what Jay Rosen calls "the illusion of themselves as bystanders." Any community journalist worth his or her salt would agree with Rosen when he asserts that such a perspective would be "devastating."[9] In community journalism, that detached attitude amounts to a death wish. "Stories generate immediate feedback," says Fran Smith, editor of the *Island Packet* of Hilton Head, South Carolina. "Knowing that we will face our sources and our subjects at the grocery store or in Town Hall or at the charity committee meeting helps keep us honest and fair."[10]

In the best cases, the conscientious community newspaper naturally practices many of the tenets of civic or public journalism. There are those who feel that the

---

[7] Thames, R. "Public Journalism: Some Questions and Answers." Hand-out accompanying session on public journalism at the ASNE annual convention, April 16, 1996. Washington, D.C., pp. 1-3.

[8] Freedom Forum. 1992 Calendar. Quote attributed to Frank E. Gannett, 1948.

[9] Rosen, J. *Getting the Connections Right: Public Journalism and What it Means to the Press*. (New York: The Twentieth Century Fund, 1995).

[10] American Society of Newspaper Editors. *Thinking Big About Small Newspapers*. (Reston, Va: Small Newspaper Committee of the American Society of Newspaper Editors, 1993) p. 3.

finest community newspapers have been doing civic/public journalism all these years at the grassroots level, quietly and without fanfare.[11] Here are some examples:

■Reporters at the *Daily Courier*, a 10,000-circulation daily in Forest City, North Carolina, write weekly personal editorial columns. The editor, Ron Paris, says this is done partly as a way to stay connected, open, accessible and human to the readers.

■The *North Hills News Record*, a 17,000-circulation Gannett community daily published just north of Pittsburgh, assigns to each reporter a "reader advisory group" that meets occasionally with the reporter to provide honest feedback. The executive editor, Rich Leonard, says this sort of accountability, or "strategic ascertainment," helps the newspaper focus on the real issues facing the community.

■The *Tryon (N.C.) Daily Bulletin*, a quarter-fold newspaper whose nickname is "the World's Smallest Daily Newspaper" and whose motto is *Multum in Parvo* (much in little), held a town-meeting-style forum titled "The Role of the Newspaper in Our Community: Spectator, Reporter, or Cheerleader?" The forum was cosponsored by the chamber of commerce and the local community college and was covered by the local National Public Radio station. Afterward, when the *Bulletin*'s editor-publisher, Jeff Byrd, was told that he had just practiced civic journalism, he said he was unfamiliar with the term.

■Cecil Bentley, the former Milledgeville, Georgia, *Union-Recorder* editor and currently the top editor of the *Macon (Ga.) Telegraph* sees that close contact as an advantage when it comes to reporting on issues and concerns. Bentley says working at a community newspaper provides "an opportunity to have an impact on the community. People see me as being involved with their concerns. At a small newspaper, you have the luxury of closely following and reporting on those issues. I think the public enjoys the connection they have with a community paper—a relationship that probably is not as strong at bigger newspapers."[12]

Perhaps it is this untethered relationship at many larger papers that helped bring about public journalism. Author Arthur Charity suggests that a "widespread professional dissatisfaction" led to the "grass-roots reform movement known as public journalism." He describes editors and reporters as becoming "increasingly restless with a style of journalism that just didn't seem to work."[13] But many successful community journalists would cheerfully take Charity to task over his blanket claim that no journalism is working.

---

[11] Stiff, C. Untitled abstract accepted for presentation to the Huck Boyd National Center for Community Media and National Newspaper Association Symposium on Community Journalism, Nashville, Tenn., March 20, 1996), pp. 1-2.

[12] American Society of Newspaper Editors, *Op. Cit.* p. 6.

[13] Charity, A. *Doing Public Journalism*. (New York: Guilford Publications, 1995), p.1.

Indeed, much of the discussion about public and civic journalism seems to begin with the unquestioned negative premise that something drastic is needed, in the words of Professor Carl Sessions Stepp, "to jump-start a tired industry,"[14] which, by inference, also includes community newspapers.

One of the founding fathers of public journalism, James K. Batten, took a more positive and therefore more useful spin on newspaper people of all walks. Writing in *Editor & Publisher*, Thomas Winship quotes Batten's words to his flagship paper, the *Miami Herald*, "I think it's good that our people realize it's not enough to just lay out the wickedness of its world . . . that they're also asking, How can I help my community? How can I help it do a better job?"[15]

Helping one's community is one of the pillars of community journalism. In his book on public journalism, Davis "Buzz" Merritt says that "helping public life go well" becomes a moral imperative for the newspaper, be it a community, civic or public newspaper.[16]

Merritt's basic tenets ("mental shifts") are so accessible and plainspoken that they provide philosophical sustenance for all public, civic, and community journalists alike:

It moves beyond the limited mission of "telling the news" to a broader mission of helping public life go well, and acts out of that imperative.

It moves from detachment to being a fair-minded participant in public life. . . . Its practitioners remember that they are citizens as well as journalists.

It moves from worrying about proper separations to concern with proper connections.

It moves beyond only describing what is "going wrong" to also imaging what "going right" would be like.

It moves from seeing people as consumers—as readers or nonreaders, as bystanders to be informed—to seeing them as a public, as potential actors in arriving at democratic solutions to public problems.

It would be easy to assume that civic or public journalism is the larger papers' spin on what the best and most forward-thinking community papers have done all along: keeping their doors open—both philosophically and physically— de-emphasizing conflict and political minutiae in news coverage, stressing problem solving and reader involvement, and keeping a weather eye on the larger picture of community change and growth. The better community papers have historically and naturally embraced their reciprocal relationship between their community (their

---

[14] Stepp. C.S. "Public Journalism: Balancing the Scales" *American Journalism Review* (May 1996), pp. 38-40.

[15] Winship, T. *"Jim Batten and Civic Journalism"* Editor & Publisher (April 1995) p. 32.

[16] Merritt, D. *Public Journalism & Public Life: Why Telling the News is Not Enough.* (Hillsdale, N.J.: Lawrence Erlbaum Associates, 1995), pp. 113-114.

public) and their mandate to provide coverage of civic and public affairs that is bold yet benevolent, success oriented and positive without pandering.[17]

Many community newspaper editors are grinning inwardly as they watch their big-city cousins strain to play catch-up. In the July/August 1996 *American Journalism Review*, Joe Meyer, a managing editor for twenty-one suburban weeklies around Columbus, Ohio, chuckles over "dailies' efforts to reconnect." Meyer is quoted as saying, "I get a real kick out of public journalism because that's what we do all the time."

However, "it would be a mistake to assume that all community newspapers are doing civic journalism," says John Neibergall, the executive director of the Huck Boyd National Center for Community Media at Kansas State University. But he agrees with the assertion that the basic tenets of quality community journalism and civic journalism are more alike than different. Both are dedicated to what Neibergall calls "community building through community journalism."

Cy Porter, writing in the Radio and Television News Directors Foundation reference booklet *Community Journalism: Getting Started*, argues that quibbling over labels is silly and counterproductive. Porter says, "Choose what name is most comfortable for you, but civic, community or public journalism is more than 'plain old good journalism.' This style of journalism not only enables you to provide your audience better coverage, but also opens an important community dialogue and creates a forum to help solve the day's pressing issues."[18]

To the credit of civic journalism, its intellectual architects have successfully and succinctly articulated the values and tenets of their discipline (in a way that community journalism advocates might learn from), thus raising to the level of a national discourse a meaningful and lively discussion about values in journalism across the board. The recent rapid growth of civic journalism has thrust community journalism into the national spotlight. In reinventing themselves as newspapers primarily dedicated to their communities' public interest, those major metro dailies practicing civic journalism are paying tribute to the good works of thousands of dedicated, involved, and conscientious community-newspaper people nationwide.

But there continues to be the nagging question of motives. Many major metro dailies seem to be turning to civic journalism for external reasons (declines in circulation, the success of nearby competing community papers, and/or orders from corporate headquarters). On the other hand, most community newspapers practice their style of journalism for internal reasons. The fire in the belly of community journalism is best captured in the motto of the *(McComb, Miss.) Enterprise-Journal*. Below the newspaper's nameplate each day is found this forthright declaration of interdependence: "The one newspaper in the world most interested in this community."

---

[17] Lauterer, J. *Community Journalism: An Instructor's Guide.* (Ames, Iowa: Iowa State University Press, 1996), p. 12.

[18] Porter, C. "Community Journalism: Getting Started." (Washington, D.C.: The Radio and Television News Directors Foundation, 1995), p. 1.

Civic journalism and community journalism are two leaves on the same branch—alike, yet distinct. One is new (scholars generally agree that civic journalism's birth can be dated to the late '80s), and the other has been around for a long time. Community journalism, exercised by conscientious professionals at high-quality, enlightened newspapers, is the obvious historical antecedent to civic journalism. The executive editor of the *Beaver County (Pennsylvania) Times*, Denny Dible, says, "Community newspapers had the answers when big city papers were still asking the questions."

To carry it one step further: community journalism is civic journalism in its original, natural, grassroots state. "These things were happening organically before someone at NYU wrote a paper about it," David Boardman, the regional enterprise editor of the *Seattle Times*, wrote in a journalism convention paper in 1996.

However, engaging in endless turf wars about who came first appears about as comical as Abbott and Costello's "Who's on First." It is time to get on with the good work of both community journalism and civic journalism: enhancing, enriching and empowering the lives of citizens so they may actively engage in public life and the maintenance of a free democratic society.

. . .

Note that not everybody is on board this train. Many are wary of editors and publishers taking strong activist roles in their communities. Especially in a small town, the editor is apt to be the publisher as well, and a prominent member of the business community. It is by no means universally held that what is good for the chamber of commerce is good for the community.

But that potential for bias aside, others argue that it is simply not the job of a newspaper to lobby for changes or to try to figure out what a community really needs—at least not on the news pages. Rather, these journalists say, the job of a newspaper is to cover a community, to provide citizens with information, and to let those citizens decide what to do. Lisa A. Abraham, an outspoken reporter who spent more than three weeks in jail rather than testify before a grand jury (see Chapter 18), sees civic journalism as a profound violation of the professional distance—the objectivity—that she believes is necessary for honest journalism.

"To me, it is absolutely wrong that reporters would be willing to sacrifice their objectivity, whether for a good cause or not," she said. "When it comes right down to it, who's going to decide what's a good cause?" Beyond establishing world peace and ending hunger, she said, "It gets all very muddy and all very local and all very political. It becomes the charity that my wife is pushing, or the publisher is pushing."

Gartner, who is now editor and co-owner of the *Daily Tribune* in Ames, Iowa—exactly the sort of small-town daily Lauterer talks about—agrees with Abraham. The chief purpose of newspapers is to inform, not to persuade or to solve problems, he said. "There is a reason that newspapers are named the *Chronicle*, the *Mirror*, the *Tribune* or the *Herald*," he said, "not the *Conciliator*, and not the *Feel Good*."

6

Privacy: How to Balance It against the Right to Know

There is no area in contemporary journalism that bothers students, and probably most other readers as well, as much as the journalist's apparent willingness to invade other people's privacy. Many believe that they see in journalists a cavalier attitude toward the sensibilities of those they write about, an indifference to—or even real pleasure in—the embarrassment and pain they cause with their probing questions, their intrusive microphones and harsh lights, their willingness to print and broadcast names and addresses and all manner of intimate details of people's lives. The question of privacy, therefore, is well worth exploring at some length.

First, it is important to recall that a free flow of *some kinds* of information is clearly and unambiguously in the public interest and essential to democracy. Most certainly, this includes the public behavior of public officials, which means the debates, hearings, votes, committee meetings, and all the other activities involving representatives of the people, who have been hired with the people's money to perform the people's business in their name and for their good. While this seems obvious, there are hundreds and probably thousands of times every year in large and small governmental bodies all across the country in which government officials try, sometimes successfully and sometimes not, to meet in secret to do the public's work. When they are caught, these public officials usually offer one of two explanations—that what they were doing was not really the public's work and therefore none of the public's business, or that there was some principle of privacy that they say should trump the right to a free flow of information. Journalists tend to view these claims of privacy superseding public access with extreme suspicion. This question of access doubtless contributes to the unease and mistrust between reporters and public officials.

There is a second category of information, which people clearly do not need to have in order to govern their own lives. Information about private citizens maintaining their own affairs in private, bothering nobody and endangering nothing, is certainly not essential to an enlightened citizen. Whether your neighbor collects stamps or coins is really no business of yours. The Supreme Court has ruled that individuals have a right to be left alone, to live their lives as they choose without the prying eyes of their neighbors poking into their affairs, as long as their affairs do not bother or interfere with others. In a seminal 1890 argument on privacy, Louis D. Brandeis, then a young man who was to become a Supreme Court Justice, and his law partner, Samuel D. Warren, laid out the case that the Lockean notion of the natural right to life had, over time, grown to include not only the right to live life, but to enjoy it, including the right to be left alone. In their argument, which has become the touchstone of the privacy debate, they expressly excluded from the right to privacy material that was in the public or general interest.

That phrase—"in the public or general interest"—is the key to dealing with the great third category of information, those things that are not clearly public but not clearly private either. The word *interest* here does not mean the mere satisfaction of curiosity. It is stronger than that. It means "claim" or "stake," as in to have an interest in a company. What if the neighbor down the hall or across the street moves from collecting stamps and coins to collecting poisonous snakes or tarantulas, something that may well affect the neighbors if the collection were were to get loose? Does the right to privacy still trump the citizen's right to know? In another form, this idea of general interest is at the heart of the debate over the recent wave of state legislation—the so-called Megan's laws—that require that neighbors be told when people convicted of some kinds of sex offenses move into their neighborhoods. Are the records of the offenders their own business because they have paid their debts to society and should be allowed to resume normal lives? Or are those records the neighbors' business —is it in their interest to know about them—because of the likelihood that sex offenders will repeat their crimes?

In another direction, political figures frequently claim the right to a private existence, one out of the public spotlight and away from reporters, with their notebooks and their cameras and their probing questions. Are public officials entitled to private lives? The answer, up until two generations ago, was a clear yes. It has become commonplace to note that President Franklin D. Roosevelt had to use a wheelchair or heavy leg braces because of the effects of polio, but that disability was rarely mentioned and almost never photographed. Perhaps more to the current point, we now know that many presidents have been unfaithful to their wives and that reporters did not write about those extramarital affairs even when they were fairly common knowledge among the press corps. It is inconceivable that journalists would behave that way today. What happened to cause the change? And, perhaps more important, are journalism and the commonweal it serves better or worse off for the change?

There are several causes for reporters' new, more intrusive attitude toward the off-camera lives of political figures. The first is rooted in press introspection after the infamous career of Senator Joseph McCarthy, the Wisconsin Republican who for four years in the 1950s parlayed his knowledge of journalism's professional standards into a cynical, but spectacularly successful, career of Red-baiting.

McCarthy understood and exploited journalists' traditional reluctance to cross over into coverage of a politician's private life. The McCarthy story is full of instances of reporters' knowing full well that the senator's public pronouncements, which they duly reported, were gross exaggerations and outright lies, but believing that they were powerless to do anything about it. McCarthy was an elected public official, after all, and he had made serious charges about suspected Communist sympathizers in the government. Reporters quoted McCarthy on what he said, even if they knew he was talking through his hat, because to do otherwise would violate the cherished goals of detached neutrality and objectivity.

A second factor is the coming of age of the professional political image maker, the spinmeister, the David Gergens and Michael Deavers of the political world, whose job it is to prevent genuine access to a key governmental official while projecting the public image of that figure most likely to curry favor with the voters. Although public relations as a profession goes back to World War I and a little beyond, it has only been since the Nixon administration in the late 1960s that political image making has reached high art. This is largely, though not exclusively, the result of the coming of age of television as the most prevalent source of information for most Americans. As recently as the Kennedy administration, reporters had regular, informal access to the nation's chief executive. But in part because of the deep suspicion Nixon held for the press and in part because of the growing unpopularity of the Vietnam War, Nixon put great distance between himself and the reporters who covered the White House. The result was what Daniel J. Boorstin has brilliantly described in *The Image:* the growing dominance of image over reality, the tightly controlled and professionally orchestrated pseudo-event coming to dominate the spontaneous genuine event. Unwilling to be full partners in this charade of politics-as-performance, many journalists have reacted by probing more, trying to get to the real person behind the façade generated by the spinmeisters and handlers.

The issue of the newsworthiness of sexual misconduct probably has at least one added impetus, the women's movement, which began in the late 1960s as one of several outgrowths of the civil rights movements of the previous decade. According to this argument, which has considerable merit, as long as a male-dominated society, and the male-dominated journalism fraternity, considered marital infidelity to be acceptable behavior, there was no need to report it. But once enough women began to demand respect as full-fledged human beings, then sexual promiscuity became more serious an offense against the public's sense of propriety.

Overall, the justification for poking around in the private lives of our public officials is fairly simple: Voters are asked to entrust extremely important things to the political system—their money, their children's education, the fate of the planet—and it is important that people know as much as they can about the character and judgment of those they are considering putting into office. Not all voters believe that a candidate's record of marital fidelity is germane to the ability to carry out official duties faithfully and with honor and integrity. Those who do not believe anything important is revealed in a candidate's marital record are free to disregard that record, just as other voters might discount a candidate's war record, and still others might vote for a candidate despite misgivings or disagreement on that candidate's stand on the progressive income tax or protection for old-growth forests. The point is that it is an absolute bedrock principle of democracy that fully informed citizens are capable of choosing for themselves whom they want to serve them in public office.

But, in truth, it is not issues that dismay the citizens, it is details of politicians' personal lives. This is not a direct result of journalists' losing their sense of decency and taste. A major reason that more politicians have been publicly vetted in the last generation than at any time before is due to a change in the major parties' methods of selecting candidates. Up until the 1960s, the major political parties went a long way toward selecting their standard-bearers without much input from the citizenry. As a result, philanderers and politicians with other embarrassing or costly bad habits were effectively, but quietly, kept from running for high office. But when popular voting replaced backroom deal making, the public began to learn of the sorts of candidates' foibles and shortcomings that the party bosses had known all along. The citizenry knocked, the door to the political back room opened, and the journalists walked in. If the door were to close again, if the political parties tried to reassert their right to select candidates for office outside public scrutiny and the primary system, would the republic be better served?

How often does it happen that good people feel driven out of politics because of either hard scrutiny or the prospect of hard scrutiny from reporters? We will never know, of course, about potential candidates who chose a different line of work altogether for fear of the disclosure of unseemly details of their past. However, the lure of political power seems to be strong enough that it takes a great deal to drive people from seeking public office. Besides, Americans are a forgiving lot, and they do not demand that their candidates be saints. During the 1992 presidential campaign, for example, then-candidate Bill Clinton as much as admitted a host of sins, including marital infidelity, avoiding the Vietnam draft, and smoking marijuana during his college days, and the voters elected him anyway and then reelected him four years later. Further, if there were something so unseemly in a candidate's past that its disclosure would keep that candidate from winning office, a strong case can be made that the sovereign voters have a right to know about it. The alternative is to argue that ignorance is better than knowledge. The political system has far worse problems than the fact that the voters know too much about the candidates. Those things that can have no bearing on a candidate's job performance have no business in the public eye, even if they are titillating. Journalists are supposed to be in the information business, not the pandering business. But the list of private vices that can have no conceivable relationship to public performance is a short one.

A related argument that has enjoyed considerable currency in recent years is that voters have become so cynical about their politicians that the whole system of citizen-run government is in danger of collapsing. If it is, what is the appropriate fix for the problem: more honorable politicians or less thorough and aggressive reporting?

What about private citizens who lead public lives, such as entertainers, sports figures, and other celebrities? Are they entitled to the same privacy afforded to the stamp collector down the block, or should they be subject to the same scrutiny that public officials get? This question is tougher, and there are doubtless occasions when the newshounds have gone overboard in chasing down reports and rumors of misdeeds. However, broadly speaking, the courts have held that celebrities are far more like officeholders than private citizens when it comes to journalists snooping around. The reasoning is that celebrities of all sorts—musicians, entertainers, athletes, and others—make their living from the public and that the public therefore in a sense employs them, just as it employs governors and presidents and police officers. Further, famous people can call news conferences to rebut accusations, whereas ordinary citizens could not draw a crowd of cameras and microphones on their name alone. Most journalists figure that celebrities voluntarily surrendered some of their privacy as part of the unwritten contract with the members of the public who pay their salaries through purchasing. This argument is weaker than the one for full disclosure concerning bona fide public officials; celebrities are typically afforded a greater measure of privacy than politicians, and rightfully so. However, if a movie star gets involved in off-screen advocacy of public policy, it seems reasonable to hold the star to the same level of scrutiny given full-time politicians.

More troubling is the question of the involuntary surrender of privacy rights. That typically concerns people involved with the criminal justice system, either as defendants or as victims. What is the justification for holding these people up to public scrutiny? They have neither earned our attention by standing for public office nor in any sense surrendered their immunity from inquiry by making a living from the public. The argument for making these people's names public against their will is weaker than that for politicians. In general, it rests on the principle that the justice system is an extremely important part of government and fully warrants our attention. An institution empowered to take away our liberty, and, in extreme cases, even our lives, is worth at least as much scrutiny as an institution that can take only our money.

But why, it may be argued, should we *identify* people, and go into full details of their backgrounds, addresses, and so on? In the case of defendants, there are two reasons. The first is for the good of society as a whole—good Millsian utilitarianism. Citizens deserve to know how well or how poorly the laws are being obeyed and what the state is doing to enforce compliance. Names make stories real in ways that little else can. The old journalistic axiom that "names make news" is true enough, but by itself the thought behind the aphorism could go either way; that is, it could apply to legitimate information that the public needs to know or could be mere pandering and titillation, a device to try to peddle a few more copies of the paper. The most legitimate reason to publish names of people in news stories is that names are the single most effective way to bring stories to life, to help readers understand and care about events going on around them.

A few years ago, the *New York Times* ran a story on the national abortion debate that illustrates this point well. The *Times* story dealt with the strategic decision of the leadership on both sides of the issue to create "poster children" of the abortion debate. Anti-abortion groups buttress their arguments with Gianna Jessen, a child born handicapped with cerebral palsy after her mother tried, but failed, to abort her late in the pregnancy. Jessen appears at anti-abortion rallies and gives testimony. Nancy Myers, a spokeswoman for the Right to Life Committee, was quoted as saying, "It means something when this really cute, outgoing teenager says she's not a lump of tissue, that this is what abortion is all about—real people." Jessen's adoptive mother, Diana DePaul, is quoted as saying that she and her adoptive daughter are out "to educate people. We're not out to sensationalize anything or raise anybody's ratings."

Abortion rights groups similarly add powerful personification to their side of the argument by including the story of Becky Bell, a seventeen-year-old Indianapolis girl who died from a botched abortion rather than tell her parents she was pregnant. For years after her death, her parents worked the lecture and interview circuits full time, putting flesh and blood and tears and pain into the story of the girl who died because she was pregnant and it was illegal to have an abortion without her parents' consent.

The second reason to identify suspects is for the protection of the defendant. The people of the United States have endured a good deal to avoid becoming a society in which the police can simply arrest people who are never heard from again. It may be embarrassing or worse to be identified in the paper as having been charged with a crime. But it would be far worse if no one knew of the arrest and thus could not rally to the defense. Stories abound in developing nations, and in poor urban neighborhoods in our own country, of people being picked up by the authorities and abused with impunity by their jailers because nobody on the outside knew of the incarceration. The tautology that the public's employees do the public's work best under the light of public scrutiny is never more true than in the area of crime. Also, there are numerous cases on record of private citizens reading of a criminal proceeding and coming forward to offer crucial information regarding the case, information prompted by recognition of the name of one of the people in the story.

Well, then, how about victims? Surely they have suffered enough without the embarrassment or inconvenience of being written up. And they have done nothing to warrant the attention. That is a powerful argument and, in many cases, has enough weight to carry the day. But there is substantial weight in the argument on the other side, which is based primarily on the journalistic value of fairness. If there are compelling grounds to use the name of the defendant, who, after all, is still presumed innocent, then fairness dictates using the name of the accuser as well. Journalists take seriously not only the First Amendment, which guarantees a free press, but the Sixth Amendment as well, which guarantees a public trial and the right to face one's accusers. If, as many journalists argue, it is part of the reporter's job to act as the eyes and ears of the public in places the public cannot go en masse, then a journalist's story should relate the most important details of what citizens who were actually in the courtroom saw and heard. On the face of it, that argument seems weaker than that dealing with other kinds of publicity, and, indeed, both law and journalistic practice have made numerous exceptions to the principle of full disclosure.

Names of defendants are usually withheld in two kinds of cases: those involving juveniles and those involving rape or other sexual offenses. In cases involving juveniles, the argument is that the potential harm to juvenile defendants by the publication of their names—which would presumably brand them as criminals in the minds of some people—outweighs the principle of full disclosure.

In sexual-assault cases, the argument is, again, that the victim will suffer unfairly by being identified. Many police departments and prosecutors have argued that the knowledge that a sex-crime victim would be publicly identified would prevent victims from coming forward. Thus, in the name of protecting privacy and of allowing the criminal justice system to work as well as it is able, most news outlets do not use the names of victims of sexual offenses. For many years, nearly every reputable news outlet adhered to this policy strictly. Most still do, although a handful of papers identify both the accuser and the accused. The *Des Moines Register* won a Pulitzer prize in 1991 for a series on a rape victim, Nancy Ziegenmeyer, which was printed with Ziegenmeyer's permission and cooperation.

Since the Des Moines case, a number of publications have altered their policies to allow for the use of the accuser's name if she (most victims of sexual assaults are female) agrees. That policy is not exactly fair, either, because it treats victims of this type of crime differently than it treats victims of other crimes, and it treats the accuser differently than it treats the accused, who, after all, would doubtless prefer not to be identified publicly as a sexual-assault suspect. But this compromise answers some of the complaints of unfairness in withholding rape victims' names altogether, while making an effort to address the principle of full disclosure.

A famous example in which the name of an accuser in a sexual-assault case was withheld at first, then published, is the 1991 case in which a Florida woman named Debbie Bowman accused William Kennedy Smith, a nephew of Senator Edward M. Kennedy of Massachusetts, with rape. The story generated massive coverage because of the connection with Senator Kennedy, who has been accused many times during his career of extramarital affairs, although never of sexual assault.

The name of the accuser in the Smith case was withheld, in accordance with normal practice, until NBC News identified her because Michael Gartner, president of NBC News at the time, believed that fairness demanded full disclosure, Gartner said in an interview. The *New York Times* used her name in a subsequent profile, saying it was pointless to withhold her name because NBC had already broadcast it. At the end of the trial, Bowman identified herself and went on talk shows to discuss her case. In thinking about whether NBC and the *Times* were fair in identifying Smith's accuser, consider this: Smith was, is, and probably will be for the rest of his life closely associated with Bowman's claim that he raped her on the lawn of the Kennedy compound in Florida. Yet the jury in the case acquitted him. Whatever actually happened that night, under the law there was no rape—Bowman is not a rape victim and Smith is not a criminal.

That raises perhaps the most powerful reason for reporting the name of the accuser in a sexual-assault case: the charge may be false. It might well turn out that she is not a victim at all. In that case, an anonymous person has been allowed to make the charge of sexual assault, surely one of the most serious charges anyone can make. Using the names of suspects but not accusers is either an acknowledged unfairness in terms of the equal application of Sixth Amendment principles, or it is a verdict in a case that has not been tried.

This is one of the most difficult conflicts in journalism, made more difficult by the powerful emotions that the crime evokes on all sides. As in any dilemma, there is no perfect solution, one that will fully satisfy all legitimate interests. But there is a middle ground that would, at least in part, address the concerns of all parties involved, Instead of identifying the accused from the very beginning and the accuser not at all, would it not be more fair to slice the identification question in another direction: to withhold all names until the matter comes to trial and then use the names of all parties to the case when they come out in open court. This solution provides some protection to the victim. When the story is a breaking police story and the scrambling for information is at its most frantic, and when stories are most prone to hyperbole, the woman's name would be withheld, as would the name of any suspect in case. But during the orderly proceedings of a trial, the press could act—with equal fairness to all—as the eyes and ears of the public, in full accordance with profoundly important principles of the First and Sixth Amendments.

Occasionally, a victim is identified, but other related information is withheld or left intentionally vague. Many newspapers and broadcast stations, especially those in big cities, provide only partial addresses for crime victims—the block the victim lives on, for example, rather than the precise street number. That is an imperfect compromise between conflicting principles. The principle of full disclosure argues that the public needs to know all about crime for several reasons. Some people will know the victim, or know of the victim, and wish to offer solace or comfort. An address distinguishes between people with similar or identical names. You need an address or description to know if the Mary Smith who got mugged is the same Mary Smith you see in church or at the P.T.A. meeting. Also, people feel entitled to know if muggers or burglars are more prevalent in certain neighborhoods or locations. On the other side, victims' advocates have argued that publishing the exact address of a crime victim, especially if the victim is an older person or lives alone, makes that person more vulnerable to another attack. Thus the compromise of publishing general addresses, rather than precise ones. Sometimes compromises in journalism turn out to be worse than either of the alternatives because they seek to find middle ground where none exists. However, in this instance, a deliberately imprecise address seems to satisfy the most serious objectives on both sides of the argument without serious harm to principle.

How much do the people involved in the story get to say concerning what is written about them? Some, of course. People can talk or not talk to reporters, as they choose. But journalists believe that they are entitled and even obliged to make independent news judgments without regard to the wishes of the individuals appearing in the story. Many people who get their names in the paper are not better off for the publicity. Some are significantly harmed, and that harm is certainly a serious reason to leave them out of a story. However, news outlets not only need to be fair, they need to be perceived as fair, which in this case means that readers and viewers need to believe that the reporter would do about the same thing next time if the circumstances were the same. Including a name in one story and leaving it out in another story of similar news value would help destroy the faith and trust that readers and viewers have in their reporters. For journalists to do the job for which their profession has been constitutionally recognized, their audience has to believe that they are telling the truth fairly and honestly.

In police stories of significant news value, therefore, the responsibility is to tell the story as accurately and effectively as possible. That usually means printing the names of the parties involved, along with other important details that provide the reader and viewer with the information they need to understand the story, both intellectually and emotionally. While embarrassment, or worse, on the part of those identified must be given weight, the stronger argument usually favors a free flow of information and having the news outlet do what it can to provide information and maintain credibility with readers or viewers. There is a price to be paid for living in any society. A society that favors order above all pays dearly in the loss of personal liberty. A society that values popular decision making pays substantially in economic and political inefficiency. And a society that values freedom pays in loss of privacy. This is not to say that journalists and others should not continue to try to draw ever better distinctions between what are appropriately public matters and what are legitimately private, but it must be acknowledged that as long as we value the freedoms of the American system, there will always be some loss of privacy.

7

How to Solve Moral Dilemmas: Balancing Competing Elements

Almost without exception, the interesting ethical decisions for journalists, as for everyone else, involve dilemmas, not mere problems or questions. A dilemma is a choice made difficult because both alternatives are unattractive. That is, in a dilemma, there is a downside to whatever choice one has to make, while a question or a problem may well have a clearly right answer and at least one wrong one. That is a point that even many serious journalism scholars often miss. The author of a recent article in *Journalism and Mass Communication Quarterly*, the most prestigious academic publication in its field, made this mistake in assuming that answers in ethical reasoning are like answers in arithmetic—that they are right or they are wrong.

The article recounts a much-discussed hypothetical situation: A television crew is covering a foreign war that involves the United States. On this hypothetical day, the crew is traveling with a patrol of the enemy of the U.S. forces when it comes upon an American squad and prepares an ambush. The question for the television crew is whether to warn the American troops or cover the ambush. In a panel discussion of the case broadcast on public television a few years ago, the ABC network news anchor Peter Jennings declared at first that he would warn the U.S. troops. Then Mike Wallace of CBS argued that the better choice would be to cover the story and persuaded Jennings to change his mind. Jennings agreed with Wallace that the television crew members had essentially already decided to be neutral observers when they first planned to travel with the enemy forces. Jennings said he had earlier "chickened out" in deciding to warn the Americans of the ambush. The *JQ* article argues that "both of these outcomes cannot be right. . . . At least one of them must be wrong."[1]

---

[1] H. Allen White, "The Salience and Pertinence of Ethics: When Journalists Do and Don't Think for Themselves," *Journalism and Mass Media Studies Quarterly*, 73:1 (Spring 1996), 26.

The point here is not to decide whether Jennings was right the first time when he decided to warn the Americans or whether Jennings was right later when he changed his mind and agreed with Wallace that the better course would be to cover the ambush. The real point here is that there is no clear right or wrong answer to the problem. For the warn-or-report problem is a true dilemma, that is, there are serious problems with both choices. The purpose of the exercises in this book is to work with the concepts of journalistic integrity and the other principles outlined in the previous section and determine what the arguments are each way.

Imagine an old-fashioned set of scales consisting of a vertical shaft on a stand or base with a crossbar attached on a pivot to the top of the shaft to form a capital T. A weighing pan is suspended on chains from each end of the crossbar. Put something in one pan and that pan goes down, raising the other pan. Put something heavier in the second pan and that pan goes down, raising the first pan, like kids on a seesaw. The way to work through an ethical dilemma is to identify the elements that go into each pan. For example, telling the truth is a substantial weight to go into one pan, the one labeled "publish." Avoiding embarrassing someone could go into the "don't publish" pan. The more familiar students or journalists are with the issues and the standards of the profession, the more comfortable they are in weighing out even complex choices and coming up with a decision that may not satisfy everyone, but can be explained and defended.

The reason no one can declare that warning the American troops is the right answer and photographing the ambush is the wrong answer, or the other way around, is that nobody can say with certainty how much each element should weigh in making the decision. Journalists are people, too, and they try to prevent harm when they can. But on the other hand, neutrality enables journalists to inform people about both sides in a conflict, and that neutrality would be jeopardized if journalists used the information they gathered from one side to warn the other side.

Determining the relative weight of each factor in the problem is up to the journalist making the decision. This is not to say that there are no standards at all and that any decision is as good as any other. The point of such documents as the Society of Professional Journalists' Code of Ethics is to spell out those basic concepts and principles that the profession has decided have considerable weight. The more familiar with the principles the journalist is, the more likely she or he is to put all the relevant weights in the appropriate pans and thus make a wise decision. Yet it remains true that two journalists of great intellect and integrity—Peter Jennings and Mike Wallace, for example—can disagree about how much weight to assign to one element or another. Reasonable people may disagree. That does not make one of them wrong.

What *is* wrong is when the journalist mimics the dishonest deli worker who puts a thumb on the scale, that is, who tries to influence the final outcome because of base, ignoble, or merely selfish reasons.

While each case that comes up has some elements to it that are unique, none is wholly original. So while each case must be weighed out on its own merits, the weighing process is not brand-new each time. Experienced thinkers, like experienced cyclists, find that much of what they do the tenth time, or the hundredth, is made easier by all the efforts that came before. Fortunately for those just starting out, journalists spend a great deal of time thinking about moral questions, weighing the pros and cons of each decision they make. And, because they are journalists, they tend to write down their thoughts, which means that there is a large body of thoughtful work by skilled writers available for study by those just starting out. Of course, what journalists have done in the past does not provide absolute marching orders for the present. Standards of taste and public morals change, technological advances bring new problems and new ways of solving old ones, and so on. But voyagers who refuses to look at any of the existing maps before starting out are bound to waste a great deal of time discovering many things that could have been easily known. They will probably also get thoroughly lost.

Thus, faced with any dilemma, the first question to ask is, What do we usually do in cases like this? Existing policy is not infallible, but it certainly counts for something. Consistency is a major element of fairness and, therefore, it takes more compelling reasons to do things differently than to do things the way they were done the last time this sort of problem came up.

The second question to consider is, What principles are involved in this case? Is privacy an issue? How legitimate a claim for privacy do the parties have? Are they innocent bystanders, or have some of them brought the attention on themselves through their own actions? Is there a public interest? Things that are important count more than things that are merely amusing. Things that are interesting fall somewhere in between. Is it newsworthy or is it pandering? Is it both? Gennifer Flowers's allegation of a longstanding affair with Bill Clinton is certainly interesting, but is it important?

The third question to ask is, Who wins and who loses? It is a blunt and unavoidable fact that almost anything a journalist does will benefit somebody and quite possibly harm somebody else. Monitoring the legal system to make sure it runs honestly and efficiently certainly works to the common good, but publishing the names of suspects certainly brings embarrassment to the suspects themselves, to their families, and often to others as well, the great majority of them completely innocent of any wrongdoing.

The fourth question to ask is, Is there a better way? If we usually provide addresses of crime victims to warn people where the dangers are, do we have to give the widow's exact address, along with the information that she lives alone and will soon receive a big insurance settlement? Maybe just a block number or a neighborhood will provide the necessary warning without telling would-be burglers the exact address of an easy target.

And last, ask, Do I have my thumb on the scales? Am I deciding the merits of the Gennifer Flowers story because I like Bill Clinton or because I dislike him? Do I think the school superintendent is incompetent because she expelled my child, or the child of a friend, for misbehavior? Many philosophers have come up with different models for tackling this sort of problem, but they all come down to this: Am I being fair and honest in assessing this case, or am I allowing my personal politics, my residence, my social or religious affiliation, or some other personal factors to distort my thinking?

Nearly all the case studies that follow present the dilemma of whether something should have been published or not. In evaluating them, think about which arguments you would put into the pan on the side for publishing and which would go into the pan on the side against publishing, and see which arguments carry more weight for you.

Part II

**Case Studies: Tough Calls
from the Front Lines
of Contemporary Journalism**

8

The Suicide of Admiral Boorda: Did the Press Hound Him to His Death?

On May 16, 1996, Admiral Jeremy M. Boorda, chief of naval operations, the top job in the U.S. Navy, got up from his desk in the middle of the day, abandoned the lunch in front of him, and abruptly announced that he was going to dine at home. He then went home, but, instead of eating, he took a .38-caliber handgun into his backyard, put the barrel against his chest, and pulled the trigger.

About the time he died, a *Newsweek* correspondent was entering the Pentagon to interview the admiral. He planned to ask whether Boorda had worn combat medals for valor that he may not have been entitled to wear.

Pentagon officials did not blame *Newsweek*, or ABC News, which also wanted to question the admiral on the medal story, but they did make it clear that he had left the Pentagon on hearing that the reporter was coming over.

According to published reports, Boorda left a suicide note addressed to the men and women of the navy, in which he said he had made "an honest mistake" in wearing the medals: two brass *V* for valor pins worn on top of rectangular service ribbons. But the error, he wrote, could have been misinterpreted and brought further embarrassment to the navy, which has been plagued in recent years by a series of scandals.

It is inconceivable that the prospect of a couple of interviews, even tough interviews with journalists questioning the admiral's integrity, could be wholly responsible for his suicide. Indeed, it was by no means certain that Boorda had worn the medals improperly, but there were legitimate questions. Boorda earned the ribbons, the Navy Commendation Medal and the Navy Achievement Medal, for serving on navy ships off Vietnam during two tours of duty, in 1965 and again from 1971 to 1973. The *V* pins are awarded to those who not only served in a combat theater, which Vietnam certainly was, but who also actually saw combat. Military researchers said there was no evidence that Boorda's vessel had ever been fired on, so he technically might not have been entitled to wear the *V* pins atop the ribbons.

But even this was by no means clear or universally agreed upon. For example, Admiral Elmo Zumwalt, who was chief of naval operations from 1970 to 1974, the time during which Boorda earned one of his ribbons, told the *New York Times* that Boorda was indeed entitled to wear the *V* pins because his ship had been in a combat zone during hostilities. Although Boorda's commendation for the ribbon underneath the pin did not specifically say he could wear the *V* pin, Zumwalt said that that had been an oversight that could have and should have been corrected. Other military brass disagreed and said that Boorda should have followed the letter of the commendation and not worn the *V* pins unless specifically authorized to do so. These critics said that at the very least, Boorda should have known he was technically not entitled to wear the *V* pins.

To civilians, the question of which ribbons may be worn with which pins may seem trivial, but to military personnel, it is not. The ribbons and medals that service personnel wear represent their résumés, and the military code of honor is fierce about questions of personal integrity. Boorda was the first navy officer to rise all the way through the ranks, starting as the lowest-ranking enlisted man and working his way up to hold the top job in the service. Top officers in the military have almost always seen combat (which is one of the reasons that women in the military seek combat duty—to make them eligible for promotion to the top ranks). Most have also either attended the Naval Academy at Annapolis or been through R.O.T.C. at college. Boorda, by contrast, was a high school dropout who lied about his age to enlist in the navy at the age of sixteen. Thus, Boorda's wearing of combat medals, if he was not entitled to them, could seem to his critics to be an attempt at something very close to fraud and, given his unusual path to the top, could, in some eyes, make him virtually ineligible for top rank.

There is considerable evidence that Boorda, even though technically not allowed to wear the medals, may have worn them for many years by mistake, an error he corrected as soon as he learned of it. The question about Boorda's medals had arisen nearly a year before the incident that precipitated his suicide. The National Security News Service, a small, privately financed research organization that examines military questions for news organizations, had raised questions about whether Boorda was entitled to wear the *V* medals in 1995. At that point, Boorda took off the medals and did not wear them again. Boorda's supporters, and there were many, cite this fact as evidence that he had made an honest error. Critics, of course, could charge that he took off the medals only when he got caught wearing them.

The question for journalists is, How much, if any, responsibility do the reporters bear for the admiral's death? Finding the answer is considerably more complicated than simply asking whether the medal story—whether any story—even if true, was worth a human life. In that equation, life is almost always more important. While it is difficult to say on a human level that one life is worth any more than any other, Boorda's death under those circumstances could hardly have come at a worse time for the service, which was struggling to polish its image and restore morale, which had been seriously tarnished after a series of scandals and embarrassments, including the infamous Tailhook sex scandal in 1991.

But the question is not whether the story was worth a life. To phrase the question that way would hardly be fair to the journalists working on the medal story. One must ask, instead, if there was anything about asking for an interview that a reasonable person would think could cause the subject of that interview to commit suicide? Probably not. Furthermore, journalists regularly ask questions, sometimes tough, embarrassing questions, in pursuit of legitimate news. That is their job, and they cannot be deterred from asking questions by threats of self-inflicted violence. If it were common practice for a reporter to quit asking questions when a reluctant subject threatened suicide, few tough questions would ever be asked, and important answers would never be found.

The real question is, Was there a story there at all? Especially in the context of the navy's recent problems, the very act of writing a story that raised questions about the medals would do the admiral harm and would do the navy harm. If the reporters had serious reason to believe that Boorda had been deliberately deceptive—had essentially lied about his war record—then it seems that they had both a right and an obligation to pursue the story. But if the reporters believed that Boorda had made an innocent error, which he had corrected a year before, then writing a story that even raised the question was irresponsible.

With a network and a major newsmagazine both on the story, and with all parties located solidly within the Washington beltway, there is more than a whiff of pack journalism to this story, and that has alarmed some critics, who maintain that the evidence seems clear that Boorda made an innocent mistake and did not deserve to be hounded for it. And Washington veterans are well aware that once a newsmagazine and a network get a story, especially a story involving some element of scandal, many more stories will be sure to follow from the competition.

It should be noted that neither *Newsweek* nor ABC had actually run their stories at the time of Boorda's death. They were still in the reporting stage. And, as later reporting on the Boorda incident made clear, the admiral had many other personal demons to contend with besides a *Newsweek* reporter. On balance, it is extremely difficult to argue that reporters should not only not write stories, but that they should not even ask questions in a case such as this.

The case is eerily similar to one involving another public figure being sought for questioning by journalists in 1988. The earlier case was in the other Washington—Washington state—and involved a local judge named Gary Little, who was based in Seattle. Little, standing for reelection as a King County Superior Court judge, seemed in many ways a paragon of civic virtue, with decades of community and local charity work in his background. Yet there were questions.

In 1985, Judge Little was transferred from juvenile court to tax court by the state Commission on Judicial Conduct after an inquiry into "unauthorized *ex parte* contact" (contact outside legitimate court proceedings) between the judge and several juvenile defendants then before him on charges. That inquiry was held in secret and its report was tightly sealed, but widespread rumors in Seattle's legal community had it that Little was coercing young male defendants into having sex with him by promising them lenient treatment from the bench. Little denied all wrongdoing and insisted that the "*ex parte* contact" was nothing more than a meal or hallway conversation.

At the time of Little's transfer out of juvenile court, KING-TV, Seattle's leading television station, ran a story featuring allegations of sexual abuse by several of Little's former students at the Lakeside School, an expensive private boys high school where Little had been a volunteer teacher in his early days in private practice in Seattle.

At the time, the state's statutory rape law specifically outlawed sex with girls under the age of eighteen but did not mention boys. Thus, even if the former students' stories were true, Little had not broken that law. The state law forbidding sex with minors has since been amended to include boys as well as girls.

Little's challenger in the judicial reelection campaign spoke in innuendoes, implying that the "dark rumors" about Judge Little's conduct as a juvenile court judge had made him ineffective on the bench and threatened the credibility of the whole judicial system. Finally, Little pulled out of the race, saying that he was retiring from public life and moving to San Francisco, where, he said, he would reenter private practice. He blamed his opponent—and the news media—for hounding him from office with no evidence of wrongdoing.

Reporters from both Seattle papers, the morning *Post-Intelligencer* and the afternoon *Seattle Times*, continued to dig for the story on Little's decision to leave the bench, looking for former juvenile defendants who could prove or disprove the "dark rumors." Eventually, the *Post-Intelligencer* conducted a final interview with Little, who again denied breaking any laws, but otherwise refused to talk about his relations with either his former Lakeside students or the young men who appeared before him in juvenile court. Little was told that a story citing allegations of molestation from his former students was scheduled to run in the next morning's paper. Little told a friend of his, a lawyer for the newspaper, that he would kill himself if the article ran, and the lawyer relayed that information to the news staff.

That night, at about 10:00 P.M., right at the start of the press run, Little went to his chambers, put the barrel of a large-bore handgun in his mouth, and pulled the trigger.

Here is his suicide note: "I have chosen to take my life. I had hoped that my decision to withdraw from the election and leave public life would have closed the matter. Apparently these steps are not satisfactory to those who feel more is required. So be it."

A close friend of Little's told journalists the next day, "He was not only driven into disgrace, but to death. He was tried out of court for suspicions about his sexuality."

Questions to Consider

1. Were the reporters in the Boorda case pushing things too far, giving too much importance to something that was in fact trivial but had the potential to cause Boorda and the navy much embarrassment? Were they looking for scandal at the expense of a man's reputation in order to get a juicy story that would serve no real purpose? Are the reporters in any way responsible for his death?

2. Both the Boorda and Little cases involved things that were over: Boorda had stopped wearing the medals a year before, and Little was leaving the bench. Does that mean those stories were no longer legitimate news? How much difference does the elapsed time make: What if Boorda had stopped wearing the medals three years before and Little had stepped down from the bench three years earlier? Explain your answers.

3. Do you see any other ways in which these stories could have been handled that might have lessened the possibility of suicide? Explain.

4. If journalists yielded to every suicide threat, we would soon be publishing only those things that upset no one. What should journalists' response be when someone threatens suicide because of a story?

9

The Haunting Profile of Meir Kahane: Should Past Sins Be Emphasized?

Just after World War II, *Time* magazine publisher Henry Luce organized and financed a major study of the American press that was designed to examine how well or how poorly news organizations were fulfilling their fundamental obligation to provide the sovereign citizens with the information they need. The study group is usually called the Hutchins Commission, named for its chair, Robert M. Hutchins, who was the chancellor of the University of Chicago. Among its many findings and observations, the commission concluded that journalists are not only obliged to report on newsworthy events, but also to put them "in a context that gives them meaning." The phrase is a deceptive one, for, half a century later, it sounds so logical and so easy, so appropriate and so obvious that one can hardly imagine any controversy surrounding it.

Yet most stories can be told in a wide range of contexts, and each context may give a whole new meaning. Take the death of Margaux Hemingway, a forty-one-year-old actress and model, at the beginning of July 1996. Following the discovery of her body in her apartment in Santa Monica, California, the obvious question for journalists was to explain how and why she had died. But in the weeks between the discovery of the body and an official coroner's report, nothing was certain. With no evidence of foul play and no suicide note, providing the needed context became an exercise in speculation. The question is not whether the facts presented as background were true, but whether they provided legitimate context, that is, gave the story not only meaning, but the correct meaning. One way to provide context would have been to note in the story that Hemingway was epileptic. That was true, and it could have explained her death. Another way would have been to explain that she was bulimic. Yet another would have been to note that she had a long history of alcohol abuse. All were true, all are possible medical explanations for her death, and all are well within the bounds of standard newsroom practice.

But many journalists put her death in another context, noting that Hemingway had only recently begun reading the work of her famous grandfather, Ernest Hemingway, and quoting friends who said she had been trying to come to grips with her family's history. Her family was rife with suicide, including that of her grandfather, who had killed himself on July 2, 1961. Thus the death of the younger Hemingway was almost on the anniversary date of that of her grandfather. These details provide a very different context. Without saying so outright, these stories about Margaux Hemingway's death implied strongly that the death was suicide.

Journalists have to deal with this sort of ambiguity all the time. One could suggest that in this case, journalists could simply have refused to speculate on the cause of death until the official report was released several weeks later. (The report did find that she had killed herself with a drug overdose.) However, journalists, whose primary job is to monitor the behavior of government, are properly skeptical of equating the official word with the perfect word. Even with all the documents imaginable and with firsthand confirmation of all of them, knowledge is imperfect. So providing meaningful context remains as much art as science.

An extraordinary and illustrative example of the question of appropriate context involves Michael T. Kaufman, who was for many years a reporter and columnist for the *New York Times,* and Meir Kahane, the founder and chief organizer of the militant Jewish Defense League, an organization loosely modeled after militant black power groups in the turbulent years of the late 1960s.

By 1971, the charismatic Kahane was a significant figure in militant Jewish politics, both in Israel and in New York City, and Kaufman, then a cityside reporter for the *Times*, spent several weeks reporting and writing a profile of him, which ran on January 24, 1971. That profile, about five thousand words long, began on the front page of the paper and filled nearly three-quarters of a page inside. In it, Kaufman wrote about Kahane's origins as the son of a highly regarded Talmudic scholar in Brooklyn, about Kahane's involvement with right-wing American politics, and about the magnetic qualities of Kahane's remarkable personality.

Kaufman also described Kahane's secret dual life as a rabbi with a wife and four children and as an ambitious writer and conservative political operative who adopted an Anglicized version of his name, Michael King, and maintained an apartment in a fashionable neighborhood on Manhattan's East Side.

About sixty column-inches into the story, Kaufman's profile contains this passage:

In June of 1966, while living as Michael King, Rabbi Kahane met a 22-year-old woman named Gloria Jean D'Argenio. The woman, who sometimes worked as a model under the name of Estelle Donna Evans, impressed Mr. King as "an unusual person." When on July 31, the woman jumped to her death from the Queensboro Bridge, the rabbi was profoundly shaken.

He attended her funeral in Connecticut and in the years after she died, he would sometimes place roses on her grave.

In early 1968, after he discarded the identity of Michael King and founded the Jewish Defense League, he established a charitable foundation in the woman's name.

Issues of the Jewish Defense League's periodicals advertise the foundation as an organization that sends money to needy people in Israel. So far, more than $200,000 has been distributed by it, Rabbi Kahane said.

Kaufman's profile then moves on to a discussion of a book Kahane wrote regarding Israel and Vietnam and does not mention the woman again.

But over the years, as Kahane became more famous and more militant, Kaufman worried about the profile and whether he should have written more, or more forcefully, about the young woman and about Kahane's relationship with her. Kahane was assassinated by a Muslim extremist in November 1990.

After the Hebron massacre in late February 1994, in which a follower of Kahane, a Brooklyn emigré named Baruch Goldstein, opened fire on a mosque full of praying Palestinians, killing twenty-nine people and wounding more than one hundred others, Kaufman devoted a column to the incident. It ran on March 6, 1994, under the headline "Remembering Kahane, and the Woman on the Bridge."

In the column, Kaufman recounted that he and Kahane had talked about D'Argenio, the woman who had jumped from the bridge. Kaufman had told Kahane that he had found the woman's former roommate, who had told the reporter that Kahane had proposed to D'Argenio but had then written D'Argenio a letter revealing his other life as a married man and breaking off their relationship. When the woman was pulled from the East River after jumping off the bridge, she had the letter from Kahane in her pocketbook.

In his column about the incident, Kaufman wrote:

I confronted the rabbi with what I had learned. He put his hand on my knee and said, "I loved her." He acknowledged everything. . . . He then began pleading with me not to publish the full account of this story. . . . He came to my office. He told me that writing about his affair would torment his ailing mother and inflict pain on his wife and his children. At one point, he promised that if I withheld the story, he would abandon public life.

In the column, Kaufman noted that he had mentioned the affair, but so discreetly that "some readers may have missed the point." There are two points here. One is that Kahane was married, yet he had an affair while living a double life. The other is that he had an affair with a woman who was not Jewish.

However, Kaufman wrote,

Years later, when racist supporters of the Rabbi's Kach movement screamed that their Israeli critics slept with Arabs or lived with shikses, [the Yiddish term for gentile women] I re-examined my choices and wished I had stressed the Estelle Donna Evans story more prominently. . . . Had I written more boldly, would the rabbi's credibility with his followers have lessened? Would young men like the then nineteen-year-old Baruch Goldstein have freed themselves from the rabbi's spell? Was that my job, to bring the rabbi down?

In an interview after the column ran, Kaufman described a remarkable ten-day period just before the original profile ran when he and Kahane "were locked in each other's minds," Kahane trying to manipulate what the story would finally say, and Kaufman trying to be thorough but fair. "I had a sense I had this man's life in my hands," Kaufman said. It was clear to Kaufman at the time, he said, that "I was in the presence of an exceedingly manipulative and evil person," but also a person who somehow wanted to be caught, including being caught in his affair with a gentile. "He wanted her to be discovered," Kaufman said. He said he recalled thinking, "Here is a man who looks for taboos and then violates them and then wants exoneration." Kaufman said he was convinced then, and remained so a quarter-century later, that the story of the affair was an important part of Kahane's life, that it revealed important dimensions about the human being behind the manipulative facade.

Kaufman's story about Kahane contains many moral issues for journalists, beginning with the fairly straightforward privacy question raised by Kahane's begging Kaufman not to include details of Kahane's affair on the grounds that it would needlessly hurt his wife and children. That question arises often, almost any time a journalist comes across embarrassing or damaging information about a newsmaker. The argument from the newsmaker may be that whatever the subject did is none of the public's business. Kahane might have argued, for example, that his girlfriend had nothing to do with his role as a leader of the Jewish Defense League and thus was none of the public's business.

According to this argument, the harm that would be done to Kahane would outweigh the good that the knowledge would provide because the knowledge of the girlfriend had no legitimate reason to be in the story at all. Next, if that argument does not persuade the reporter to kill the story or to kill that part of the story, the subject often argues that on grounds of human decency, the reporter should protect the subject's family, who, after all, did nothing wrong and who, this argument goes, should be spared the embarrassment of reading embarrassing things about someone they love. Kahane did use this argument, which carries more weight. Kahane's family had done nothing wrong, and they would certainly have been hurt by the disclosure. Journalists do not want to harm the innocent, so the reasons to publish must be strong if they are to outweigh such a consideration.

However, think what would happen if the don't-hurt-my-family argument routinely carried the day. Almost nothing negative would ever be written or broadcast about anyone, and journalism would be abdicating its most profound obligation, which is to monitor the behavior of public officials. While Kahane was not an elected public official, he clearly met Cato's or Wortman's standards for public scrutiny because Kahane thrust himself into the public consciousness, and his behavior was of both interest and importance to the citizenry. To go along with a public figure's plea to say nothing damaging on the grounds that it would embarrass an innocent family member would be to yield to a form of journalistic blackmail. Although it may sound callous, it is Kahane's affair with the young woman, not Kaufman's reporting, that was the real cause of the pain and embarrassment to Kahane's family. It is Kahane, not Kaufman, who bears the responsibility for it. Kahane was certainly not a media naif—he was an expert manipulator of journalists for his own ends.

Does this mean that whatever happens, the journalist bears no responsibility? Not at all. Journalism is a powerful institution and what journalists do has profound consequences, for good and for ill. Kaufman did bear some responsibility for the pain that Kahane's family suffered as a result of the story, and had he played the affair more prominently, and therefore caused more pain, he would have borne greater responsibility still.

Yet Kaufman was haunted by the possibility that by playing down the extramarital affair, he inadvertently bore some responsibility, however obliquely and indirectly, for the massacre at Hebron. That seems unduly hard on Kaufman, yet the Kahane story serves as a reminder that most of the time, the results of our behavior are unknowable. To provide truthful and complete information about a legitimate subject of news is the journalist's primary obligation. If something bad happens as a result, the journalist bears some responsibility, but not nearly so much as if something bad happens because the journalist deliberately withheld information.

There are other dimensions to Kaufman's story as well. One is his observation that there may be some things that daily journalism simply cannot do. Kaufman echoed what Walter Lippmann reminded his readers of in *Public Opinion* back in the 1920s: Journalism simply cannot do everything, even in the hands of the most skilled and gifted reporter. "I felt I had met my Dostoevskian figure. I don't know if journalism can deal with Raskolnikov," Kaufman said, referring to the haunting central character in Dostoevski's *Crime and Punishment*, who was driven to break all the taboos and then seek atonement for them. Kaufman's point about this extremely complex and highly nuanced literary figure serves as a useful reminder that journalism, even at its absolute best, is not a substitute for all other learning.

Finally, and most chilling, is a point that Kaufman mentioned in the interview, but one he did not bring up in his column. "The only thing I liked about him was that he loved her," Kaufman said. "He really loved her. Do you destroy a man with the one thing you like about him?"

Questions to Consider

1. Did Kaufman make the right decision on how to handle the information about D'Argenio, the woman who killed herself, in the profile of Kahane? Why or why not?

2. If a reporter encounters a person in the public arena who appears to be evil, does the reporter have an obligation to try to destroy that person? Why or why not? If so, how should the journalist go about that? If not, what obligation does the journalist have?

3. What kind of reasons could justify the publication of material that would cause great emotional pain to a person's family?

4. Does Kaufman bear any responsibility—as a journalist or as a person—for the massacre at the Hebron mosque by Goldstein?

5. Was Hemingway's death a legitimate news story? Why or why not? What kind of context, if any, was justified in the coverage? What if the story concerned the unexplained death of a high-ranking White House official?

10

A Candidate's Past: News, Political Manipulation or Mere Pandering?

The line between what people need to know and what is merely interesting or titillating is never fixed, and responsible journalists are forever trying to nail it down, at least for the current news cycle—tomorrow, they will have do it again. The following story is a prime example of trying to stay on the responsible side of a moving boundary. Along the way, it raises issues concerning the confidentiality of sources, manipulation of the press by politicians, and economic pressures to pander in a battle for readers' attention (and, by extension, advertisers' dollars), a battle that sometimes seems like a race to the bottom. It takes place in the northeastern corner of the country, in the state of Maine, supposedly far from the salaciousness and tawdriness of big cities. The leading characters are both conservative Republicans, and the major journalistic player is the *Boston Globe*, the very epitome of respectability, even before it was bought in 1993 by the *New York Times*.

In June 1996, three Republicans were involved in a close race for their party's nomination for the U.S. Senate seat being vacated by retiring Senator William Cohen. They were Susan Collins, the most liberal of the three (recognizing that "liberal Republican" no longer means a Rockefeller Republican); Robert A. G. Monks, a longtime conservative political operative in Maine Republican circles; and W. John Hathaway, a former poor boy who made a fortune in real estate in Huntsville, Alabama, during the go-go years of the 1980s. Hathaway, back in Maine after an abrupt departure from both politics and business dealings in Alabama, was running as the most conservative of the three.

Collins enjoyed an early lead, but Hathaway stayed in the race, spending hundreds of thousands of dollars of his own money, stressing "family values" and his close connection to conservative Christian organizations.

Then, in the final days before the June 11 primary, the *Boston Globe* got a tip about Hathaway's past that changed the race and quite probably inaugurated a new era in New England politics. The *Globe* was told that Hathaway had abruptly moved back to Maine from Alabama because of a sex scandal involving a twelve-year-old girl. The *Globe* sent its two-time Pulitzer Prize-winning reporter, Stephen Kurkjian, to Huntsville to nail down the story. In a day, Kurkjian had the story. On Wednesday, June 5, six days before the primary, Kurkjian had a front-page story outlining allegations of an eighteen-month sexual affair between Hathaway and the family baby-sitter, who was twelve when the affair started. The child was not identified. No legal charges were ever filed, but local and state prosecutors from both political parties were quoted, by name and for the record, as saying that they had been thwarted in their efforts to prosecute the case as statutory rape only because the family of the girl had refused to allow the case to go forward. As the paper's assistant managing editor, Walter V. Robinson, explained later in a telephone interview, the girl's parents, who were well-heeled friends and business associates of Hathaway's, "did not want to put the girl through the ordeal of a trial and instead essentially drove the guy out of town."

When confronted with the accusation by *Globe* reporters, Hathaway would not acknowledge at first that there had ever been an investigation. Later, he called the charges groundless and said the girl "was in a mental institution" when she had accused him. Essentially, Hathaway "said the girl was crazy," Robinson explained. Hathaway later said he had misspoken in saying she had been in a mental institution. In fact, according to the *Globe*'s story, the girl had begun showing signs of increasingly serious emotional problems within months after she starting baby-sitting for the Hathaway children. Eventually, her parents moved her to a California school for emotionally troubled students. Five months later, according to the *Globe*'s story, the girl told a counselor at the California school of her affair with Hathaway, saying that she loved Hathaway.

Hathaway then accused Monks of being the source of the damning background data on him, a charge that a Monks staff member initially denied. But Monks later acknowledged that he had hired a new breed of political consultant to conduct opposition research on Hathaway. The *Globe* did not say who had tipped the paper, and Robinson would not say unambiguously later, but the paper repeatedly noted, with such phrases as "widely held perception," that many believed Monks had put reporters onto Hathaway's past. The paper also noted that the opposition researcher whom Monks admitted hiring had looked into Hathaway's years in Alabama.

For the balance of the week, Hathaway and Monks traded insults, while Collins stayed out of the fray. Some of the slung mud apparently stuck, for Collins won the primary the following Tuesday and went on to win the general election in November.

This case raises a number of interesting questions for journalists. The first, and most basic, is whether the sex scandal in Alabama was a legitimate news story at all. The scandal had nothing to do with the concerns facing Maine voters, and it effectively brought to a halt any serious discussion of the real issues. By breaking the story, did the *Globe* raise the legitimate issue of the moral character of a candidate for high office, or was it just a "gotcha," albeit an especially powerful one, since the hypocrisy it exposes involves a candidate who was running as a Christian conservative on a family-values platform having had a longstanding sexual relationship with, not only a child, but his own baby-sitter and the daughter of a friend?

This story is not just about morals, though moral turpitude in a candidate is usually considered a legitimate area of voter concern. This story is also about a crime. One can argue that whether a candidate has an extramarital affair is a private matter and nobody's business beyond the people personally involved, but having sex with a twelve-year-old is statutory rape, which is a felony. It is hard to imagine building a case for an informed electorate, the foundation upon which our republic rests, that would exclude voters knowing about felonies in a candidate's past, especially the recent past. Robinson said that if Hathaway had been found to have had an affair with a twenty-five-year-old in Alabama, and all the other facts had been the same, "there would have been no story."

The second question raised is, What if the story is not true? After all, no legal action was taken and no charges were filed. Yes, state and local prosecutors—the local district attorney and Alabama's attorney general—both went on the record saying they thought they had a case worth prosecuting, but an opinion is not a prosecution and a prosecution is not a conviction. The old shibboleth about being presumed innocent until proved guilty is not true in the sense that it is often used,[1] but criminal charges were never even brought in this case. One purpose of a criminal trial is to give the state a chance to prove a suspect's guilt; another is to give the defendant a chance to establish innocence. The printing of the story did not put Hathaway in prison, but it may well have kept him out of the U.S. Senate.

Although no charges were ever filed, the *Globe* was convinced that the story was true, and prosecutors, both Democratic and Republican, in Alabama were willing to go on the record and say so. Robinson said that "there was lots of stuff our reporter knew but which we didn't publish" that convinced him and other editors at the *Globe* that the charges were true. "We were absolutely convinced, as were the prosecutors," he said.

The story's newsworthiness aside, the third question is whether its subject matter is simply too unseemly to discuss in a respectable publication. Robinson lamented what he called the "tabloidization of the entire culture. Everybody seems to be fair game." He noted that the *Globe* was "the responsible broadsheet in this town" but that not only newspapers, but "especially television, even the networks, have gone down-market." Readers, "whether we like it or not, have more and more of an appetite for salacious stories. Societal values have changed about what ought to be put" up for public discussion, he said. And, especially given the increasingly intense competition for readers, Robinson added, "You and your readers are not in this hermetically sealed cocoon anymore."

---

[1] As many lawyers have tried to point out, a presumption of innocence holds true only within a courtroom and only after a trial starts. It is a legal fiction designed to protect those defendants who happen, in fact, to be innocent. But in the broad sense in which the phrase is commonly used, it makes no sense at all. If suspects were really thought to be innocent, there would be no arrests and nobody would ever be held on bail.

This shift is not entirely a degredation of culture and a decline in public taste. If it were, it would be easier to know what to do. The shifts Robinson described also reflect a healthy candor in discussing publicly—and thus condemning publicly—a great deal of sexual and other kinds of abuse that flourished in the secrecy of earlier times. Many topics that are now openly discussed—calmly or breathlessly, for noble reasons or base—would not have been mentioned in polite company even a few years ago. At one time, tuberculosis was never mentioned as a cause of death in respectable circles, including the obituary pages of most major newspapers. While this doubtless prevented discomfort to those who had been acculturated to find the mention of the disease embarrassing, the policy of not talking about the disease almost certainly contributed to the deaths of many people who could otherwise have been saved. So it was later with cancer and then AIDS, and so it is with a great many topics. One of the functions of journalism, as Walter Lippmann pointed out more than sixty years ago, is to shine a searchlight on first one issue then another. Such illumination focuses attention on an issue and can generate the public interest to address it. On balance, the evidence seems strong that if the question is one of knowledge and discomfort or embarrassment on one side and ignorance and serious harm to either justice or health on the other, knowledge must win out. There was certainly nothing salacious about the content of the paper's reporting of the accusations against Hathaway in Alabama.

Fourth, there is a question of news manipulation. Although it was never stated unequivocally that the leak came out of the Monks campaign, all the evidence suggests that it did. Even if it did not, it seems certain that the leak came from a political enemy of Hathaway's, someone with an agenda other than high-minded public service. Given that, was the *Globe* merely acting as the tool, witting or not, of a partisan in a political race? The answer lies in the adverb *merely*. Yes, there is almost no doubt that the story was initially leaked to the *Globe* to do Hathaway political harm. And, since he subsequently lost, there is little doubt that the story accomplished its intended purpose. But, no, that is not why the paper ran the story.

As Daniel Boorstin pointed out a generation ago in his seminal book *The Image*, very little news happens spontaneously. Sometimes planes crash and hurricanes blow, but most newsworthy events occur because someone, somewhere makes them happen, and usually for the purpose of getting those events. Effective protest organizers try to do or say something unusual enough, and often outlandish enough, so reporters will cover the event and then explain whatever more serious point the organizers want made. Similarly, the point of a ceremony in the Rose Garden at the White House is for reporters to come and take notes and then spread the word about whatever policy the White House wants promulgated. In this regard, the hard part for a journalist—but a critically important dimension of sound news judgment—lies not in making news decisions based on why wants what covered or ignored, but in making such judgments independently, apart from anyone else's agenda. In the Hathaway story, the responsible journalistic position is to assess the newsworthiness of the information about the events back in

Alabama *without regard* to whether it sinks Hathaway's candidacy or revives that of one of his opponents.

Finally, the Hathaway story deals with a special journalistic form of promise-keeping, that of keeping a confidential source confidential. In this area, the current legal principle, and with it professional standards, comes from a 1991 U.S. Supreme Court case involving a situation very similar to the Hathaway story. The case began in Minneapolis in 1982, during the last days of the gubernatorial campaign that pitted the Republican, Wheelock Whitney, against the Democrat, Rudy Perpich. A local public relations executive named Dan Cohen, who was working for the Republicans, offered local television and newspaper reporters copies of court documents that indicated that the Democrat's running mate, Marlene Johnson, had many years before been arrested for shoplifting six dollars' worth of sewing supplies. (Eight months later, a judge expunged the conviction from her record, which is why an ordinary records check had not turned up the petty theft.)

Cohen offered the documents to, among others, Bill Salisbury of the *St. Paul Pioneer Press* and Lori Sturdevant of the *Minneapolis Star Tribune* on the promise that the reporters would not identify Cohen as the source. But editors at both papers overruled their reporters' promises of confidentiality and decided to identify Cohen anyway, a practice known in the trade as "burning a source." The editors argued that it was at least as newsworthy that the Republicans were resorting to such smear tactics at the eleventh hour as it was that Johnson had once pocketed some needles and thread. When the two papers printed Cohen's name, the P.R. man sued for breach of contract, essentially arguing that the reporters were speaking for their respective newspapers when they promised to keep his name out of their stories. Thus, when his name was printed anyway (over both reporters' vehement objections, but that is beside the point), Cohen argued, the papers violated their verbal contracts with him. Eventually, the case wound up before the Supreme Court, which held, in a vote of five to four, that Cohen was right.

Many reporters, Salisbury among them, have complained that as a result of the Cohen case, it is harder to get sources to talk to them, for fear that the reporters will burn them, too. To the degree that that is true, neither journalism nor the citizenry has been well served by the Cohen case. However, many reporters, again including Salisbury, have said that reporters are now much more careful than they used to be in making promises to sources. And editors and reporters seem much more likely than before the Cohen case to have a clear understanding about when a reporter can and cannot offer confidentiality. The result, in short, is better and more accurate communication between reporters and editors and the same between reporters and sources. The only thing punished under the Cohen ruling is the breaking of a promise. And under virtually every journalistic precept, that is, and should be, a punishable offense.

In the Hathaway case, Robinson briefly had a serious dilemma. On one hand, his paper had promised anonymity to the tipster who had first revealed the information about Hathaway. On the other, the identity of that tipster became part of the story. Robinson acknowledged that "we have an obligation to a source" not to reveal that source's identity if the promise of anonymity was made. Yet, he said, "We have a larger obligation not to mislead our readers." He would not like to burn a source, he said, but "there are higher moral obligations." Then, he said, "We will not allow a lie to appear in the *Boston Globe*."

He said he had "a little bit of a problem" with the first-day story in the *Globe*, when Monks denied being the source of the leak, even though the evidence presented in the *Globe* in that story strongly suggested that Monks had been behind it. Then Monks admitted hiring an opposition research firm, and many Republicans in New England began accusing Monks of the leak. At that point, Robinson said, "we were off the hook."

Robinson kept his promise to his tipster—he did not identify him in the paper, nor would he name him later in telephone interviews—but he made it clear that rather than allow a lie to stand in the *Globe*, he would tell the source to figure a way out of the problem. It was in that context that Robinson had much sharper criticism for Maynard Parker, Joe Klein's boss at *Newsweek*, than he had for Klein himself. (See the discussion of the uncovering of the author of the political novel, *Primary Colors*, published with "Anonymous" as its author, in Chapter 21.) While Klein verbally denied to many colleagues that he had written *Primary Colors*, Parker ran several small stories in *Newsweek* suggesting that other writers had written the book. Parker knew all along that Klein was the author.

Questions to Consider

1. If you had been the editor, would you have found the accusation against Hathaway to be newsworthy? Would you have published the accusation, even though no charges had been filed? Would you have published the name of the girl involved? For all of the above, why or why not?

2. If the prosecutors had been willing to confirm the accusation but had not been willing to have their names used, would you have gone forward with publication? Why or why not? What if the prosecutors said they did not want their names used but would go public to testify for you if you were sued for libel and the case wound up in court?

3. If you had been the editor and the accusation turned out to involve a twenty-five-year-old woman, would you have found that newsworthy and suitable for publication? Why or why not?

4. In the Cohen case, was the editor ethically correct in overruling the reporters who had offered to keep the name of the tipster secret? Why or why not?

5. How could the use of an anonymous tipster have posed ethical problems for the *Boston Globe*? Should journalists rely on anonymous sources, keeping in mind that much news about politics, and even crime, is available only in that manner? Why or why not? What ethical pitfalls should journalists try to avoid in dealing with confidential sources?

11

Peeking at Tonya Harding's E-mail: Serious Invasion or Trivial Excess?

During the 1994 Winter Olympics in Lillehammer, Norway, far and away the biggest story centered on two American women figure skaters, Nancy Kerrigan and Tonya Harding. During the final practice days leading up to the American trials, which picked the U.S. skating team, an assailant had attacked Kerrigan, hitting her just above the kneecap with a metal bar. Eventually, Harding was implicated in the assault. Harding was never charged with arranging the potentially career-ending attack on her skating rival, but her former husband, Jeff Gilooley, was, as was one of Harding's bodyguards.

For weeks, it was doubtful if Kerrigan would be able to skate, and if so, whether she would be in peak condition, given her forced layoff because of the attack. Then there was great attention given to whether Harding would be allowed to skate in the Olympics because of her connection with the assault.

Eventually, both women were put on the team, and the soap opera that had been the Nancy-Tonya story moved to Norway. Journalists and their reading and viewing publics seemed to be insatiable in their pursuit of any and all scraps of information, however unseemly and however irrelevant to the athletic competition. The story had all the requisite elements for intense interest, if not genuine importance: glamour, intrigue, and huge sums of money, for although Olympic winners get no prize money, the commercial endorsements available are worth millions of dollars, and sometimes tens of millions. Harding was the tough kid who did her own auto engine work; Kerrigan was the sweet-tempered, hard-working ice angel from blue-collar Boston suburbs with a mother who was legally blind. Kerrigan was clearly a victim, but Harding became something of a victim-hero as well, as details of spousal abuse by her ex-husband came out.

There was a breathless run-up to the opening of the games, as it was doubtful almost until the opening ceremony that Harding would be allowed to skate. And after the games opened, the waiting continued. Figure skating is one of the great glamour events of the winter games, so the Olympic schedulers and the powerful forces of ratings-minded television save the women's figure-skating events until near the end of the two-week competition. There were other good stories during the Olympics, but they were minor sideshows compared with the morality-on-ice running story of Kerrigan and Harding.

Then, at about 2:00 A.M. on Tuesday, February 22, a small handful of reporters returning from a midnight trip for pizza got to talking about the E-mail system that the Olympics organizers provided to all the athletes. On a lark, as they later described it, they decided to see if they could log on to Harding's account, just to see if they could. It turned out to be easy to do. Each athlete at the games was given a unique logon, or user identification number, which was printed on the identification cards that the athletes had to show at various security checkpoints around the site of the games. Each athlete was also given a password, which was the four-digit number representing the athlete's birthday. All the athletes were told to change the password to one of their own choosing the first time they logged onto the computer system.

Several reporters from different newspapers huddled around as one of them logged on as Harding, using her athlete-identification number, which they apparently read off of a photograph of her in which her credentials were clearly visible on a chain around her neck. For the password, they tried 1112, representing December 11, Harding's birthday. It worked. At least four of them—Michelle Kaufman from the *Detroit Free Press*, Jere Longman of the *New York Times*, Ann Killion of the *San Jose Mercury News* and Dave Barry of the *Miami Herald*—had at least a glance at a directory of Harding's incoming E-mail, although there were reports of at least a dozen, perhaps as many as one hundred, others who knew of the hacking to one degree or another. Everybody involved denied reading any of the mail.

Looking at a listing of Harding's E-mail is hardly the smarmiest element of the Harding-Kerrigan story. Indeed, that story produced a virtual casebook of ethical problems all by itself. One of them was the issue of composite pictures. *Newsday* made a composite picture of Harding and Kerrigan that made them appear to be skating together, when, in fact, they were not (see Chapter 32). Another unseemly occurrence was when an unwarranted tie-in was made between a news show and entertainment programming. Connie Chung, then coanchor of the *CBS Evening News,* flew with Harding to Norway and secured an interview, which many critics said contained no news at all, but which made for good promotional material for the Olympics, which CBS had paid hundreds of millions of dollars to broadcast.

And checkbook journalism became an issue. At least two tabloid television shows paid big money—reported to be several hundred thousand dollars each—for interviews. Bill O'Reilly, anchor of *Inside Edition*, explained in a somber op-ed piece that paying for interviews was the only way shows like his could compete with each other and the networks, which do not pay for interviews but which can offer an audience of millions and a chance to be interviewed by a star, a Barbara Walters or a Chung.

Against this ethical backdrop, the cybersnoops in Norway tended to dismiss their misstep. Kaufman, a *Free Press* reporter who was one of those caught, said,

"It's really a non-story that a bunch of bored journalists are trying to turn into a huge story."

San Jose's Killion said she had really been looking for the bus schedule.

Barry, the humor columnist, told a reporter from the *Chicago Tribune*: "This is being held up as some kind of criminal thing. In fact, it's no different than a reporter reading someone's mail upside down on a desk."

Barry's boss, Tom Shroder, executive editor of the *Herald's Tropic Magazine*, compared his columnist's actions with seeing mail sticking out of someone's mailbox. "You might read it to see what it is," Shroder was quoted as saying. "It depends on what you do with it."

Note that both Barry and Shroder are talking about reading what is visible, not opening somebody's mail. Barry made the analogy to reading documents that are lying face-up on someone's desk. Shroder made the comparison to looking at the outsides of envelopes. That is essentially as far as the reporters in Norway went. They looked at a directory of Harding's mail—the return addresses—but, if they are to be believed, did not open the envelopes and read the letters inside.

To a journalist, Barry's observation, and that of his boss, seems reasonable enough. Reporters are curious by nature and nosy by training. They know that they have access to truly frightening amounts of information,[1] and that the determination of which information they use is not what they have access to so much as their own and their employers' judgments about what is fit for public dissemination.

In this context, many journalists see nothing wrong with learning potentially newsworthy information by an extremely wide array of means. Bob Greene, the two-time Pulitzer prize–winning investigative reporter for *Newsday* who now teaches journalism at Hofstra University, gives his students full instructions, complete with handouts, on how to collect and sift through people's garbage after it is put out for collection. (It is perfectly legal.) Many journalists see these practices as part of the job. In a world of perfect integrity and candor, there would be no need for this sort of snooping, but in such a world, there would be no need for the police or judges or any of the other institutions that exist largely to make people do what they should do anyway.

But to many people outside journalism, such prying is an unconscionable invasion of privacy, one of the more distasteful of the many bad traits journalists are accused of having. For many years, the rather smug journalistic response was that journalism is not a popularity contest, that it performs a public service whose value far outweighs any animus—or fondness, for that matter—that readers and viewers may have for those who practice it. Many no longer voice that bit of arrogance. Readers and viewers are no longer considered inevitable, and most news organizations have in recent years taken the tastes and appetites of the audience very seriously indeed. In some cases, this has led to shorter stories with prettier

---

[1] One of the country's leading investigative reporters, Louis Rose of the *St. Louis Post-Dispatch*, even wrote a book called *How to Investigate Your Friends and Enemies*, rev. ed. (St. Louis: Albion Press, 1982)

pictures and widespread accusations of deliberate dumbing down of the news content, with more fluffy stories of questionable importance and less serious work patrolling the perimeter of the commonweal.

But even in this reader-friendly world, journalists sometimes do unseemly things to gather and verify information that is of public importance. As with most quandries, there is no perfect solution, but the best chance for doing the right thing is to weigh what is at stake against what is the possible outcome.

In the case of Harding's E-mail, was anything of value likely to come out of the exercise of using guile to get into her account? Almost certainly not. It seems inconceivable that anything either incriminating or exonerating could have be found. Titillating, perhaps, but titillation does not count for much, not enough to offset the clear privacy invasion that breaking into Harding's E-mail involved.

Serious journalists have and always will have a number of intractable conflicts between themselves and their readers and viewers. There is no point in squandering valuable goodwill on a venture that will, at best, yield trivial results. The late-night notion to hack into Harding's E-mail account was not based on a serious cost-benefit analysis. Enough pizza, washed down by whatever, and a reporter's natural curiosity could easily overcome good judgment. That appears to be about all that happened here. It is no coincidence that it took place at a tiny town where ten thousand or so journalists were hanging around on expense accounts with not much to do between stories.

That is not to say that a reporter should never go through a mobster's garbage or scan the desk of a politician suspected of being a crook. Examining someone else's mail, printed or electronic, is a more serious act, both legally and morally, than going through garbage, so it takes more compelling reasons to look at it at all, even from the outside. But it would be easier to defend looking at an envelope than opening that envelope and reading its contents.

Questions to Consider

1. If you had been the supervising editor for one of the reporters who logged onto Harding's E-mail, would you have published the information gained (assuming it was of some interest)? Would you have reprimanded the reporter? In both cases, why or why not? What if the E-mail involved had been that of a highly placed U.S. official, and the E-mail addresses showed an incoming communication from Fidel Castro that was labeled as a reply to a message from the U.S. official (a label like that would show up on a list of incoming E-mail even without opening any files)?

2. Journalists like to say that they act on behalf of "the public's right to know," but the law gives them no more right to information than any other members of the public. So if they break a law—anything from trespassing to libel or violating a governmental secrecy act—to get information, they are criminally liable. Would you ever break the law to get information? If so, what kind of laws and what kind of information? If not, would it trouble you to let a violation of the

public trust go unreported because you could get the information about it only by breaking the law?

3. How much stealth—or sneakiness—can be justified for journalists seeking legitimate information? What about surreptitiously reading mail or other papers (maybe even upside down) on someone's desk? What about staking out someone's home or business, following the person, or going through her or his garbage? Ignoring the legal ramifications (state laws vary), is it ever ethical to tape someone without that person's knowledge or consent? To answer these questions, you will need to decide on the factors that should go into each decision and what weight you will give to each factor.

4. What case can you make against checkbook journalism, which is the practice, eschewed by most news outlets, of paying sources for interviews?

5. Can you make a case, based on sound journalistic principles, for why the Kerrigan-Harding story deserved coverage?

12

Central Park Assault Victim: We Know Everything but Who She Is

In midafternoon on Tuesday, June 4, 1996, New York experienced one of those crimes that captures the attention not only of famously blasé New Yorkers, but of the whole nation. A young woman walking alone in one of the most fashionable sections of Central Park, just off the glitz and money of Central Park West, was attacked and beaten savagely, her head repeatedly slammed into the concrete walkway. Her assailant fractured her skull in multiple places and left her for dead.

She was in a coma for weeks before she slowly began to recover from the brutal assault. She did not have a wallet in her possession when she was found, and for several days her identity remained a mystery. On the third day after her attack, the *New York Times* ran a story about her condition, detailing how the hospital staff cared for and spoke to the woman over and over again, but how troubled they were because they did not know her name. Marilu Espiritu, a nurse at New York Hospital-Cornell University Medical Center, said nurses talked to comatose patients as a way of humanizing them. "We're used to calling someone by name," she told the *Times*, "and we still don't have a name to call her."

Dr. Jamshid Ghajar, the neurosurgeon who almost certainly saved her life (and who himself became the subject of major stories in prestigious publications, including the *New Yorker*) was quoted as saying, "As New Yorkers, we treasure our independence and we like our anonymity. But when something like this happens and there's no neighbor or co-worker who notices her missing, you begin to think, 'Have we lost our sense of community?'"

Eventually, the woman was identified, but because police believed that she might have been sexually assaulted as well as savagely beaten, news organizations did not release her name.

For weeks then, readers and viewers were treated to the bizarre unfolding spectacle of every conceivable detail of the woman being brought to light except her name. The church that she sometimes attended offered prayers for her, and her mother recorded a message of thanks to the congregation, which was also broadcast across the city. Neighbors in her apartment building were interviewed and quoted at length, as were former coworkers at the Steinway piano store where she had once worked. Readers learned that she was thirty-two years old, that she was of Armenian descent, and that she had written passionately about the massacre of thousands of Armenians by Turks in 1915. They learned that she had been on staff at a music magazine in California and that she was a classical pianist and teacher who dreamed of playing Carnegie Hall. Her piano technique was lauded by her former music teachers. She liked Schubert, and recordings of her favorite pieces were piped into her hospital room. Relatives and friends visited her in the hospital and talked to her for hours in an effort to bring her out of her coma.

New York took the woman to its heart, except, as nurse Espiritu put it during those first dark days, "We still don't have a name to call her."

Why not? And does it matter? The first question is fairly easy to answer. News organizations routinely make an exception in their full-disclosure policies when it comes to victims of sex crimes. The principle has considerable merit. The standard reasoning goes like this: There is a social stigma associated with being a victim of a sex crime, as if somehow the victim must be at least partly at fault for what happened—that she said or did something, went somewhere or wore something that, in some measure, invited the assault.[1] Since such a belief is so widespread, there is a natural reluctance on the part of rape victims to come forward for fear that they will be similarly stigmatized. Therefore, many rapes go unreported and many rapists are never arrested because they are never sought. District attorneys have long asked news outlets to voluntarily withhold the names of sex-crime victims as a matter of policy, precisely so that subsequent victims will be assured that they can come forward without fear of being publicly identified. Thus, for the journalist trying to weigh the question, the normal policy of full disclosure of all newsworthy information is justifiably breached by the greater weight of helping the system of law enforcement work better by deliberately withholding a small, albeit important, amount of information.

Not everyone agrees. Some women's rights advocates agree that there is a stigma attached to victims of sex crimes but argue that the stigma is caused at least in part by the secrecy that surrounds the reporting of sex crimes. By making an exception to the normal policy of full disclosure, this argument goes, the news organizations themselves help perpetuate the false perception that the woman has done something shameful. Only by treating this crime like other crimes, they say, will it ever be thought of as being like other crimes, with a perpetrator and a victim.

In the case of the Central Park pianist, there was no possibility that by withholding her name, her friends would be tempted to think ill of her—they were all told who she was and were encouraged to spend time at the hospital in an effort

---

[1]The feminine pronoun is used here because most victims of sex crimes are female, while most assailants are male, even though same-sex rape is not unheard of, and there are cases of women raping men, although almost always in the latter circumstances it is so-called statutory rape, that is, the male was underage.

to aid in her recovery. What evolved was a bizarre case in which those who knew the victim, whole congregations and apartment houses full of people—everyone, in short, for whom the name would be meaningful—knew her identity, but the public did not. There certainly seems to be no possibility that a stranger would think ill of her if her name were to be made public.

It could be argued that in this case, the sexual assault, if there was one, was but a trivial part of the story, and therefore not powerful enough to keep the woman's name a secret. But that argument invites all manner of problems for the future. Reporters and editors would then be put in the position of having to determine case by case if the victim had been primarily beaten or primarily sexually assaulted—tasteless business indeed, and almost certainly fruitless.

The choices, then, are but two: One is to stick to the current standard policy of publishing the name of suspects but not their accusers' names—an unfairness in itself—even when, as in this case, events like the broadcast from the church and the interviews with the neighbors make such withholding something of a bizarre game of journalistic peek-a-boo. The other is to rethink the policy with the goal of achieving greater fairness, while acknowledging that sexual assault is still very much a special case.

Questions to Consider

1. Are there legitimate journalistic reasons to identify people accused of crimes? To identify their victims? Does it change the equation if the victim in a case has a good reason to wish to remain anonymous—e.g., suppose business partners would look foolish and not very competent if it were known that they had been tricked and defrauded—or should a crime victim's preferences ever affect the decision on disclosing her or his name?

2. How does your answer to the first question change, if at all, if the crime involved is a sexual assault?

3. Should journalists be as concerned with fair treatment for crime suspects as for crime victims? Does that change if the crime is a sexual assault?

4. How much information should be made public about the victim of a sexual assault (independent of whether a name is used)? Most journalists would say a woman's sexual history is generally not relevant and should not be reported. Are there ever times when it might be relevant? Would you report it if the woman had filed spurious sexual-assault complaints before? What if the woman had been drunk or on drugs at the time of the assault?

5. News outlets' policies vary on identifying those involved in crimes. There are many possibilities: You can identify the victim when a crime is reported, wait until the trial, or not identify the victim at all. You can give the victim some privacy—and protection, if there is a possibility of a further attack—by withholding an exact address. You can identify a suspect when an arrest is made or hold off until the person is formally charged in an arraignment, or is

indicted. (And, sometimes, as in the infamous Olympic bombing in Atlanta in 1996, suspects are identified before an arrest is made.) Or you can wait until trial to identify a suspect or, of course, never identify the suspect. You can have one set of policies for crimes in general and another for sexual assaults. If you were setting policy for a newspaper, magazine, or television or radio station, what would you do and why?

13

The Brilliant Student with the Dark Past: How Much Is Relevant?

The first week of April 1995 was an emotional roller coaster for Gina Grant, a nineteen-year-old honor student and star athlete at the prestigious Cambridge Rindge and Latin High School just outside Boston.

On Sunday, April 2, the *Boston Globe*'s Sunday magazine ran a glowing story about her, depicting her as an orphan who had triumphed over adversity: She was cocaptain of the tennis team. She tutored poor children in biology. She was an honor student with an IQ of 150. And she had won perhaps the nation's most coveted high school academic prize—an offer of early admission to Harvard.

Then, it all began to fall apart. The offer of admission was withdrawn because a package of old newspaper clips, mailed anonymously, had arrived at Harvard. Similar packages arrived at her high school and at Boston's newspapers. The stories, by then nearly five years old, were news accounts from Lexington, South Carolina, of how Grant, then fourteen, had bludgeoned her mother to death with a candlestick and then, with the help of her boyfriend, had tried to make the death look like a suicide by slitting her mother's throat with a kitchen knife and then wrapping the dead woman's fingers around the handle.

The defense called the killing self-defense against an alcoholic and abusive mother, a woman who had blamed the girl for her father's death from cancer three years before, who had fought with her daughter the night of her death, and who was drunk that night (her blood-alcohol level was 0.30, three times the level defined as intoxication for drivers). The prosecution called it a vicious murder, spoke of the thirteen blows with the lead crystal candlestick, the clumsy attempt at a coverup. Grant pleaded no contest to manslaughter charges and spent six months locked up in a juvenile center before being released into the custody of an aunt and uncle living in Cambridge.

The *Globe* profile said that she had had a falling out with the aunt and uncle and had been on her own in Cambridge since the age of sixteen, living on a trust fund she had inherited at her mother's death. What the profile did not say was how Grant's mother had died, instead quoting Grant as saying it was "too painful" to talk about. For her part, Maria Karagianis, a freelancer regarded highly by the *Globe*, did not press Grant on the issue of her mother's death because she was writing a child-overcomes-adversity story, not, as she told reporters, a story about "the Mafia or political corruption."

Walter V. Robinson, assistant managing editor of the *Globe*, said Karagianis, a former staff writer for the paper, "felt taken in" by Grant, but, given the nature of the story, she had seen "no need to do a clip check" on Grant's background.

When Harvard withdrew its offer of admission, it gave few details, saying only that it sometimes did so if it turned out that an application contained false information.

Over the next two days, her story was all over the country, making the national wires, the front page of major newspapers, ABC's *Nightline* program and more. Since Harvard did not go into detail, reporters were left to try to figure out what had happened. Speculation centered on Grant's having answered no to a question about whether she had been on probation. As part of the terms of her release from the juvenile facility, Grant had been on probation until she reached the age of eighteen. But the question was worded ambiguously and could be read as asking only if the applicant had been in any academic difficulties, including academic probation. A Boston-area lawyer, Margaret Burnham, whom Grant's Massachusetts friends had found to represent the student, told reporters that Grant should not have had to disclose anything that had happened while she was a juvenile. Grant's trial lawyer from South Carolina, Jack Swerling, agreed, telling the *New York Times*, "This girl has paid her debt. That chapter in her life should have been closed and she should have been able to start over."

This last issue, whether Grant should have had to disclose anything that happened while she was a juvenile, goes to the core of the ethical question for journalists in this case. At the time the case broke, Grant issued a statement though her Boston attorney saying that she was "deeply disappointed" that Harvard had withdrawn its offer of admission, saying she was worried that her collegiate career had been jeopardized, and noting that "the promise of a juvenile justice system" was a fresh start. "I deal with this tragedy every day on a personal level," she said in the statement. "It serves no good purpose for anyone else to dredge up the pain of my childhood."

Similarly, Judge Marc Westbrook of Lexington County, South Carolina, who had ordered her to be released to relatives in Massachusetts, told reporters that it had been in Grant's best interests to release her. "There was nothing else in her record that indicated any other problem," Westbrook said. "She was on the right track, by what society deems to be the right track. What's happened since then bears that out. She was certainly not a menace to anybody."

The notion of allowing juveniles "a fresh start" lies at the heart of most of the many judicial restrictions on what can be reported out of the juvenile justice system. Most judicial records are sealed and most proceedings are closed to the public, which means that the names of many juvenile defendants are never made public. The reason to withhold the names of juveniles is to avoid tagging them with their offenses, labels that could follow them around for the rest of their lives.

However, John Allard, the reporter for the *State* in Columbia, South Carolina, who covered the Grant trial, cautioned against being overly concerned with protecting the identity of juveniles. In the great majority of cases, he said, "who in ten years or twenty years is going to remember" the name of this or that defendant?

His paper identified Grant at the time even though she was still a juvenile. And Allard said the Grant case was one of the few that would not be forgotten. "Her story will probably follow her all the rest of her life," he said. "And maybe that's as it should be." For Grant's name to get into Allard's newspaper, it had to pass two gatekeepers, the local sheriff's office and then Allard and his editors at the paper. The sheriff "was so outraged by the brutality of the crime that he said it was his duty to release her name," Allard said. The second hurdle was the paper's own staff. "We handle it on a case-by-case basis," Allard said. A juvenile is more likely to be identified in the paper "if it is a very serious crime, especially one involving violence, and it generates a lot of community interest and concern." The Grant case certainly qualified on those grounds.

But it is not just reader interest that justifies putting a story or a name in the paper, especially if the story may cause some harm. And the widespread publicity surrounding the Gina Grant case, arguably even in this book, could well cause her harm. It is the details of individual cases that interest citizens and focus badly needed attention on whole systems of government.

"People don't know what the justice system is like," Allard said, "and this is more acute with juveniles because so few of the proceedings are covered and so much of the record is sealed." Allard agrees with many journalism professionals who believe that the problems of the juvenile justice system are exacerbated by the lack of public scrutiny. While the Grant case generated a great deal of attention from reporters, "it was in many ways very atypical. She had wealthy relatives. She had strong advocates in the community, people who got her a good lawyer." Allard argued that if more attention were paid to the more typical cases, those that do not involve brilliant students and high-priced attorneys, the public might have a better understanding of the system of juvenile justice.

In the argument of the authorities in Lexington, South Carolina, the apparent viciousness and brutality of the slaying justified the release of Grant's name. That is, the crime was so unchildlike that the normal extra protection afforded children was forfeited in this case. But that issue, however legitimate it is, is primarily a question for law enforcement, or perhaps for society at large. "We don't know whether we want to rehabilitate or to punish them," Allard said. Publishing a defendant's name tends to add to the punishment. Withholding it would tend to support rehabilitation. This ambivalence is behind the mixed response to such arguments as Judge Westbrook's, who said it had been in Grant's best interests to release her to relatives in Massachusetts. Grant's supporters agreed and expressed dismay at all the coverage the case received. Her critics asked, in effect: What about the mother whom she beat to death and then stabbed? (It should also be noted that releasing Grant to Massachusetts was also, in part at least, in Judge Westbrook's best interests, too. Grant had strong support in the community, and South Carolina was under a federal court order to reduce the number of juveniles in detention in its state facilities, Allard said.)

The question for journalists is: Could the story have been told, or told as effectively, without using the defendant's name? The answer is, in truth, no. As has been argued above with the example of the "poster children" in the abortion debate, names and faces and the living details of a case are what make it real and significant and memorable to readers. "To get a full picture of the story," you have to have a name to go with the events, Allard said. "Without a name, there is a distance" between the subject and the reader. "If there is a name, and maybe a picture, then you, as a reader, have to confront the issues the story raises."

Allard sees a particular significance in his paper's decision to identify Gina Grant at the time of the slaying. It was copies of his stories, after all, that were sent to the schools and the newspapers in Boston, bringing the whole story to light. But even if foresight were as good as hindsight, he would still identify her. "If I had to do it over again, I'd do exactly what we did," he said. "I have no qualms about what we did."

Did identifying Grant cause her harm? Allard does not think so. "I'm not at all sure that the publicity from having named her has harmed Gina in any way," Allard said. "She clearly has had to deal with this at a very personal level every day."

The final chapter of this story has not occurred yet, so it is impossible to say with finality whether Gina Grant was irreparably harmed by the two rounds of publicity surrounding the case. However, after her early decision offer was rescinded at Harvard, she was admitted to Tufts University, also in Boston, where, as of this writing, she is still a student. John A. DiBiaggio, the president of Tufts, told reporters that Grant had served her sentence and had not lied on her application or in an interview. "We didn't see any reason why she should be denied the opportunity of pursuing a college degree," he said. She finished her first year at Tufts successfully, and while student records are strictly confidential, a university administrator said unofficially that she had done "wonderfully."

Questions to Consider

1. Did it serve a legitimate journalistic interest to identify Gina Grant in news articles at the time she killed her mother? Would it serve a legitimate interest to identify all juveniles accused of crimes? If a news media outlet adopts a case-by-case policy on identifying juvenile suspects, what problems could arise from that?

2. Did it serve a legitimate journalistic interest to identify Grant and publicize her crime nearly five years later? Was the reporter who wrote the glowing profile of children who had overcome adversity remiss in not investigating Grant's background more thoroughly?

3. Do you see any violations of Grant's right to privacy in any of the coverage? Did she weaken her right to privacy through her actions in 1990 or in 1995? If a reporter were to resurrect this whole case twenty-five years from now, publicly linking Grant to her crime again, would her right to privacy be violated by that?

4. Assume you were the reporter who interviewed Grant to profile her, and you found out about Grant's criminal past—either because Grant told you about it or because you did a background check. Would you include her in your article about children who had overcome hardships? Would you write about her at all?

14

Sex in an Elevator: Legitimate News or Sophomoric Titillation?

O n a Monday morning in November 1993, after a big home football weekend, Penn State University students reading the student campus newspaper, the *Daily Collegian*, found this item leading the police log, a standing roundup of the weekend's police activity on and around the campus:

> A man and a woman were charged with disorderly conduct Saturday night after police found them having sex in an elevator.
> The State College Police Department was called to Park Hill Apartments, 478 E. Beaver Ave., because an elevator was stuck between floors.
> When the doors were opened, a gust of hot wind was emitted and two people . . . were found partially dressed having sexual intercourse. The officer reported the couple was practicing safe sex by using a condom.

The ellipsis in the third paragraph above represents where the two students' names were printed in the newspaper story. Obviously, while the *Collegian* felt comfortable using the students' names, this author does not.

Amy Zurzola, a journalism student who was the midlevel editor at the paper responsible both for running the item and for using the names of the two students, says she did the right thing, although she does not see the incident as particularly important.

"This was not anything major—this was not a big deal," said Zurzola, now a reporter for the *Asbury Park (N.J.) Press*. "It was funny. If you are going to have sex in an elevator, then you'd better be prepared to take whatever happens.

"This is what happened. I would say that, by some of the language that was used, which came directly out of the police reports, that the police probably thought it was pretty funny, too."

Zurzola freely acknowledged that the primary purpose of running this story was entertainment. "On a Sunday after a big football weekend, strange things happen," she said. "People pick up the *Collegian* on a Monday after a football weekend and go directly to the police log. They know they are going to find stuff like this. We did one where a guy was dressed in a cow suit, standing in the middle of College Avenue making obscene gestures with the udders, things like that. And the reporters know this when they go off to look for things like that because it's interesting stuff."

Note that the news judgment was made on the grounds of "interesting stuff," as opposed to "important stuff." This distinction has been a real and important one for centuries, and both kinds of "stuff" have been staples of journalism since at least the beginning of mass-market newspapers in the 1830s. The profile—a long, supposedly revealing article about a single person—was essentially invented by James Gordon Bennett in 1835, when his *New York Herald*, then a brassy new paper, ran a profile of a madam whose brothel had been the scene of an especially titillating murder.

In reporting a case of sex in an apartment-house elevator, the story has no great news value, but a great deal of entertainment value—albeit collegiate humor at the expense of the students involved, at least one of whom was deeply embarrassed by the report. While the possibility of embarrassing a newsmaker does not usually warrant leaving a name out of the paper, the people in this story are not newsmakers in the ordinary sense.

Many police stories run in the *Daily Collegian*, as in other papers, for sound reasons. The police department is an extremely important arm of government, and the sovereign people have a right to know what their employees are doing in their name. This is especially true with the police because the police are armed and authorized to use deadly force if necessary. There is another reason as well. People need to know what is going on around them; they need to know whether their neighborhoods are safe. Police news has long been a staple of journalism, and properly so.

But in this case, there was little real news value. Zurzola pointed out that the story told readers that people having sex in an elevator could be cited, something that she had not known. In that regard, the story served a valid informational purpose, especially, perhaps, in a college town. But that seems to be something of a reach. Primarily, this police story is in the paper for the same reason that Bennett put police stories in the paper: people like to read them. While there is nothing inherently wrong with a news outlet publishing items that its readers, listeners, or viewers want, as opposed to things they need, a story without significant news value should be much easier to knock out of the story lineup when other issues against publication arise. The embarrassment to the students is a significant factor weighing against running the story. Serious news might justify the embarrassment; trivia is less likely to.

The author of this book has concluded, for example, that even though the students' names have already been published, there is little added value in repeating their names here, certainly not enough to get past the threshold of the potential extra embarrassment to the students and their families. Because the question of reprinting information arises in journalism all the time, it is worth noting that the relative significance of the questions related to publication changes over time. The argument for identifying the two students in a news story in November 1993 in State College, Pennsylvania, is different, and greater, than the reason that could be given for identifying them in a retelling of the story many months or years later.

Beyond the question of publishing the names of the students, there is the question of whether to run the story at all. The case for running the story can be made this way: The story is news. It happened both locally and recently and involved both local residents and the police. Arguably, in a college town of nearly forty thousand students, a reminder is warranted that having sex in public places can lead to a disorderly conduct charge. And, while it is not a major story, it certainly will be read by a great many people. Zurzola is doubtless right that students eagerly look to the police log, especially after a big party weekend, to see who did what (or, more accurately, who got caught doing what). True, journalists should be in the information business, not the pandering business, but a story is not automatically *not* newsworthy just because it has the high-readership elements of risqué humor.

A century ago, the *New York World*'s publisher, Joseph Pulitzer, whose cherished editorial page was a marvel of thoughtfulness and reason, was asked why he filled his news columns with salacious trivia. His answer: "Because I want to talk to a nation, not to a select committee." To print or broadcast a story *solely* to attract readers (or sell more papers, or attract advertisers) is morally indefensible because journalism is not just a profit-making business, although it is that, too. As has been argued above, the First Amendment protections afforded the press are there for a reason and bring with them an obligation to perform the essential public service of conveying information the sovereign citizens need to govern themselves.

What are the reasons, then, not to run the story at all? As a police story, it is a trivial offense. Not all such trivia makes the paper, even in the police log, so in the name of fairness and evenhandedness, there is a good case for not publishing. Further, the story, at least as written, is in somewhat poor taste, even by the standards of college students, who tend to be more ribald than the population as a whole. The story will almost certainly offend some readers, which is not a factor with veto power over a story, but is a significant factor nonetheless. It is worth noting that the young woman involved in the incident withdrew from the university immediately afterward without finishing the academic semester. It is impossible to tease apart fully the embarrassment of being caught in the elevator and the mortification of having the story appear in the paper, but it seems undeniable that the publicity played some part in her decision to drop out of school.

The primary reason not to run the story at all is that, try as we might, we cannot come up with very much news value in the story to offset the pandering and bad taste inherent in it. The primary reason to run the story is that it will have high readership, which will, theoretically at least, keep readers interested in the news and the newspaper, so the paper can go about its business of providing its readers with useful and important information to allow them to make rational decisions concerning the world around them.

Questions to Consider

1. Would you have run the item in the police log? Why or why not? If you would have run it, would you have used the names?

2. In making your decision, how much consideration would you give to the embarrassment caused to the students? What if the embarrassment was likely to be significant enough to cause some harm to one or both of the students?

3. Should a newspaper police log carry all items handled by the police? If it usually does, should some items be withheld at times, when circumstances seem to justify it?

4. The decision on whether to use the item was made by a student journalist. (It might have been made by a student in any discipline since journalism training is not necessary to work on a college newspaper—or in any other area of journalism.) And the decision had serious consequences, at least for one student. Should college student newspapers have some sort of supervision, by faculty or professional journalists, to handle these kinds of questions? What about high school newspapers? Should some kind of training or proficiency—in ethics and libel law, for example—be required for student or professional journalists, given the potential for harm?

5. How much should a news outlet's audience affect its decisions on propriety? Should college papers have different standards than a city or community newspaper? What about college broadcasting outlets?

15

Suicide: Important News or a Grotesque Invasion of Privacy?

S uicide presents journalists with a number of ethical problems. Emory University journalism professor Loren Ghiglione, formerly the editor and publisher of one of the country's most thoughtful small newspapers, the *News* of Southbridge, Massachusetts, wrote this column in the *News* about journalists' conflicting responsibilities concerning the coverage of suicide. In it, he raises a number of important questions and gives his answers.

SHOULD SUICIDES BE REPORTED?[*]

The day after Thanksgiving, Bonnie Mataras, a funeral director at the F. A. Sansoucy & Son Funeral Home, telephoned *News* reporter Michele Morse with an obituary about a 24-year-old Sturbridge man.

Morse, who had gone to high school with the man, asked Mataras the cause of death. She replied, "Just say that he died."

"As soon as she said that," Morse recalls, "I knew that it was a suicide." Though a medical examiner ruled a self-inflicted gunshot the cause of death, *The News* reported only that the young man had "died early yesterday morning."

"People always lie about suicide," a newspaper editor instructs the cub reporter in novelist Benjamin Cheever's *The Plagiarist*. "The family lies. The police lie. Even the medical examiner will lie if he has to."

The newspaper, too, lies. Or it unquestioningly reports the lie or dissemblance of the victim's funeral home.

A review of death certificates from area towns for the past 15 years reveals that medical examiners have ruled almost 100 of the region's deaths to be suicide. But,

---

[*] By Loren Ghiglione. Reprinted, with permission, from the *(Southbridge, Mass.) News,* Wednesday, December 23, 1992.

with few exceptions, those self-inflicted deaths have not been described by *The News* as suicides.

News obituaries, based on information provided by funeral homes, often have misled readers. A 65-year-old Southbridge man who shot himself in the head with a .22 caliber rifle, *The News* reported, "died today in his home." A 79-year-old Southbridge man who hanged himself, the newspaper wrote, "died Saturday afternoon in Harrington Memorial Hospital."

In other instances, *The News* has hinted at suicide but has failed to report the medical examiner's ruling. A Charlton man, 26, was "found dead in his car near his home." A 20-year-old Woodstock man "died of carbon monoxide poisoning at his home."

Debate rages over press coverage of suicide. "It should not be reported," says Robert W. Bullard, director of Bullard's Funeral Home. "Word gets around. It doesn't have to be printed for the archive. The family doesn't have to pick up a clipping 10 years from now and read that somebody blew his head off."

"When it's suicide, I refrain" from telling reporters, says Elaine Sansoucy, owner of F. A. Sansoucy & Son Funeral Home. "It's for the survivors—if it is 10 people that don't know about the suicide, that's 10 less people they have to deal with."

But Stanton C. Kessler, acting chief medical examiner for the Commonwealth of Massachusetts, believes accurate disclosure—not grisly, gory reporting—"is really important. I would report fully. The more the news gets out, the better things are. How can you not report suicides?"

What should a small-town newspaper—any newspaper—do about reporting suicides? The local standard has changed over the last century. In 1888, when the weekly *Southbridge Journal* deemed Sylvanus Davis' purchase of two cows newsworthy, a suicide guaranteed front-page coverage.

The *Journal* detailed the suicide of a Charlton farmer who stood on an old chair and hanged himself in his barn. "When found the chair was turned over and his palmleaf hat, with a red bandanna handkerchief in it, was lying near the chair," noted the *Journal*.

Suicide began to be reported more discreetly at the beginning of the 20th century. The humiliation felt by surviving family members, the false belief that suicide "runs in the family," the religious attitude of condemnation—all worked to encourage understatement, if not nonstatement.

George Grant, owner of the weekly *Southbridge Press* between 1891 and 1938, never reported suicide. "He ignored it because he was an old-fashioned type who didn't believe in a certain kind of news," recalled Andrew Tully, who got his start in journalism as a $7-a-week *Journal* sportswriter and proofreader. "Of course, everybody loved him."

The News, founded in 1923 and published by Virgil McNitt and Frank McNitt between 1931 and 1969, downplayed suicide. A suicide at home was "left up to the readers," Tully said. In 1957, a 64-year-old optical worker hanged himself. *The News* merely noted that he "died at his home yesterday morning."

A prominent person's suicide in a public place might result in a tiny article, recalled George A. Anderson, *News* managing editor during 1945–50 and 1964–69. In 1953 an automobile dealer, missing for six days, was found dead in his car on a cart path off Eastford Road.

The News kept the word suicide out of both the headline and the lead of the two-paragraph news brief. But the second paragraph listed the medical examiner's finding and concluded, "A hose had been run from the exhaust pipe of the car into a rear window."

The News in 1976, by then under ownership of this editor, announced a policy change in reporting suicide: The newspaper would describe the medical examiner's finding—for example, "suicide by carbon monoxide asphyxiation"—even if its reporters could not learn that finding until after publication of the victim's obituary.

To remain silent, *The News* editorialized, threatens the newspaper's credibility and "risks making suicide into an invisible death." Suicide patterns that deserve public scrutiny, the newspaper warned, would otherwise go undetected and undiscussed.

The new policy failed on four fronts.

First, more than three-fourths of suicides still went unreported. Of 17 deaths termed self-inflicted by medical examiners in the next four years, 1977–1980, *The News* reported only four as suicides. Medical examiners and funeral directors often had kept the cause of death from *The News*.

Second, the ethics of the newspaper, which spoke of its duty to try to tell the truth, ran into the ethics of readers. Some attacked the new policy as, in the words of Sally Kalis, a 1980 letter-to-the-editor writer, "tasteless and totally lacking compassion." Others criticized it as an invasion of privacy that threatened a victim's right to a Christian burial.

The harder *The News* tried to track the cause of death, the louder readers protested. In 1982 *The News* reported that a 17-year-old student had died "in Worcester City Hospital." The funeral director and medical examiner refused to tell *The News* the cause of death. *The News* spent two weeks locating the death certificate, which confirmed suicide.

Without mentioning the student's name, *The News* editorialized about the need to provide the facts that would encourage readers' understanding of adolescent suicide locally. "A newspaper shouldn't seek to sensationalize suicide," *The News* said, "but it should at least report the truth."

A letter signed by three residents of the victim's hometown sided with the medical examiner and funeral director: "They realize the family involved has to live with hurt every day of their lives. After weeks have gone by, you just had to let your readers know the truth about [the young woman's] unpleasant death. For what purpose?"

Third, *The News* began to worry about the impact of reporting suicide on those who might themselves be considering suicide. Dr. Richard L. Fowler, the medical examiner for the region, said, "I personally would prefer that suicides wouldn't be reported. When a prominent person commits suicide, usually two or three others follow. Apparently it stirs people thinking of something of that sort."

The notion of an account of one suicide causing—through suggestion or imitation—another suicide dates from at least 1774. Johann Wolfgang von Goethe, inspired by a diplomat's suicide, wrote a novel, *The Sorrows of Young Werther*. Goethe declined to discourage reports, since refuted, that his novel's publication led to a wave of suicides. In studies between 1974 and 1979, sociologist David P. Phillips found what he called the Werther effect: Newspapers' suicide stories were followed by statistically relevant "excess suicides."

Fourth, the manner in which an understaffed newsroom tried to carry out *News* policy encouraged the newspaper, like most media, to focus its feature reporting on certain suicide patterns while ignoring others.

If a young person's cause of death was not made available, the *News* staff, logically, pushed for the cause. But the death of a 70-year-old failed to attract as much staff attention. Aware of teen-agers killing themselves, *The News* devoted lengthy articles to local teen-age suicides and the response of the health establishment.

Suicides of older people, however, went unreported. A review of local death certificates suggests *The News* missed an important story. Of the region's 21 suicide victims between 1976 and 1980, for example, none was a teen-ager. But 11—more than 52 percent—were men between the ages of 60 and 79.

Since 1985, *The News* has returned to reporting the cause of death as provided by the person's family or funeral home. In effect, suicides have gone unreported for the past seven years: Of 11 Southbridge deaths that medical examiners have ruled self-inflicted, not one has been reported by *The News* as a suicide.

Reporting policies by New England's major metropolitan newspapers provide no simple answer to what the policy of *The News* should have been or should be. Newspapers everywhere find it virtually impossible to report suicides evenhandedly. Some families, doctors and undertakers go beyond hiding the truth.

Daniel Warner, editor of the *Lawrence Eagle-Tribune*, caught a police captain—aided by a coroner—falsifying the death certificate of his father-in-law, a suicide victim. Edward Patenaude, veteran Webster reporter for the *Worcester Telegram & Gazette*, remembers a millworker's obituary submitted by undertaker Bernard Shaw. "Shaw said the man 'died after a short illness.' He had hanged himself."

But reporting of suicide by *The News* and other media suggests a "do" and "don't" list:

I. Don't report suicide as entertainment, glamorizing or glorifying suicide as the ultimate flight from life, the great getaway for eternity.

If Shakespeare had his Romeo and Juliet, newspapers and magazines have their leaping suicides. The *Worcester Telegram & Gazette* publishes a large photo atop page one of a man in Toledo, Ohio, swinging from a 200-foot-high bridge girder, threatening to jump. *New York Magazine* features Theodora Sklovar, "a remarkable woman" who sees her solution to life's problems as a leap to her death from a ninth-floor midtown Manhattan apartment.

A *New York Times* profile of the 900th suicide off the Golden Gate Bridge romanticizes the jump from "the beautiful span that is San Francisco's signature." The article ends with a quote from the sister of the dead man, Ron R. Berst. Berst's leap from the bridge, she says, "has eloquence to it, and maybe that's what he wanted to say."

II. In a society fixated on the young, don't suggest by the frequency and quantity of prominent coverage that suicide almost exclusively befalls people—especially bright people—in their teens and twenties.

Suicide "epidemics" and "copycat suicides" among the young are staples of press coverage. Even the staid *New York Times* gives page-one tabloid treatment to adolescent suicides: "4 Jersey Teen-Agers Kill Themselves in Death Pact."

Reporters, who often are young and who often see themselves as brilliant, write there-but-for-the-grace-of-God-go-I profiles of young, brilliant suicide victims: Frank Aller, Bill Clinton's "brilliant" roommate at Oxford; Emily Ann Fisher, "a brilliant" Harvard Phi Beta Kappa; James Dallas Egbert 3d, a "brilliant" computer student who entered Michigan State University at age 16; Paul Leahy, one of the "most brilliant students" at Conestoga High, Berwyn, Pa., and Eddie Seidel Jr., "a sometimes brilliant boy" from St. Paul who jumped 200 feet to his death.

III. In reporting the news of suicide, don't appear to sell the so-called "rational suicide" and "assisted suicide" as ultimate civil rights appropriate for all.

Headlines like the *New York Times'* "In Matters of Life and Death, The Dying Take Control" may suggest suicide is a simple, rational act. Media attention focuses on Derek Humphrey's best-selling suicide manual, *Final Exit*, on Dr. Jack Kevorkian, the Michigan doctor who has helped eight people commit suicide, and on initiatives in California and Washington state that would have authorized doctors to assist in suicides.

But most suicides, say psychiatrists, are far from rational. They are desperate, often irrational, acts of depressed, despairing people. The hopelessness that leads to those suicides often can be reversed through medication, hospitalization, therapy and support. But, in a statistic that the press should take to heart, two of three Americans with serious depression will not seek help. They do not see treatment, which receives little coverage, as a choice.

IV. Do demand that vital sources of information about suicides—autopsies and the state's annual cause-of-death survey—are continued and be sure to study them.

Budget cuts and staff reductions statewide threaten the compilation and publication of death data. Dr. Kullikki K. Steen, the area's primary medical examiner for the past eight years, warns, "for one and a half years [1990–91] we were not autopsying all suicide cases." When asked about annual Massachusetts reports on causes of death, Kessler, the state's acting chief medical examiner, says, "We haven't been doing them."

Of significance locally, perhaps, a federal survey last year showed that suicides among the elderly, which dropped between 1950 and 1980, have risen in recent years. Indeed, the rate of suicide for people ages 75 to 84 is almost double the rate among young people—in 1990, 26.1 suicides per 100,000 vs. 13.6 per 100,000 for people ages 15 to 24.

Kessler reinforces the data's message by repeating an acronym he uses when lecturing medical students about suicides—MA'S SALAD. The letters, he says, stand for middle-aged and older people with previous suicide attempts, males who are single, alcohol users and abusers—lonely, alone and divorced.

V. In reporting suicides, do put the emphasis on the living—on those who might be able to help a suicidal person, or on the bereaved who are trying to cope with their loss.

Two articles earlier this year by Jane E. Brody of the *New York Times*— "Suicide Myths Cloud Efforts to Save Children" and "Recognizing and Rescuing Suicidal Youths"—deftly described signs of depression, suicidal triggers and overlooked hints to recognize the seriously suicidal. Such reporting is all too rare.

The media need to make the public aware of sources of help: the American Suicide Foundation (regionally, 1-617-965-2664, and a national survivors' referral line, 1-800-531-4477); The National Institute of Mental Health Depression Awareness, Recognition, Treatment (DART) program (1-800-421-4211); Samaritans hotlines (1-875-4500 and 1-617-247-0220), and the Samariteens hotline, 3-9 p.m. (1-800-252-TEEN).

VI. Do acknowledge the possibility that reports of suicide—possibly even this column—may encourage people at risk to question their shaky hold on life.

Caution should push newspapers to question photos, extensive page one coverage, headlines that use the word suicide, detailed accounts that suggest suicide is easy, and intimate, romanticized reconstructions that invite readers to identify with heroic victims eulogized by their communities.

However hard-nosed the self-image that journalists wish to perpetuate, they need to recognize the emotion—the anger, even terror—that surrounds suicide. It symbolizes society's failure. Parents, ministers, counselors and other safety nets have not worked. That "frightens the horses in the street," as Virginia Woolf wrote before killing herself.

Painful for survivors, suicide, nevertheless, remains newsworthy. It should not be allowed to disappear, slipping silently back into the community's closet. But it may be most usefully as well as most sensitively reported not in a details-and-drama profile about a victim. And not in a medical examiner's one-sentence finding or in an obituary code phrase like "died suddenly."

It may be best reported in an annual review of the region's suicides that, without identifying victims by name, draws attention to patterns and issues that should concern us.

So this scribbler will add one item to his list of New Year's resolutions: To report at the end of each year on those in the area who killed themselves. Perhaps those who died can provide a lesson or two for those who live.

. . .

In considering how to cover suicides, if at all, Ghiglione raises a point that is easy to overlook from the classroom, but which every successful professional knows well: You must, absolutely must, know your readers or viewers. What is acceptable as good journalism in New York or Los Angeles may not be considered good journalism at a weekly or small daily. The responsible journalist might, for example, give more weight to the potential for a family's embarrassment in a small town than in a metropolis. Some details of a story might lend themselves to a written description but be too gory for television footage.

The strongest reason for covering suicides is the newspaper's obligation to cover the community it serves—in this case, to inform the sovereign citizens of that part of the Commonwealth of Massachusetts of events and patterns of events going on around them so that they may be able to make informed decisions about how to govern their own lives. It is important to note that this coverage is, in Ghiglione's mind and in the mind of most thoughtful journalists, not a mere right, but a positive obligation. That was Ghiglione's point when he announced in 1976 that the *News* would henceforth cover suicides.

But as time went on, he discovered that his policy was difficult to carry out. The first problem he encountered was that despite his and his staff's best efforts, he could not find out about most area suicides to report them. Funeral home directors and others in the community would not tell the newspaper about suicides. True, the cause of death is a public record, which means that the cause of death can eventually be reported, but certainly not in a timely enough fashion to include in a news story about the death. That raises a fundamental question of fairness. A policy, however high minded, is seriously flawed and unfair, if it is uneven in its application.

The unevenness of the coverage was Ghiglione's first problem. It was also the fourth in his list, though as he describes this further flaw in his policy, it stemmed from an inevitable unevenness resulting from making editorial decisions about marshalling scarce resources to cover the news. That meant that some suicides, young people's in his example, were covered, while an important element of the story, suicides among the elderly, were not being covered.

Ghiglione's ethical "duty to tell the truth" clashed with the ethical sense of the readers who wanted the newspaper to respect the privacy and taste of the families and friends of suicide victims. Readers are not required to buy and read a newspaper. Ghiglione could not fulfill his primary obligation of conveying information to his readers if he chased them all away from his paper with repeated violations of their sense of probity and good taste.

The other thing Ghiglione mentions as a reason for not covering suicides is the fear of generating copycat behavior, prompting disturbed people to follow suit. That could certainly amount to doing harm needlessly.

Many newspaper publishers would have given up at that point, and part of what sets Ghiglione apart is that he did not. In his judgment, the obligation to cover his community is a powerful one that is worth finding a way to accommodate. The solution he found is not perfect—by definition, a compromise never is. Ghiglione no longer covers a suicide as breaking news, which robs it of timeliness, a significant dimension of news by anyone's definition. But he has found a way to cover the issue still, which is a clear plus. His new policy, of covering suicides as part of a year-end wrap-up, is farther from the journalistic ideal of full disclosure than the old one, but that old policy did not work. Hence Ghiglione's attempt to fulfill his responsibilities as a journalist while respecting the feelings of the community he serves. One can ask no more of a journalist.

Questions to Consider

1. Just why would we want to report suicide as the cause of death, anyway? What is the point?
2. Is Ghiglione's new policy on suicides the best you can envision for small newspapers or broadcast outlets? Why or why not? Does your assessment of the policy change when you consider it for larger news outlets? Why or why not?
3. If the policy at your newspaper was to report suicides and there was a string of suicides by teenagers in your circulation area, would you change that policy? Why or why not? What if it was your policy *not* to report suicides and there was a string of suicides by teenagers in your area?
4. How should the issue of assisted suicide, with or without Dr. Jack Kevorkian, be reported? Is it possible to report on this issue without encouraging more assisted suicides? Do we have an obligation to make this information available so more people can avail themselves of suicide assistance?
5. What did Ghiglione mean by this statement: "Do acknowledge the possibility that reports of suicide—possibly even this column—may encourage people at risk to question their shaky hold on life"? What good does it do to acknowledge that?

16

Unnamed Accusers: Sex, Abuse of Power, and an Election, Too

In early March of 1992, the *Seattle Times* had a major story that everyone agreed was missing a major component. Largely because of the political calendar—it was early in the campaign season of an election year—the paper ran the story anyway and, in so doing, deliberately ended the political career of one of the Democratic Party's most powerful senators. The incident inaugurated a journalistic debate that has still not been fully resolved.

On Sunday, March 2, the *Times* devoted most of the front page and three full pages inside to a package of stories in which eight former political aides, lobbyists, and business associates accused Senator Brock Adams of sexual harassment, molestation, and, in one case, rape.

The headline stripped across the front page read: "8 more women accuse Adams." Below it was this subhead: "Allegations of two decades of sexual harassment, abuse—and a rape."

The missing component was the identity of the women making the charges. All eight had refused to be named in the newspaper, so the paper was left running a story, which senior editors knew would end Brock's political career, based on charges made by accusers it did not identify. Adams had earlier announced that he would seek another term in the Senate, but he pulled out of the race the day after the story ran. He denied the allegations and denounced the newspaper for running such charges by anonymous people, but said he would not put his family and loyal staff through the inevitable agonies of running a campaign in the climate the story engendered. He said the story was part of a political vendetta.

This case raises a host of important issues for journalists. The most obvious is the fact that Adams's accusers are not identified. The paper dealt with this enormous hole in the story in the third paragraph of the main story: "The women, fearful of being thrust into the public spotlight, all spoke to the *Times* on the condition their names not be published. Seven have signed statements attesting to the truth of their stories and another has said she will. They all acknowledged they could be required to testify in court should Adams sue the *Times*, as his lawyer has threatened."

The paper acknowledged that withholding the names of Adams's accusers seriously weakened the story's credibility. Michael R. Fancher, the paper's executive editor, explained in a note to readers that editors and reporters had been working on the story for more than three years and "were convinced the allegations were true. Our dilemma was that none of the victims would allow us to use her name, despite our ongoing attempts to persuade them to go on the record."

The paper then had to decide whether "to publish nothing of these allegations or to publish a story without naming the women," Fancher wrote. "We decided that a responsible approach was to publish the claims of women who were willing to sign statements affirming the truth of their allegations and acknowledging they might have to face him in court should he sue us. Eight of the women agreed. Other women the paper had interviewed would not agree to the stipulation, and their stories were not told in any detail.

"We would have preferred to publish a story with all parties named. Because that wasn't possible, we believe what we did was the only responsible course we could follow," Fancher wrote.

In an interview, Fancher said his reporters had verified the accusers' information as far as possible—comparing accusers' reports of dates against the senator's travel itineraries, for example, and interviewing third parties whom the accusers said they had told of the assaults—and had found that those parts of the accusers' accounts checked out.

In several places, the newspaper outlined the steps it had taken to verify the charges—talking to the co-workers and friends whom the accusers had talked to, comparing accounts from women who did not know one another, and trying, on several occasions, to let the senator answer the charges. Each time, Adams declined.

Thus, faced with competing obligations—that of publishing a seriously flawed but important story, versus giving that story as much credibility as possible—the *Times* found a creative way to bridge at least part of the gap between what it published and what it would have liked to publish. The paper was unable to persuade the women to go on the record with their names, despite repeated efforts. The paper acknowledged that this weakened the story and ran a long sidebar quoting psychologists explaining why women would be reluctant to become known publicly. By getting the women to sign statements attesting to the veracity of their statements and acknowledging that they might have to testify in court, the paper did as much as it could to replace the normal badge of credibility: names. And, even though their names were not given, the accusers were described in enough detail that it seems inevitable that Adams could have figured out who the accusers were, at least in several cases.

In an interview after the story's publication, Fancher acknowledged that some of the women would be easily identifiable to political insiders close to Adams, while others insisted on concealing details that would allow Adams or others in politics to figure out their identities. "Some of the women were willing to allow more descriptive material than others," Fancher said. Some "just didn't want to be writing a check at the grocery store and have someone ask, 'Aren't you one of the women in the Brock Adams story?'" while others, Fancher said, were more concerned with protecting their political careers and wanted to keep their identities secret within the political world as well as on the outside.

The problem of the anonymous accusers was enormous, as Fancher had predicted it would be. At his news conference the next day, Adams emphasized the anonymity of his accusers, and he maintained that the stories had no credibility as a result. Prominent journalists weighed in with their analysis of the *Times's* decision, which the paper carried as a sidebar. The columnist George Will said basing the article on anonymous sources ws "an open license for character assassination." The retired *New York Times* columnist Tom Wicker noted that papers often had to rely on anonymous sources, but he added, "I don't think it is ever justified when criminal charges are hanging over someone's head, and that's the case here." Other journalists and press critics supported the paper's decision.

Putting the question of relying on anonymous sources aside, was this a story at all? Was it simply a case of sexual dalliance—lurid perhaps, but eventually one that might well be considered a matter between Adams and his wife, Betty? Fancher addressed this question, too, in his note to readers. "Even if true, was this information that readers and voters needed to know? Or was it a matter of private sexual behavior that had no place in the public discourse?" Fancher answered his own questions this way: "The alleged incidents described were not consensual love affairs or 'womanizing' but abuses of power and of women. As such, they raise questions about Adams's character, both personal and political, that we believe voters should have an opportunity to evaluate."

There are other problems with the story. Some of the accusations against Adams went back decades, and the standards defining outrageous behavior and what is merely boorish have changed enormously in the last generation. The story also dealt with this moving-target issue. The story quoted women as saying that male politicians made unwanted sexual advances all the time but that the charges against Adams involved behavior far more serious than misguided or unwanted excessive flirtation. In an interview, Fancher said, "This was behavior that was way, way beyond what anybody could call reasonable or acceptable."

It is also instructive to look at how the story first came to light. In September 1988, a woman named Kari Tupper, then a twenty-four-year-old friend of the Adams family and a former Congressional aide, filed a criminal complaint against Adams, accusing the senator of drugging and molesting her at his Washington, D.C., home a year and a half before. The District of Columbia police sought a warrant to arrest Adams, but no criminal charges were ever filed. The federal prosecutor for the district said the case was without merit. Up to that point, nothing had appeared in print, and Fancher said the whole story might never have been published if it were not for Adams's own attempts at political damage control. In late summer 1988, rumors circulated within the Washington, D.C., political scene that a local magazine, which deals heavily in political gossip, was about to print a story about Tupper's allegations against Adams. Adams's staff tried to defuse the threatened upcoming story by putting out the story that Tupper was merely trying to extort money from Adams on trumped-up charges. The rumors and the spin control spread from the nation's capital to Adams's home state of Washington. Thus alerted, the Seattle paper did a story on it.

"In essence, Adams put the story in play," Fancher said. "His spin control sort of blew up on him." Since the criminal complaint had been dismissed as groundless, the story might never have broken had Adams not gone public with his reaction, Fancher speculated.

Because of the attention, the *Times* decided on a story. Usually, in cases involving a sex crime, the *Times*, like most papers, will not identify the accuser. But in this case, Fancher and his top editors decided, after much debate, that "it was no longer a case of a sexual assault" so there was no longer any reason to withhold Tupper's name from the story. "It could have as easily turned out to be a story of a woman trying to extort money from a U.S. senator," Fancher said. "If you know who's telling the truth, it is real easy to figure out what to put in the story," he said. But in this developing story, his paper decided to identify all parties concerned, on the grounds of full disclosure and fairness.

After Tupper's case became public, other women began calling the *Times* with stories of their own, saying that they, too, had been molested, and, in one case, raped, by the senator. So, some of the women who were eventually quoted in the 1992 stories had volunteered their stories. The paper said it had begun investigating the story after the calls and had found most of the accusers on its own, through its own investigation.

It was a case, common in journalism under circumstances like this, of one person's story encouraging or emboldening others with similar tales to come forward, either by volunteering on their own or by being newly willing to talk to reporters when questioned. That is what happened here. Over the next three years, several women came to the paper with similar stories, and *Times* reporters found still others.

Veteran editors are fully aware of this phenomenon and are careful not to exploit it by printing half-cooked stories, figuring the rest will come out of the woodwork by itself once the first part of the story is published. Editors are also aware that among their readers are people seeking attention, people who, seeing a tale of one person's adventures (or, even more likely, misadventures), will come forward with made-up tales.

For more than three years, Fancher's staff pursued the Adams story. The paper was committed to adhering to its policy of not running the story without attributable information—that is, without names to go along with the accusations.

Many political insiders, Fancher said, expected that Adams, notorious in rumor circles for many allegations of sexual abuse of women, would simply not run for reelection. But in spring 1992, Adams announced that he would seek another term. The announcement, Fancher said, brought more accusers forward, people who might have let the matter die if Adams had decided to retire but who were determined not to let Adams have another term in office.

Once Adams announced that he would run again, the pressure was on to publish the story soon or abandon it, probably forever. Fancher said he would not have considered running the story late in the campaign season, near Election Day.

Was Adams guilty? The evidence strongly suggests that he was, although it is not likely that anyone except those directly involved will ever know for sure. If he was guilty, did the paper do the right thing? There is something disturbing about the nature of the charges. Most were many years old; some were nearly twenty years old. Standards of acceptable behavior had certainly changed during that time. Many unwanted advances that outrage people today were look at as hardly more than boorishness in Adams's formative years. If the allegations had concerned chance encounters, unwanted advances, and the like, there would have been far less of a story and far less reason to publish it. Probably no woman has ever gone through a career without receiving unwanted sexual attention. But the charges against Adams are far worse than excessive flirtation, or even drunken Christmas-party lechery. They include numerous allegations that he had deliberately spiked women's drinks with drugs to send them into a haze from which it was difficult or impossible to resist his groping. And they include a full-fledged rape in which Adams is accused of tossing two hundred dollars at the woman on his way out. These accusations involve felonies, not misunderstandings. Voters are certainly entitled to know about that sort of behavior—if they are not, it is hard to imagine what they are entitled to know. But are they entitled to know about *anonymous charges* of that sort of behavior?

Questions to Consider

1. If you had faced Fancher's dilemma about whether to publish the accusations against Adams, would you have run the article? Why or why not?

2. Fancher said he would never have run such an article near Election Day; he gave that as the reason for wanting to publish early in the campaign. Why does that make a difference?

3. When people give information to reporters without allowing their names to be used, they could have less than honorable motives for doing so and for not wanting to be held accountable. But much important information—the Watergate scandal, for example—would never have come to light without the use of anonymous sources. What should the policy of a newspaper or broadcast station be on the use of anonymous sources? When should exceptions be made to that policy?

4. If Adams had decided to retire instead of running for reelection, should the newspaper have dropped its investigation? Why or why not?

5. Do you agree with the way the newspaper handled the initial article about Tupper's allegations? Why or why not?

17

In Politics, How Far Back Is It Fair to Go?

By mid-October 1992, just three weeks before the presidential election, the reelection campaign of incumbent President George Bush had faltered seriously. Bush, whose popularity had been at record levels at the end of the Gulf War in 1991, saw his approval ratings plummet, and along with them the likelihood that he would be reelected. Normally Bush was extremely civil in public, but during the campaign's closing weeks, the president began calling into question many details of the personal life of his Democratic challenger, Gov. Bill Clinton of Arkansas.

Bush, the first president since John F. Kennedy to be known as a World War II hero, made a great deal of his record as a Navy bomber pilot in 1944. And he more and more blatantly challenged the patriotism of Clinton, who had been of draft age during the Vietnam War but who had managed to keep a student deferment under questionable circumstances and had participated in antiwar demonstrations while a Rhodes scholar at Oxford in England. Bush challenged Clinton to "come clean" on how Clinton had managed a draft deferment by promising, falsely as it turned out, to join the Arkansas National Guard.

In the last frenetic run-up to Election Day, a freelance writer named Paula Ogburn offered journalists documentary evidence that called into serious question Bush's war record. The evidence suggested, but did not prove conclusively, that in 1944, as a twenty-year-old ensign on his first bombing run, Bush may have committed a war crime.

Official navy records that Ogburn offered to reporters indicate that Bush may well have strafed—that is, machine-gunned from the air—a lifeboat containing the crew of an armed Japanese fishing trawler that his plane had just bombed and sunk. The bombing of the armed vessel off Palau on July 25, 1944, was the first "kill" for twenty-year-old Ensign George H. W. Bush, and contributed substantially to Bush's case for being a war hero.

There is no question that the bombing was a legitimate act of combat, but once the boat's crew were in lifeboats, international conventions of war forbade firing on them. To fire on them could be considered a war crime, although, as historian John W. Dower pointed out in a recent telephone interview, such things happened frequently on both sides. Dower, who teaches at MIT and has written a book, *War without Mercy*, on the war in the Pacific, said, "This was the nature of the war."

The evidence is inconclusive in other ways as well. First, the official navy record of the mission does not state unambiguously that Bush fired on the lifeboats. The navy document, an after-action report, describes an attack from the air on a Japanese trawler anchored in the lagoon by two navy planes, one piloted by Bush, the second piloted by Lieutenant R. R. Houle. "First run . . . resulted in two misses. On second low-level runs, Ens. G. H. W. Bush, U.S.N.R., scored hit on stern of trawler. Lt. R.R. Houle, U.S.N.R., dropping his bomb closely alongside the bow of the trawler. The trawler sank within five minutes, with its crew taking to two life boats, which VT strafed."

"VT" in the quotation refers to the squadron of which Bush and Houle were part. It is not clear if "VT" is used as a singular or plural form, although the term is used as a plural earlier in the document. Thus, the "VT" that did the strafing could be Houle alone, Bush alone, or both, but the best guess is that it means both.

The report of the incident became part of the official navy record, where it remained, unnoticed, for nearly half a century. A researcher working on federal documents came upon the report in 1991 during the course of his own work, but did nothing with it, not wanting to undercut Bush during the Gulf War. But when Bush made an issue of comparing his own war record with Clinton's lack of military service, this researcher, who has never been publicly identified, wanted to get the strafing story out. He took it to Ogburn, who passed it along to several major news organizations, none of whom ran it before the election. In September 1993, *Harper's Magazine* ran a story on the strafing incident and on the news organizations' refusal to run the story before the election.

This case is an interesting reversal of one of the most common charges against the press: that reporters will rush anything into print, whether substantiated or not. Editors who looked into the matter said they had passed on the story because of the ambiguities in the information. Harrison Rainie, of *U.S. News & World Report*, told ABC's *Nightline* that although *U.S. News* had tried to check out what it thought it would be "a hell of a story" if it could be corroborated, the ambiguities about whether Bush was included in "VT" had caused the magazine to kill the story.

The timing was also an issue. A major scandal in the final weeks of a campaign could prove fatal to a candidate or, just as conceivably, create a backlash of support for a candidate who appears to be pursued unfairly. Evan Thomas, *Newsweek*'s Washington bureau chief, said, "Obviously, if you're on the verge of a national election and you may tip the election one way or the other, you'd be crazy not to think about that."

But Mark Hertsgaard, who wrote the article for *Harper's*, disagreed. In an interview, Hertsgaard argued that it is not only the right but the duty of journalists to publish legitimate news whenever they get it. Anything else, he said, is news management. Even in the waning days of the campaign, he said, "it is a legitimate question that Bush should have been made to answer." He acknowledged that the navy document suggested, rather than proved, Bush's complicity in a war crime, but he noted that the document's authenticity was not in question.

Hertsgaard is the author of *On Bended Knee*, a book about the Washington press corps during the Reagan administration. In it, he argued that journalists were too timid and too easily cowed by the White House. Would he have run such a story just a few weeks before the election? "Absolutely," he said.

While it has been convincingly argued since Cato's time, more than 250 years ago, that irresponsible rumormongering has no place in legitimate journalism, it is just as true that public officials are responsible for their behavior.

Had Bush not made a campaign issue of his war record—and Clinton's lack of one—the question about his actions as a rookie pilot nearly half a century before would be of marginal newsworthiness. In that case, the ambiguity about who "VT" included, coupled with the fact that there were no official charges of wrongdoing, either at the time or later, would probably have combined to outweigh the possibility of Bush's machine-gunning of the boat's survivors. Indeed, in the judgment of the newsmagazines, that is how the factors deciding the question weighed out. But to Hertsgaard and *Harper's*, the incident was worth raising, even though there were no definitive answers.

"It's not a question of the media accusing the president," Hertsgaard told *Nightline.* "The document accuses the president. And if the media does not report that document, it's withholding that information from the public."

Questions to Consider

1. Would publishing an account that said that George Bush might have strafed a lifeboat have served a legitimate journalistic purpose? What arguments could be made for withholding the information?

2. If the information had clearly shown that Bush had committed a war crime, would publishing that account be giving the public relevant information or just scandalmongering? What if he had committed a misdemeanor as a young man?

3. In deciding whether to publish such information, how much consideration should be given to the possibility of affecting an election? Could the decision not to publish affect an election as much as the decision to go ahead? Should journalists even think about the possible effects of their decisions on politics?

4. How can journalists be sure that they are not putting a thumb on the pan—inappropriately steering the decision one way or the other—because of personal political leanings or personal feelings toward the people involved?

5. To avoid a conflict of interest that could lead to bias, should journalists avoid all personal political activities, including registering to vote and voting? How much political activity, if any, can be justified? What about community service? Should any restrictions apply only to journalists with a direct connection to political coverage?

18

When the Law Asks for Help: What Is an Independent Journalist to Do?

One morning in June 1993, Lisa A. Abraham, a reporter at the *Warren (Ohio) Tribune-Chronicle*, stood at one end of a newly paved bridge, looking first at the county engineer out on the bridge, then at her watch, then down at her new red shoes, then back at the wet, sticky tar. It was just a couple of hours until deadline and the man on the bridge was James Fiorenzo, who had some explaining to do. What the hell, she said to herself, and out she marched, unavoidably mindful of the tar but trying to ignore what it was doing to her new shoes.

It seems that Fiorenzo, having ridden Bill Clinton's coattails to victory in Trumbull County, a Democratic stronghold in northeastern Ohio, had been sprucing up the office he had inherited from his rather frumpy Republican predecessor. Just that morning, the county commissioners had held a news conference to announce plans to look into $25,183 worth of remodeling work. The figure was important because, by law, anything over $10,000 had to be put out for bids. What Fiorenzo told her on the bridge that morning, and what she put in the paper for that afternoon's edition, was that the engineer had hired three different contractors, each, as he explained it, doing less than $9,000 worth of work. Voilà. No job over $10,000, no law broken, no problem.

But, as so often happens in public scandals, Fiorenzo's dealings could not withstand the scrutiny focused upon them. There were charges of cronyism—hiring friends and old business partners for work that was unneeded and sometimes went undone—plus other problems with the remodeling job. One of the remodeling contractors was subsequently indicted for submitting phony and inflated bills, and as part of his plea bargaining with prosecutors, the contractor agreed to wear a wire to secretly record conversations with the other two. That led to charges that there were not three contractors after all, just the one who had induced two other friends and fellow contractors to submit phony paperwork to sneak under the $10,000 no-bid ceiling.

As months went by, other shady dealings came out, involving Fiorenzo. "He was your basic corrupt politician," Abraham summed up in a July 1996 interview.

As details of the bogus remodeling emerged over the summer, Fiorenzo changed his story, professing ignorance of the scam and blaming any irregularities wholly on the contractor. As Fiorenzo explained it, if the contractor whom Fiorenzo had hired turned out to be crooked, why, that was terrible, but Fiorenzo surely had not known of it. Abraham wrote a news analysis pointing out the inconsistencies between his latest version of events and what he had told her back on the newly paved bridge.

Eventually, a special prosecutor from nearby Lorain County, Jonathan Rosenbaum, came to Warren to handle the case.[1] Then the sheriff's office called Abraham at the paper, asking for clips of her stories on the case. Abraham complied. "I'm always happy to give people copies of what I've written in the paper," she said in an interview. After all, copies are readily available at the local library and even at the paper's front desk, she said. Then the sheriff's office called back, asking if she would discuss the stories and their preparation with the detectives investigating the Fiorenzo case. This time, she declined. "We're not cops," Abraham said by way of explanation. "It's not my job to go out and catch criminals. It is my job to say, 'Hey, look. This is what's going on, Trumbull County public.'"

Rosenbaum persisted, maintaining that the conversation back on the newly paved bridge was crucial to his case. Abraham still refused, and she was eventually subpoenaed to testify before the grand jury investigating the case. She went to the grand jury room and was sworn in, but she refused to discuss anything about the story.

She was ordered to testify, again refused, and after more legal wrangling, was cited for contempt on January 19, 1994. She was handcuffed and led in a standard "perp walk" past a gaggle of reporters, most of them friends, and off to jail, where she spent twenty-two days in the lockup. She was released only when the grand jury's term expired, an event which meant that she could not be legally held any longer.

The grand jury indicted Fiorenzo without Abraham's testimony. As the trial date approached, Abraham was again called to testify, this time in the trial's open courtroom, not behind the closed doors of a grand jury probe. That made a significant difference. The first time Abraham was called to testify, she argued that since grand jury proceedings were secret, the prosecutor could ask her about all sorts of cases unrelated to the Fiorenzo case. "I didn't want to open myself up to a fishing expedition," she said. But in the open court of a criminal trial, she said,

---

[1] Trumbull County, like many local governments, brings in an outside prosecutor if the local prosecutors have some connection with the case that would raise questions about conflicts of interest. In this case, the Trumbull County prosecutor's office had sat in on discussions with Fiorenzo early on.

she felt a little better, believing that the public scrutiny would keep the proceedings more focused on the topic at hand. Still, the idea of testifying was abhorrent to her.

To Abraham, the closed nature of the grand jury proceeding was actually secondary to her fierce belief that journalists must maintain their independence, even from law enforcement. But to her newspaper, the difference between the closed grand jury room and the open courtroom was so important that the paper changed its policy on paying her salary while she was incarcerated. Abraham said she drew her regular paycheck for twenty-two days the first time around, and she wrote many stories from the inside on inmate grievances, living conditions, and so on. And while the newspaper paid her legal bills throughout, the *Tribune* management said it would put her on unpaid leave if she were locked up again, saying the openness of the trial changed things entirely.

There were other differences between going to jail in round one and getting locked up in round two. In the first case, she was literally in jail, that is, the local lockup. And that was for just over three weeks. Criminal contempt—the charge that would result from refusing to testify in Fiorenzo's criminal trial—would mean up to three months and in state prison, a far scarier place than the local jail.

Abraham fought the order to testify, without, she said later, ever coming to a final decision about whether she would go to prison. On one hand, she did not look forward to life in prison, especially without the support of her paper. On the other hand, she sees herself—a single person unencumbered by family responsibilities—almost perfectly situated to make such a sacrifice. "I don't even have any pets," she said. In the end, she didn't have to decide, for she was excused from testifying under court order.

She said the prosecutor had been angry at what he saw as her apparent inconsistency—she was willing to point out problems but unwilling to help solve them. "There is an attitude that says, 'Well, you tell us all this, but then you won't help us get him,'" Abraham said. "And that's exactly right because that's my job, to tell you all this, so you can get him yourself. Or not.

"That's what being a watchdog is," Abraham said. "I'll bark and tell you there's somebody on the property, and if you want to get worried about it, that's up to you."

Abraham's case is unusual but not unheard of, and it raises an interesting moral question. Over the years, many reporters have been pressured by law enforcement people to share information with them. There are powerful reasons, both practical and principled, to do so. At a practical level, there is a tendency toward a natural give-and-take between reporters and police sources. However fair journalists try to be, there is simply no precinct stationhouse where the bad guys hang out, and there is no muggers' association with press releases and a public relations department. And, it is always easier—and less dangerous—to get information from the police than from those whom the police are chasing.

And, not to put too fine a point on it, it is fun to hang out with the cops. Most police work is not as exciting as it is on the cop shows on television, but it has its moments. It has been a staple for rookie reporters for generations to spend a shift riding around town in a squad car, reporting a feature called, "A Day in the Life of Officer Somebody." Or, better yet, "A *Night* on the Beat with. . . ."

It is undoubtedly true that developing sources through chatting with police officers or hanging around the squad room produces a payoff in the journalist's two most valuable currencies: reliable information and a good chance to get it first.

Beyond the camaraderie and the relative ease of access to cops, at least when compared with access to robbers, there is a natural affinity between the police and the prosecutors, and reporters. Law enforcement and journalism both play crucially important roles in enabling a free society to function. On principle, journalists and the authorities are, at least in very general terms, on the same side.

Yet the two institutions play very different roles. "I know it is sort of a fine line, and a lot of people don't get it," Abraham said, "but to me, reporters simply can't work for the government. If what we do gives the government a good blueprint for what they need to do, then we're being a good watchdog. But we're not the ones to go and slap the cuffs on, and I'm not the one to help you indict Mr. Fiorenzo."

On the other hand, an equally principled reporter, faced with the same case and the possibility of the same prison term, agreed to testify. Janet Rogers, a reporter at WFMJ-TV in Youngstown, said, "I'm not above the law." Ohio law makes it clear that citizens can be compelled to give evidence. Rogers said she, too, would not testify at the grand jury stage of the proceedings because of the secrecy of the grand jury process. But she figured out a way to refuse to give testimony without landing in jail. While grand jurors are under oath to maintain secrecy about the proceedings, witnesses are not, "and I made it very clear that I would do a story about everything that went on," Rogers said. "I don't believe in secrecy."

But at the trial, "everything is in the open," she said. "It is not a secret proceeding. There is a document," that is, the transcript of the trial. "People can see what they want to. People can hear everything that goes on." Rogers noted that the Fiorenzo case had not involved a confidential source. Had it, and had the prosecutor tried to force her to break a confidence, "I'd still be in jail," Rogers said flatly. As it was, she testified to the truth of the story she had done on Fiorenzo, which related much the same information as Abraham's newspaper story had.

Rogers said she thought it was inconsistent for journalists to try to expose lawbreakers and yet maintain that they themselves do not need to obey the laws. "The First Amendment is very important, and it gives us very important rights," she said, "but it does not give us the right to break the law. I am a citizen of Ohio and I am obliged to obey its laws, just like anyone else."

Both reporters in this case cited high principles in deciding whether or not to testify for the prosecution in the Fiorenzo case. Both stood firm on testifying against secret. Abraham went to jail rather than testify, and Rogers threatened to do a story for her television station on what transpired in the closed grand jury room, a threat that kept her out of that room. At trial, Rogers testified in open court, but she said she gave little more than the cliché of "name, rank and serial number" that prisoners of war are supposed to tell their captors. Neither reporter was willing to become an unofficial deputy for law enforcement, even though each is profoundly committed to the principle of law in a democratic society.

Rogers is confident that she satisfied the demand to obey the law by testifying, without ruining her journalistic reputation for independence and integrity by sharing secret notes with the prosecution. Abraham was spared having to decide whether to testify when the stakes were at their highest, but she is sure of what the right choice would have been: refusal. Her only doubt was whether she had the personal courage to follow through.

Questions to Consider

1. Which course would you have chosen—Abraham's or Rogers's—or perhaps a third choice altogether? Why? If Abraham had been forced to make a decision on testifying in court, what decision should she have made? Why? Do you see any other courses of action that could have been taken?

2. Why did both reporters see such a difference between testifying before a grand jury and testifying in open court? If a reporter testifies in open court, is it ethical for that person to give information about the case that did not appear in any of her or his stories about it? Why or why not?

3. Is it ethical for journalists to become friendly with police officers? Often, journalists need the cooperation of the police to get their coverage—tagging along on drug raids or other arrests, getting permission to ride in squad cars to do feature articles, etc. Do we compromise ourselves by accepting such favors from the police? Are we hypocritical if we accept favors from the police but refuse to do favors for them?

4. Are the principles of journalism, as you interpret them, important enough to you that you would choose to go to jail rather than violate them? Why or why not?

19

The Graffiti Artists: Turn 'Em In, Get the Story, or Both?

For the attention paid to the following story to make sense, it is necessary to know two things about New York City. First, it has an extraordinarily activist population. The number of protest marches, demonstrations, and sit-ins has dwindled significantly since the 1960s and early '70s, but every day still brings new rallies, marches, and protests of all sorts. A great many of them are announced by fliers pasted on the sides of buildings, on light poles, and on almost any other vertical surface.

The second thing to know about New York is that it has a longstanding and persistent graffiti culture, a peculiar form of urban blight that some in the hip art world occasionally try to elevate to the level of modern art, but that most New Yorkers consider an ugly and irritating plague of urban vandalism. The modern graffiti era dates from 1970, when "Taki 183" began showing up on street signs, subway cars, bridge supports, and eventually almost any flat surface in the city. As it turned out, Taki was the nickname for a Greek-American teen-ager from Brooklyn named Demetrius (his last name is still not publicly known), and 183 was a shortened form of his street address. Taki's particular form of self-expression was quickly copied by dozens, then hundreds, of fellow New Yorkers, who spray-painted their names, nicknames, and sometimes entire street scenes on any and every surface available.

For a generation now, the city has been in a running war with the "taggers," as some of the vandals call themselves. New York City spends millions of dollars every year erasing and painting over graffiti and trying to develop new surfaces for the subways and other public spaces to make graffiti less likely to adhere and easier to clean off.

In the fall of 1994, a new wave of defacement/announcement swept into the city. Hundreds, and then thousands, of paper fliers appeared all over the city, most bearing a single cryptic word, either "REVS" or "COST," sometimes both. For months, more and more of the miniposters showed up, stuck to almost any surface that would hold them. Occasionally, *REVS* and *COST* were also painted onto walls and the sides of buildings.

The New York City Police Department sought whoever was plastering the cryptic graffiti all over the city, but months went by and thousands of the fliers went up without an arrest. New Yorkers went about their business, but even in a city that seems to pride itself on a blasé tolerance of the latest urban nuisance, many eyebrows went up and many faces scrunched up quizzically at this bizarre new message, so obscure that it was impossible even to categorize as either vandalism or political protest.

Then two days after Christmas, the New York edition of *Newsday*, the most restrained and respectable of the city's three tabloid dailies, ran a story about the rash of postings and an interview with those responsible: two young men who called themselves Revs and Cost. The *Newsday* reporter recounted meeting the two in a diner near the Queensboro Bridge, which connects Manhattan to Queens across the East River, and discussing their "artistry" and their philosophy. The story did not give their real names.

By the time the story ran, one of the two had been arrested and identified as Adam Cole of Queens. A warrant had been issued for the arrest of the other man, but he had not been caught and was not identified by the police.

While graffiti is not a crime of violence and certainly not as serious as many other crimes, it was still against the law and was an urban irritant important enough to prompt the creation of a new graffiti vandalism unit in the city Police Department. The police had declared whoever was behind the *REVS* and *COST* signs to be their most-wanted target.

Thus, the *New York Newsday* reporter, Julio Laboy, had an interesting and common journalistic dilemma—a quick game of "Whose Side Are You On?" He found out the whereabouts of two wanted criminals and, according to his story, chatted with them in a diner before they were arrested. Was Laboy acting morally and responsibly when he interviewed the two wanted men without tipping off the police as to their whereabouts, or should he have told the police what he knew, which might well have led to the arrest of both men? Instead, the police spent several days trailing the pair and wound up arresting only one of them.

For the journalist, there is a clear dilemma based on the conflicting obligations of the several roles the reporter has to play. One the one hand, the journalist is a citizen and, like other citizens, has an obligation to uphold the law. In fact, it could well be that since reporters are far more interested and knowledgeable about public affairs than most citizens, the journalist-citizen has an even greater obligation to perform the duties of citizenship than others.

The journalist-citizen certainly has a greater than average awareness of the importance of obedience to a government of laws. The journalist's most fundamental political role—the reason for the First Amendment in the first place—is to help democratic self-government work. It seems that a journalist, in the role of citizen, would be obliged to help the police in any way possible. True, the journalist also has an obligation to monitor the role of the police, who, as public employees, report to the sovereign people, but in this case there was no hint of impropriety on the part of the police and no suggestion that the suspects were in any way victims of any miscarriage of justice. The general societal good that journalists take as their most basic raison d'être would seem to suggest that the reporter should tip the police about where to find the graffiti squad's most-wanted characters.

On the other hand, the journalist was able to provide his readers some understanding about who "Revs" and "Cost" were and why these two people wanted to plaster the city with their graffiti nicknames. The two do not appear in the *New York Newsday* story to be particularly insightful or profound, and the story is no great stirring example of urban insight; the two men are quoted as advocating a vague nihilism, a do-your-own-thing sort of anarchy. To the question: "What do all those 'REVS' and 'COST' signs mean?" the best answer, it turned out, was: not very much. Still, the readers learned what there was to know—and that this campaign fell into the category of graffiti vandalism, not some oblique protest against the high price of ministry. Of course, the reporter could have tried to time events so that he would have had the interview with Revs and Cost just before the cops showed up to arrest them.

So far, this seems to be a fairly strong case in favor of telling the police of the planned rendezvous between the reporter and the pair of vandals. By not notifying the police, the reporter did get an interesting but not very profound story, but the reporter failed in the obligation to help an orderly society function. There is, however, more to the problem of whether to turn in Revs and Cost, which has to do with the independence of the news media and—perhaps even more important—the public perception of that independence. Journalists have a special bond of trust with their readers and viewers. It is not necessarily a stronger bond than many of the other bonds between the different parts of a society, but it is a powerful and an important one. And it is unique. It is not the same, say, as the relationship between the citizenry and its police force, or between the citizens and the judiciary. For the public to trust news organizations, the public must believe that journalists are bound to nothing but the truth and are not a secret, or not-so-secret, extension of law enforcement.

Under the best of circumstances, it is difficult to keep journalism independent of the police. The criminal justice system provides a large segment of our daily news diet, which is probably as it should be, and the police are far more helpful in providing information about crime than are the criminals. Reporters spend a lot of time with police officers and generally like them, often seeing them as natural allies, as in a sense they are.

Yet it is important to maintain journalistic independence, especially as it relates to monitoring the police force itself. In this case, the police have done nothing wrong, but once in a while they do. The temptations of being a police officer are enormous. We give the police guns and sticks and great latitude in their actions. We ask them to confront all kinds of danger and unpleasantness in our name and for our well-being. They are subject to bribes, to intimidation, and to a range of pressures, both physical and mental, yet we expect split-second judgment and flawless behavior. We have, and should have, high expectations of the police, and the best way to keep confidence in the police is to know what they are doing.

One of the greatest deterrents to malfeasance is knowing or suspecting that you will be found out. It is as true for a police officer as it is for a politician or a college student or a reporter or a kid eyeing the cookie jar. The best way to have a scrupulously honest police department—which is in the best interest of an overwhelming majority of police officers as well as the rest of us—is to monitor police behavior closely. And the way to do that is to make the public know that journalists are independent agents, not an extension of law enforcement. On those rare occasions that someone in a police uniform does abuse the public trust, it is important for the citizenry to have someone to call whom they can trust.

Suppose that the reporter had arranged the meeting with the two vandals and then tipped the police, who then showed up at the diner and made the arrests. Several things would have happened, none of them good for journalism and none of them good for the principle of honesty:

First, the journalist would have been fundamentally dishonest in dealing with the graffiti vandals. Behaving dishonorably to anyone—good guy, bad guy or, like most of us, some combination of the two—is, on the face of it, the wrong thing to do. Other principles, such as saving a life, might sometimes be more important, but good journalists consider themselves obliged to be truthful and honest unless extraordinary circumstances warrant otherwise. The absolute core foundation of what they do is based upon the expectation that what they say and write will be as truthful as they can make it.

Second, at least two people, and probably a great many more before it was all over, would have learned that reporters are not to be trusted. In the case of Revs and Cost, this might or might not seem particularly important, but, as every investigative reporter knows, the journalist's reputation for independent integrity is very important. The chances of people telling journalists of abuses of power in the future are greatly diminished if it is known that reporters sometimes act as extensions of the police. The reporter who is tempted to set up Revs and Cost has to consider the harm that will be done to all reporters at all stations and newspapers.

Third, the police would learn that at least some reporters would lie on their behalf. That would inevitably lessen the deterrent value that comes from having police work—the public's business, after all—conducted under public scrutiny. A police officer who feels less likely to get caught is more likely to yield to the pressures and temptations that arise every day.

In this light, there was a great deal in favor of meeting with Revs and Cost without informing the police and much less to recommend tipping the police of their whereabouts. Another, less satisfactory, course would have been to pass on the story altogether. That would have avoided the problem of deliberately refusing to help apprehend wanted men, which would be a plus, but it would have not fulfilled the journalistic obligation to tell the public about the world around them.

Under this analysis, the worst choice would have been to do what at first glance seemed the most attractive course: to help the police apprehend their vandals.

This is what is means by the often-heard journalistic exclamation, "I'm not a cop."

Questions to Consider

1. Would you agree to interview two criminals without telling the police who and where they are? Why or why not? Would the type of crime involved make any difference in your decision?

2. What would have been the obligation of the *New York Newsday* reporter if, during the interview, he had found out the vandals' plans for more graffiti? What about if he had found out that they were involved in crimes that were even more serious?

3. If a police reporter at a crime scene spots physical evidence related to a crime, should that reporter notify the police?

4. Journalists generally keep their distance from all law-enforcement agencies, including the FBI and the CIA. Why do journalists protest when those agencies allow their agents to pose as journalists?

20

Connie Chung: Did She Sandbag the New Speaker's Mom?

During the months between the general election in November 1994 and the opening session of Congress in early January 1995, no politician in the country was more the center of attention than Newt Gingrich, the conservative and often caustic Republican from Georgia who was about to become Speaker of the House of Representatives, the most powerful member of the House, and the first Republican to hold the post in forty years. He was the subject of many profiles in major newspapers, and his views were sought avidly by print and broadcast reporters on every conceivable topic.

During inauguration week in early January, journalists were scrambling to provide comprehensive coverage of the juggernaut rolling in from the right with Gingrich at its head. It was a massive story and an important one, with profound implications for the nation's domestic, foreign, social and economic policies. As part of this story, the CBS television network secured an interview with Gingrich's mother, Kathleen, and stepfather, Bob, for the news program, *Eye to Eye with Connie Chung*.

In the interview, Chung first asked Gingrich's stepfather if his son had ever said anything about President Bill Clinton. Bob Gingrich replied, "The only thing he ever told me is that he's smart. That he's an intelligent man. That he's not very practical, but he's intelligent."

Chung turned to Kathleen Gingrich, and asked, "What has Newt told you about President Clinton?"

The Speaker-designate's mother answered, "Nothing. And I can't tell you what he said about Hillary," referring to Hillary Rodham Clinton.

Chung then said, "You can't?" and Kathleen Gingrich replied, "I can't."

Chung persisted, saying, "Why don't you just whisper it to me, just between you and me."

In a stage whisper, the new Speaker's mother said, "She's a bitch." Then, back in her normal voice, Kathleen Gingrich added, "That's about the only thing he ever said about her. I think they had some meeting, you know, and she takes over."

Chung prodded, "She does?"

Kathleen Gingrich nodded and continued, "But with Newty there, she can't."

The cameras were rolling and the exchange was included as part of the broadcast, and excerpts were used during the network's nightly newscast as a teaser for the *Eye to Eye* program shown later that evening.

The next day, both Clintons shrugged off the comment, but the new House Speaker demanded an apology from both CBS and the interviewer. Appearing on another CBS program, *This Morning*, Representative Gingrich said, "I think it is unprofessional and frankly pretty despicable to go to a mother, who is not a politician, not in public life, and say, 'whisper to me' and then share it with the country."

Instead of an apology, the president of CBS News, Eric Ober, defended his star in a statement. "Approximately midway through the two-hour uninterrupted interview in front of three CBS News cameras, Mrs. Gingrich volunteered an unsolicited view that she said her son had expressed regarding Hillary Rodham Clinton. While broadcasting Mrs. Gingrich's comments may have been perceived by some as unfair, CBS News does not believe withholding those comments would have been appropriate."

The network also said that seeing the exchange in the context of the full interview had made it clear that Chung had not ambushed the Speaker's mother.

This case sets up a common confrontation between the obligation of the journalist to have unassailable personal integrity and the public's right to be informed of important events and trends in the public arena. First, is what the Speaker's mother had to say news? While not earth shattering, the information is useful. The Speaker of the House is the most powerful member of that chamber of Congress. Given that Gingrich would be the first Republican to hold that office in forty years and that he has a reputation as a combative, caustic politician, relations between the Republican Congress and the Democratic White House are certainly a matter of legitimate public interest. This is the people's business.

It is less clear whether it is the public's business to know whether the people's representatives get along with each other on a personal level. On one hand, personal enmities seem likely to have a bearing on how political decisions are made. On the other hand, these are professional politicians. Their public behavior is not automatically tightly tied to their personal feelings and personalities. On balance, most journalists today would probably argue that the public interest is well served by examining politicians' personal likes and dislikes. That is especially true in the context of a combative Republican taking over the leadership of one house of Congress, while the White House is held by a Democrat. If CBS had interviewed the Speaker's mother instead of talking to Gingrich himself, it could have been faulted for missing the story or for trivializing the news. But as part of extensive coverage about the vanguard of the Republican revolution, interviewing the Speaker's mother seems fully appropriate.

But how sure can we be that Kathleen Gingrich is a credible source in describing her son's feelings about Clinton and his wife? Again, she appears to be.

Wouldn't a more direct, and therefore more even credible, approach be to put such questions to Gingrich himself? Probably not. Asking Gingrich directly is almost certain to produce an answer that Gingrich believes to be in his political interest at the moment. That is not necessarily an honest answer. Political figures are rarely fully candid, and close relatives may well provide better information. There is no guarantee that Newt Gingrich said what his mother quoted him as saying, but there is little reason to doubt it, either. On both grounds, the quote is newsworthy, especially during inauguration week, when the new Congress was just getting down to business.

Next, the question has to be whether Chung used improper or unethical methods to get Kathleen Gingrich to quote her son. Is there merit to Newt Gingrich's claim that CBS ambushed his mother? If his claim is valid, that would be a strong argument against publishing (in this case, publishing through broadcasting) the statement. True, as the network's statement said, Kathleen Gingrich brought up the subject of her son's views toward Hillary Clinton unbidden. However, according to the transcript, she was very reluctant to quote her son and did so, in a low voice, only when Chung implored her to "whisper it to me, just between you and me." Chung did not promise not to use the quote, and certainly Kathleen Gingrich had to have been aware that the interview was being recorded. The question becomes: Was it reasonable for Kathleen Gingrich to believe that Chung's statement "just between you and me" was a promise not to use the whispered quote?

That illustrates one of the differences between law and ethics. Legally, there is no question as to whether the statement was safe to publish, but the question of whether it was ethical to publish it is harder to answer. Neither Chung nor Kathleen Gingrich invoked the magic words "off the record," nor did Chung promise not to use the quoted material. However, as the contemporary philosopher, Sissela Bok, points out in her book *Lying*, morally speaking, lying is the intent to deceive rather than the technical accuracy or inaccuracy of words, whose meaning can be the subject of much interpretation and debate.

Did Chung intend to deceive Kathleen Gingrich into thinking that the "bitch" quote would not be used? There is no way to absolutely certain, but every indication is that she did, indeed, believe that the broadcast would not include that statement. She twice refused to quote her son, then did so only in a whisper. Chung is a skilled interviewer, and journalists frequently resort to various tricks to get interview subjects to open up, particularly on television, where paraphrasing and other devices are less workable than they are in print. In this case, it appears that Chung deliberately misled the speaker's mother into believing that the quote would not be used. That is lying, by Bok's definition. Few people are as absolute about never, ever lying as was Immanual Kant in discussing his categorical imperative, but most ethicists believe that lying is morally indefensible. As such, it is a powerful argument against publishing.

What about Representative Gingrich's observation that Chung's duplicity involved not a politician, but a private citizen? Do journalists have different standards for politicians and for nonpoliticians? Most journalists would say yes. Politicians spend their lives around journalists; indeed, they exist in today's mass media world only because of journalists. They develop a keen sense of journalistic propriety and are aware of the naturally adversarial relationship that exists between reporters and politicians. Some yearn, or say they yearn, for easier, simpler days when journalists did not seem always to be looking for a "gotcha!" but, in fact, both politicians and reporters constantly use each other for their own purposes, and each is constantly aware of the symbiotic relationship that they share.

Private citizens are considerably less aware of the ways of reporters. They tend to be less guarded, more open, and more susceptible to a journalist's techniques for drawing a person out, for getting an interview subject to come up with the quote the journalist knows will make for a better story. Professional politicians are very wary of what they say to a journalist, particularly on camera, but a private citizen is less cautious. Most journalists recognize the difference and hold the politician more accountable. In this case, Newt Gingrich is right: the interviewer did at least bend the rules in a way that seems unfair to Kathleen Gingrich and, by extension, to her son.

The danger is not that Kathleen Gingrich will feel angry, or abused, or even deceived by Chung. At a personal level, that may be important, and she may be more wary the next time a reporter asks for an interview. The danger is that journalism may have lost just a bit of its institutional integrity. Politicians regularly complain about reporters, and Gingrich himself has made something of a career out of complaining about journalists, who he says have a liberal bias against him and against his conservative agenda. Chung's small deception almost certainly was not politically motivated. Reporters can and do wheedle quotes out of people without any particular grand scheme in mine. However, anything that lends credence to a politician's accusations of unfair or unsavory behavior by journalists tends to diminish the entire journalistic institution and makes it that much harder for reporters to maintain the Lockean contract with the people they serve to bring them honest and timely information about the world around them.

The network has a good point in arguing that a full viewing of the interview strengthens its claim that Kathleen Gingrich should have expected Chung to use the quote. In apparent good humor, Chung and Kathleen Gingrich had resorted to stage whispers "just between us" earlier in the interview, adding weight to the network's argument that Chung had done nothing improper. However, the network violated its own call for context when it showed the exchange in question during the network newscast as the teaser for the full interview. That made the network seem ingenuous when it later defended the quote by calling for viewing the exchange only in full context.

Just as in the NBC truck case (see Chapter 24), the brief controversy over whether or not Chung had unjustly misled the unwitting Kathleen Gingrich clouded the story and moved public attention away from the topic at hand. If the ethical question had not arisen, viewers would have been left with a slightly clearer picture of Newt Gingrich—largely a validation of the Georgia congressman's image as combative—and a further suggestion that citizens take note of whether Gingrich's abrasive personality would lead to more or less effective government. One way to have headed off the controversy would have been for Chung to have tried to get Kathleen Gingrich to agree to use the quote, since the request for a whispered response "just between you and me" was ambiguous at best. If she had agreed, the new Speaker of the House would have been denied the chance to do what he did next: bash the press once again, with considerable righteous indignation, and in so doing divert attention away from his own combativeness and vulgarity, potentially significant traits in the new occupant of a position of considerable power and dignity.

Because of ethical questions about Chung's behavior, Gingrich was able to turn the question away from his own behavior and once again blame the messenger. Every time a reporter steps out of line just a little bit, those with things to hide pounce gleefully on the appearance of journalistic sin thereby turning public attention away from the issue at hand and onto questions about the shortcomings of the reporter. Charlatans in public life like nothing better than for the public to lose confidence in its watchdog. On balance, it seems that too little information was gained and too much public trust risked to make the use of the quote worthwhile. Even less credible is the network's decision to pull the exchange out of the very context it claimed was important and use it during the newscast to draw viewers to the later show.

Questions to Consider

1. What are the arguments for and against using the quotation in dispute? What would you have done?

2. Is a politician's mother a legitimate interview subject? How about the person who cuts the politician's hair? The person who rents the politician videotapes?

3. Does Kathleen Gingrich have as much right to privacy as any other ordinary person, or has her right to privacy been affected by having a famous son? Has any of her own behavior affected that right?

4. In this case, a reporter appeared to have made a promise to a source not to use a piece of an interview. Reporters often make promises to sources to consider material off the record (cannot be used) or not for attribution (material can be used but the source's name cannot be associated with it). How binding should such promises be? How can such promises compromise the reporter?

21

Primary Authorship: Can You Lie about Your Other Job?

For most of the first half of the presidential election year of 1996, the strange world of political Washington—part trivia, part gossip, and part deadly serious politics—was abuzz over a new novel called *Primary Colors*, a thinly disguised account of Bill Clinton's 1992 presidential campaign. The buzz was not just over how much was literally true and how much was literary license, but also over who had written it. For in the book, published by Random House, the author was listed as "Anonymous."

The book was a spectacular success, spending twenty weeks on the *New York Times* best-seller list, the nation's most credible list of book sales. For nine weeks it was number one, the best-selling fiction book in the country. It sold more than a million copies and fueled a fascinating game of sleuth played inside the beltway and among political junkies beyond.[1]

The mystery was a publisher's delight, for speculation about the author's identity prompted talk of the book, and when books are hot topics of conversation, people buy them, if only to see what the fuss is about. Plus, the mere presence of a mystery suggested that someone high inside the Clinton administration might have written the book. The political intrigue was as high as as it had been since Deep Throat kept Bob Woodward and Carl Bernstein on the trail during Watergate. The book was so successful that the film director Mike Nichols bought the movie rights for more than $1.5 million, according to published reports, and cast major Hollywood stars for the leading roles.

---

[1] Literally, the term refers to the District of Columbia and its immediate surroundings that lie within the 66-mile ring road of I-495 that circles the national capital. In common usage, it refers to the whole national political establishment, including politicians, lobbyists, hangers-on of all descriptions—and journalists. The term is sometimes used derisively to suggest that those inside the beltway become so absorbed with political minutia that they lose touch with what the rest of the country is thinking.

Periodically, speculation centered on Joe Klein, a prominent Washington political columnist for *Newsweek* magazine, as the author, but Klein denied it—vehemently, categorically, and unequivocally. He denied it when asked by friends and competitors in the press corps, and he denied it when asked by CBS, where he moonlighted as a political consultant. He denied it in February 1996 when *New York Magazine* reported that a Vassar professor with a computer program that analyzes writing styles had identified Klein as the author. And he denied it when a *Washington Post* staffer asked him if he would stake his journalistic reputation on his denial. Each time, the questioning went elsewhere—toward a mole in the White House or a one-time speechwriter for Mario Cuomo, the former governor of New York. But as it turned out, Klein's denials were lies. He had written the book, a fact that emerged only in July when the *Post* took off after the story again, this time hiring a handwriting expert who compared the handwriting on an early draft of the manuscript with several submitted writing samples and concluded, without question, that Klein was the writer.

Random House held a news conference to 'fess up and say, Oh, by the way, the book will be out in paperback in a couple of months. The initial press run: another 1.5 million copies.

Klein wrote his *Newsweek* column on the matter the next week, repeatedly referring to his "little white lies" and "fibs" and maintaining that he had been "almost relieved" when he had been found out. He wrote that he had figured that nobody would believe his initial denials and that the charade would be quickly over. Ha, ha. No harm done. Meantime, next year's tuition for the kids is taken care of.

But journalists in Washington and elsewhere were outraged, not amused, at Klein's duplicity. The *Philadelphia Inquirer* said he should be fired along with *Newsweek*'s editor, Maynard Parker, who knew that Klein was Anonymous but kept the secret. Parker even ran several short pieces in the magazine that directed speculation on the identity of Anonymous toward various other people. CBS dropped Klein immediately, and *Newsweek* gave him a couple of weeks off to let things cool down.

So what? Is this a serious breach of ethics, or is the anger directed at Klein by his friends in the press corps just grousing that he tricked them—even gave them bald-faced lies—even though what he did was essentially harmless? Klein describes the matter as a little joke that got out of hand so quickly that he had seen no graceful way to get out of the deceit he had begun. He said he had been caught between "two ethical systems—book publishing and journalism." He said he regretted having been so categorical in his denials, rather than dodging the questions, but he noted, by way of explanation, "I was on the spot and Von Drehle (from the *Washington Post*) wouldn't let go."

It was, he said, just a novel and therefore not important, and he complained about the attention his unmasking received. "This is the kind of overzealous, bloodthirsty, witless pursuit, over a very trivial matter, that does far more damage to journalists than anything I've done," he said in a published interview.

Besides, he said, his agent at Random House insisted that he keep his commitment to them to remain anonymous. And no wonder. For while there may be some credence to Klein's argument that he had initially wanted to write anonymously so his book's harsh portraits of the Clintons would not affect his subsequent White House coverage, it is doubtless true that Random House's marketing people realized full well that mystery in Washington translates into news copy, which translates into sales.

Klein has something of a point when he describes the Washington press corps as highly aggressive. The primary focus of journalism is politics, and as Washington is the political capital of the nation, so Washington is the epicenter of political reporting. Journalism's strengths and weaknesses stand out in starkest relief in Washington. The "feeding frenzy," as one popular book of press criticism called it,[2] is at its fiercest in Washington, but so are the political efforts to use journalists for partisan ends. The stakes are at their highest in the capital and so are the egos, the salaries and the perquisites of both journalists and politicians.

Doubtless, some of the reporters who gave Klein a hard time at his confessional news conference were personally angered—and may even have felt betrayed—at having been lied to, especially by a friend and colleague. But there is a good deal more at work here than personal pique. What gets journalists in a lather more than almost anything else is hypocrisy.

As a journalist, Klein's primary job is to tell the truth as well as he knows it and to make those he covers do the same. Journalists do not issue a free pass to those who say that the story is not important, as in: "It's only a multimillion-dollar book-and-movie deal." Besides, it is important. It is not a life-or-death issue, but a White House staffer falsely accused of being Anonymous would certainly have lost her or his credibility and reputation for loyalty, highly regarded traits in political Washington. The book showed keen insight and great familiarity with the 1992 presidential campaign. If it had not been written by a member of the press corps, then it almost had to have been written by a member of the campaign staff. And, given the unflattering portrait painted of Clinton, such a staff member, if discovered, would be in for a serious dressing down, if not worse.

Both Klein and Random House made millions from the book's popularity, which was greatly enhanced by the guessing game and the suspicions that this was an inside job. Reporters who called for sanctions against Klein and his magazine saw his categorical denials as a betrayal of the most sacred trust in journalism: to tell the truth.

For Klein to excuse his dishonesty by saying that the *Washington Post* reporter "wouldn't let go" is dissembling in the extreme. A reporter is supposed to get at the truth and not take evasive answers. Klein is good at his craft and knows the rules.

---

[2] Larry J. Sabato, *Feeding frenzy: How Attack Journalism Has Transformed American Politics*. (New York: Free Press, 1991).

Once the *Post* reporter made it clear that Klein was staking his journalistic reputation on his answer, he could be taken at his word. Klein's "little white lies" and "fibs" could well end his career. A reporter, whose core principle should be telling the truth, instead first got rich by evading the truth (when he published anonymously) and then got richer by lying about it, even when others' reputations stood to be seriously harmed by being mistaken as the book's writer. And Klein's editor went along with the ruse, to the point of putting several stories in the magazine that he knew were not true.

The damage to journalism may well exceed that to Klein personally, who, after all, could live out his days on the estimated $6 million he has made on the book. It is hardly convincing for journalists to say that their duty is to expose—and, in so doing, condemn—dishonesty born of greed when one of its major-league writers does exactly that.

The damage Klein has done to the profession's reputation, and thus its ability to do its most basic job, may well exceed that done by another Washington reporter, Janet Cooke, in 1981. Cooke, as a twenty-six-year-old reporter for the *Washington Post*, wrote a story about an eight-year-old heroin addict whom she called Jimmy. It was a powerful piece of writing, and after it appeared, the police began a massive search for the child but could never find him. The story, called "Jimmy's World," was nominated for, and was awarded, a Pulitzer prize. But the prize and the consequent fame were extremely short lived. When the Pulitzers were announced, reporters localizing the Cooke story found holes in her résumé—colleges she had not really attended, degrees she had not really earned. With the author of "Jimmy's World" now suspect, her story soon fell apart. Jimmy did not exist. He was a "composite character," a notion that enjoyed a brief run of popularity during the late 1970s and early 1980s, when *new journalism*, or *literary journalism*, which adapted fiction techniques to nonfiction writing, came into vogue. Defenders of composite characters, internal dialogue, and other literary devices taken from fiction writing maintained that while there was no particular eight-year-old child named Jimmy, heroin addiction was an increasing problem among younger and younger children. There were, according to the defenders of composite characters, lots of children who resembled the portrait of Jimmy that Cooke painted in the *Post*.

The practice of relying on composite characters suffered an enormous and well-deserved black eye in the Cooke case. The defense of such practice usually gets around to some version of claiming some larger Truth, even at the expense of some garden-variety truth.

Cooke was a fast-rising young reporter who was under staggering pressure from her own newspaper to come up with an actual person to illustrate the true and important story of young kids and hard drugs in the nation's capital. Unable to produce the perfect child to illustrate the story she wanted to tell, she reached for a journalistic technique then in high fashion among the most celebrated of the country's journalists. She got caught, embarrassed her paper mightily, and left both the *Post* and journalism altogether.

By contrast, Klein was a highly paid and well-connected member of the journalism establishment's inner circle. He was reaching for no literary device. In *Primary Colors,* Klein had no particularly important story to tell. And the deception he undertook for half a year, lying with indignant vehemence to friend and colleague alike, served no purpose beyond personal enrichment.

Philip E. Meyer, professor of journalism at the University of North Carolina at Chapel Hill, posted a message on the Internet that sums up Klein's case admirably. "'Anonymous' was a clever marketing ploy to make the book seem more authentic, i.e., more of an inside job, than it really was," Meyer wrote. "You have to admire that. But it also means that the lie was much more than a white lie; it was created for the purpose of enriching the liar, and it did so with spectacular effect—at the expense of all those who bought the book thinking they were getting the inside scoop." Meyer's conclusion was, "Anyone who lies to enrich himself at the expense of others should not be in journalism or any other form of public service."

Questions to Consider

1. Some might argue that *Primary Colors* had nothing to do with Klein as a journalist and that it should have no effect on his reputation as a journalist. Do you think it was related? Why or why not?

2. If there had been no deception involved about the authorship of the book, would *Primary Colors* have been an acceptable thing for a journalist who covers national politics to write? Why or why not?

3. Journalists hold politicians to a high standard in their personal lives. Should journalists have to meet these same high standards? Should they make public their investments, speaking fees or any other factors that could be seen as a conflict of interest for them in covering certain stories or beats? Why or why not?

4. If you accept the premise that journalists should be personally honorable in order to be worthy of public trust, does that mean they should be drummed out of the profession if they cheat on their income taxes? Engage in activities that some might consider immoral? Just what kind of standard of behavior do journalists need to meet?

5. Klein wrote a book of fiction and lied about writing it. Cooke tried to pass fiction off as nonfiction, but she said it reflected an underlying truth. Do you see one as more of a transgressor than the other? Why or why not?

22

A Reporter with AIDS: Depth
of Understanding or Obvious Bias?

As the horizons of legitimate topics for news continue to broaden, so, too, do the possibilities for a conflict of interest. In the days when most hard news came off the police and political beats, it was fairly easy for reporters to know, and for their editors to know, whether they had any biases that might jeopardize their ability to cover stories fairly. But hardly anyone considers such a narrow definition of news to be adequate any longer, and justly so. In the following piece, a powerful testament by Jeffrey Schmalz, a gay reporter infected with AIDS, the journalist is forced to confront the most basic questions of his existence. Only in doing so can he deal with the painful tensions between his life as a gay man and his life as a reporter.

COVERING AIDS AND LIVING IT: A REPORTER'S TESTIMONY*

Two years ago tomorrow, I collapsed at my desk in the newsroom of the *New York Times*, writhed on the floor in a seizure and entered the world of AIDS.

I had been, as far as I knew, absolutely healthy, and it took the doctors a few weeks to reach their diagnosis: full-blown AIDS, with a brain infection often fatal within four months.

That I have lived these two years is a miracle. How long my luck will hold, no one knows. But for now, I am back working, a reporter with AIDS who covers AIDS.

I've thought a lot about my dual identity since the death last Sunday of Ricky Ray. I wrote about him and his family in 1988, about their new life in Sarasota, Fla. It was a year after their home was destroyed by arson in Arcadia, Fla., a town

---

*By Jeffrey Schmalz. Reprinted, with permission, from the *New York Times*, December 20, 1992.

where many people hated Ricky and his two younger brothers because they were infected with H.I.V., a town where pickup trucks bore the bumper sticker "This vehicle protected by a pit bull with AIDS."

I recall my late-summer evening with the Rays vividly. Three barefoot boys in jeans and T-shirts, scrambling on the floor with their hamster. A sooty Garfield the Cat, himself a survivor of the fire, looking down from the china cabinet. "I'm only human," Garfield said when his string was pulled, and the Ray boys would turn giggly.

How proud I was of myself. How noble of me to write about these people nobody wanted to touch. How smug I was that I, a gay man, had escaped AIDS. (I know now that I was already infected. But I had not been tested; I felt great.) And how ambivalent I was about the Rays, these people who had parlayed personal tragedy into celebrity—they seemed just a little too available for interviews—and who talked so glibly of death.

Now, four years later, at the age of 39, it is I who talk matter-of-factly of life and death and who have used my affliction to advantage, to obtain interviews and force intimacy. Does that make me feel guilty? You bet. But to have AIDS is to live with guilt and shame.

So many tensions are at work on those of us with AIDS that it's hard to chronicle them. My mother, seemingly healthy, died last year at 73, a few months after my sister told her of my AIDS. A coronary? A stroke? Who knows? In my mind, it will always be a broken heart.

I make sure everyone with AIDS whom I interview knows that I have it, too. To be sure, that is an interview ploy; I'm hoping the camaraderie will open them up. But there is more to it than that; I want them to take a good look at me, to see that someone with full-blown AIDS can carry on for a while, can even function as a reporter. Much of the time, it works. Their faces light up. There is hope.

'You'll Be Here Soon'

But sometimes it fails, and I am the one changed by our chat, overcome by guilt that I have lived these two years when so many of my friends and hospital roommates and people I've interviewed have died. At times, I think my fellow AIDS sufferers are laughing at me, looking up from their beds with eyes that say, "You'll be here soon enough."

Endlessly, I fret about my interviews. I know the buttons to push with people with AIDS and I push them well. Do I cross the line, pressing too hard for the sake of a good quote?

"I wish it wasn't true," Bob Hattoy said of having AIDS just before he addressed the Democratic National Convention. "But it isn't overwhelming me. Really, I don't know why."

I knew from my own experience the nightmares of waking up in a coffin, of wondering whether every cold was the big one that would do me in. I challenged him for not being honest, and he broke down. I wanted to hold him. I wanted to apologize. Then he hit me as hard as I had hit him.

"I think I will probably die of AIDS," he blurted out. "Won't you?"

Yes, I expect so. In my gut, I know it. Yet in the back of my mind, I just can't believe it: Maybe, just maybe, I'll live to see a treatment breakthrough.

How different these AIDS interviews now are from the one four years ago with the Rays, when all was well and I was just a spectator to the train wreck, not riding in one of the cars. It was simple then: A quick goodbye. A shake of the hand. A perfunctory wish for the future. Then off into the night. Now, it's embraces and tears and whispers from me and for me: "Stay well," "Don't give up," "God bless." And always there is that one futile question: Have you found the magic cure?

To have AIDS is to be alone, no matter the number of friends and family members around. Then, to be with someone who has H.I.V.—be it interviewer or interviewee—is to find kinship. "I'm so glad they picked you to do this," Mary Fisher said in an interview just before she spoke at the Republican National Convention as a woman with H.I.V. With her, as with Magic Johnson and Bob Hattoy and Larry Kramer and Elizabeth Glaser, who spoke at the Democratic Convention, the talk was the same: of anger and courage and politics. We talked of that deep nausea in the pit of your stomach when even cancer patients pity you and when a doctor, who should know better, puts on latex gloves just to shake your hand.

There are timeouts in each of the interviews for both of us to get tissues, for both to pop our AZT, for both to laugh and always to hug. "I will see you again," Magic Johnson said pointedly, in what was not a social nicety but an affirmation of life between two people with H.I.V. Like each of the other interviews, ours was therapy for him. It was therapy for me.

"Who are you?" a TV reporter asked me at a funeral march in Greenwich Village for an Act-Up leader dead of AIDS. The reporter knew full well who I was: the guy from The Times with AIDS.

The lid of the coffin had been removed, the open box carried on shoulders in the rain, led in the dark by mourners with torches, the dirge of a single drumbeat setting the pace of this, a funeral turned protest against President Bush's handling of AIDS.

"Are you here as a reporter or as a gay man with AIDS?" the TV correspondent persisted, shoving a microphone in my face. His camera spotlight went on.

I didn't respond. People in the crowd moved closer; they wanted to know the answer. I wanted to know it, too. Finally, it came out: "Reporter." Some shook their heads in disgust, all but shouting "Uncle Tom!" They wanted an advocate, not a reporter. So there I stood, a gay man with AIDS out of place at an AIDS funeral, an outsider in my own world.

I walked back to the office in the rain, thinking along the 30 blocks about how tough it must be for blacks to report about blacks, for women to report about women. Yet that kind of reporting is the cutting edge of journalism. Some people think it is the journalism that suffers, that objectivity is abandoned. But they are wrong. If the reporters have any integrity at all, it is they who suffer, caught between two allegiances.

Don't misunderstand; it was I, not my editors, who pressed me to write about AIDS. For 20 years, I had been a by-the-book Timesman, no personal involvement allowed. But now I see the world through the prism of AIDS. I feel an obligation to those with AIDS to write about it and an obligation to the newspaper to write what just about no other reporter in America can cover in quite the same way. And I feel an obligation to myself. This is the place where I am at home. This is the place where I must come to terms with AIDS.

I didn't write an article about the funeral march, judging it worth only a picture and a caption. I passed the journalism test that afternoon in the rain by failing the activism test. To turn activist would mean that AIDS, not reporting, would define me. It would be to surrender totally to the disease.

But no matter how neatly it works out in the mind, that doesn't make it any easier, even when I'm reporting on issues besides AIDS.

Breakfast in Iowa

Traveling the country to interview voters about the Presidential election, I dropped by an Iowa cafe where, as a reporter from New York, I was hailed as a mini-celebrity. Asked to say a few words at a breakfast of 30 leading citizens, I wanted to tell them I had AIDS, to watch the stunned look on their faces. But I didn't. That would have crossed the line between reporter and activist. Yet I do tell some politicians I interview. In my mind, that's O.K. I can't explain why. I left the breakfast in Iowa feeling hypocritical, a disciple who professes to carry the message of AIDS but is most comfortable preaching to the converted.

"Why are you here with me?" Jerry Brown asked when, while I was covering his Presidential campaign for a few days, the conversation turned to AIDS and I told him that I had it. "I'm here," I said, "because it is what I do."

He leaned closer to me, asking quietly, "Don't you want to be off getting in touch with your spirituality?"

Religion. How I have wrestled with that one. I had wanted to stop in church the day before brain surgery. But to me it would have been the height of hypocrisy to turn to God in desperation after years of turning away.

Yet I have become more spiritual. I think often of the dozen friends who have died of AIDS, and I feel them with me. It's not that I am writing editorials, avenging their deaths. It's that I feel their strength, their soothing me on. They are my conscience, their shadows with me everywhere: In the torchlight of the march. Over my shoulder. By my desk. In my sleep.

It's Still News

On its surface, life is much the same as before: I walk into the newsroom, sit at my desk, work the phone. But it is a through-the-looking-glass world. Sitting in my doctor's office, listening to the latest update, I can't help thinking, "This is a good story."

An interview with Clinton on gay issues and AIDS was the oddest I've ever had. He had been briefed that I had the virus, but we never discussed it. It seemed self-centered for me to bring it up, and I guess he thought it rude for him to do it. So there we were, talking about AIDS. I knew that he knew that I knew that he knew.

Before me on the desk are the letters—a hundred of them this year, some from people who read that I had AIDS, others from people who figured it out between the lines of my pieces. Those are the ones I am proudest of. "Consider this letter a giant hug," wrote a man from Philadelphia. I have killed the message on my phone tape from a man dying of AIDS who had called begging me to save his life, to give him some nugget of information that would keep him alive. "Please!" he cried. I called him back to say there was nothing I could do except recommend doctors. I kept that tape for weeks, playing it over and over. "Please!" I wonder if he is dead now.

Oh, I have come to understand the Rays—those people who seemed so glib. Now, I see that they are like all of us with AIDS, trying to go on about their lives but caught up in this nightmare. They do what they have to do. We all do. I think about them. I am one with them. And I think about Ricky, the newest shadow looking over my shoulder.

My editors keep an eye on me, I am sure, to make certain that AIDS has not yet weakened my reporting. But I suspect I will be the first to say when it is time to call it quits. As I write this, I feel tired but sharp. The AZT is holding for now. The brain infection, though diminished, is still present, making the fingers of my right hand stiff and clumsy on the keyboard. I use a tape recorder; my short-term memory isn't what it was.

I hold a different job—one that is supposed to be less stressful. But I am sitting in my old spot in the newsroom to finish this, the same spot where I suffered the seizure. As I look up, I can see the wall clock clearly. I couldn't that Dec. 21 when failing vision was the first sign of trouble. Now, two years later, I see things more clearly than ever. And I am alive.

. . .

Twelve months after Jeffrey Schmalz wrote this piece, in December 1993, he died of AIDS.

In this piece, Schmalz puts in sharp relief, with honesty and poignancy, how he dealt with a danger that all beat reporters either experience or fear they will—getting so close to their subject that they lose the professional distance that makes them credible reporters. Schmalz did not lose that distance. His moment of truth came when he had to stare into a television light and declare that he was, first and foremost, a reporter. Having AIDS came second.

But the same sort of question arises on a much less powerful scale in newsrooms all over the country. Should a gay man cover gay issues (or substitute almost any affiliation, condition or circumstance you can imagine—blacks, Hispanics, Italians, suburbanites, Democrats, born-again Christians, parents with children in the public schools)? On the one hand, members of a group are usually more knowledgeable about that group's goals and principles. They can bring insight and understanding to a story that a newcomer could not. They are less easily lied to and less likely to make major mistakes.

One of the arguments heard most often for cultural diversity in newsrooms—making the ethnic and racial composition of a newsroom, and the number of men and women, more closely reflect the demographics of the audience or readership—is to introduce different points of view into the news process. The assumption is that membership in certain ethnic or racial groups will—and should—change the way one functions as a journalist. When that argument is used as justification for assigning, for example, only Hispanic reporters to cover the Hispanic community, it could be seen as a wedge that forces segregation upon the newsroom, forcing reporters to cover only certain beats.

On the other hand, members of a group are inevitably torn in their allegiances. Schmalz became an outsider in his own world when he declared that he was a journalist before he was an AIDS activist. That is a painful thing to do and very difficult to deliberately inflict upon oneself.

But if you are a member of a group that you cover as a reporter, there are some very powerful forces acting upon you to make you slant the coverage of that group, consciously or unconsciously. If it is a group to which you belong by birth, there is a strong likelihood that you feel a deep bond or kinship, perhaps literally, with such a group. If it is a group to which you belong voluntarily, then you probably believe that the group is right, or more right than wrong, and more right than down-the-middle coverage would indicate to readers. Such groups, advocates would argue, deserve better-than-neutral coverage. Either way, there is a strong tendency to become an advocate, not a reporter, and to believe that you are justified in doing so.

This might seem to be the stronger argument; the dangers arising from advocacy may be more powerful than the dangers arising from ignorance. Yet Schmalz and his editors at the most respected paper in the country allowed him, a gay man with AIDS, to cover those very issues. A moment's reflection will help explain why. There are two reasons. First, trying to attain utter neutrality by not allowing reporters to cover things they are close to or connected with in some way will almost certainly fail. Take the example of politics, in some ways the simplest area to deal with on this issue. If you will not let liberal Democrats cover liberal Democrats for fear of bias, how much better is it to let conservative Republicans cover them? The biases of affinity are no more likely to occur than the biases of enmity. If parents of public school students are too biased to cover schools, how much more fair are the parents of private school children or childless reporters apt to be? And that brings up the final reason, one that Schmalz makes in passing in his piece. In the final analysis, it is the integrity, not the personal bias, of the journalist that makes for honest copy. As long as the journalist is fretting about bias, she or he is probably staying on the right side of the line.

Questions to Consider

1. Should Schmalz have covered AIDS after he found out he was infected? Should Schmalz, a gay man who was a political reporter for most of his career, have covered issues affecting homosexuals? In both cases, why or why not? Was the coverage of AIDS and gay issues better or worse in the *New York Times* because Schmalz was on the beat?

2. Schmalz said that he used his disease tactically at times, telling interview subjects he also had AIDS to get them to open up about their real feelings. He felt somewhat guilty about that, but he continued to do it. Was that an ethical tactic for him to use? Is it ever ethical to push people's emotional buttons to get a better interview? Is it ever ethical to point out what you have in common with an interview subject (e.g., a similar background or similar experiences) to get a better interview? How do you justify your answers?

3. How important is it for newsrooms to reflect the demographics of the areas they cover? Should black reporters cover the black community, for example? Should reporters of other backgrounds not be allowed to cover the black community? What does the newspaper or broadcast station gain by having members of ethnic or racial groups cover their own groups, and what does it lose? If reporters cover their own racial or ethnic groups, in what ways could that help or hinder their careers in journalism?

4. It seems obvious that expanding the racial and ethnic makeup of the newsroom and getting a balance of men and women in various areas will expand the number of points of view that go into defining what is news. But is that necessarily true?

5. This book deals with what is called mainstream journalism. Is there a place for advocacy journalism, journalism in which a position is openly taken in news coverage? If so, what is that place? If not, why not? Do mainstream journalists have anything to learn from advocacy journalists, and vice versa?

23

How Close Is Too Close When the Subject Is a Scared Little Girl?

For good reasons, journalists usually try to stay out of their own stories. In the name of neutrality and objectivity, journalists usually consider themselves obliged to keep from becoming part of the stories they cover. The thinking behind this premise is simple and straightforward: The journalist is morally obliged to be as honest as possible, both with the subjects in the article and with the readers or viewers. One of the great journalistic sins is getting too to close a source, that is, becoming so friendly with a news source that personal feelings impede the reporter's ability to report honestly and fairly. It is relatively rare that journalists actually fabricate stories out of whole cloth on behalf of news sources-to do that would be such a blatant violation of the principle of honesty that few reporters are seriously tempted. It is much more common—because it is much less clearly wrong—that a journalist will play down a negative aspect of a story because of personal friendship or loyalty.

This wariness about reporters getting too close to news sources is behind the policy at many papers and stations of rotating reporters from beat to beat on a regular basis. The idea is that after some period of time—a year, two years, or sometimes longer—the reporter is apt to have made personal friends among the regular news sources on the beat and be unable to cover them objectively, that is, with neutrality and fairness.

(By the way, this apprehension leads to the chronic creative tension in newsrooms over beat assignments. At the other end of the rope is the realization that most beats are complicated matters and that it takes time to understand the dynamics of any area of public affairs. Each beat inevitably has its own players, its own issues and its own institutions, which have their own unifying forces and divisive fissures. Almost any beat worth covering will have its own set of publications and its own jargon. It takes time to come to understand all these things, and a neophyte is likely both to make serious mistakes and to be manipulated deliberately.)

Sometimes it can be very hard to stay out of a story, as Michael Dillon, now a Ph.D. and a journalism professor at the State University of New York at New Paltz, found. He was a reporter at the *Bloomsburg (Pennsylvania) Press-Enterprise* in 1988 when he wound up at the very center of a story he was covering, a spot made all the more uncomfortable because it was a bitter custody battle. Here is his account of what happened:

THE DAY THE NEWS CAME TO THE REPORTER*

It's not often the news comes to you, and rarer still when you wish it hadn't.

On a quiet Friday morning in October 1988, frantic voices on the police scanner reported a little girl abducted from the County Courthouse with police in pursuit of two suspects. The newsroom was still relatively empty, but before I could alert colleagues and join the chase, there was a commotion at the receptionist's desk. There was no need to go looking for the little girl, 8-year-old Amanda Petock, because she was standing in the lobby with her grandparents, sobbing and shaking while they cast nervous glances out to the highway.

Before Amanda left the newspaper several hours later, my newspaper and I would be drawn into the center of an ugly story involving allegations of child abuse and judicial neglect. Not only were we covering the story, we were also negotiating the conditions under which police and social workers could take the girl out—they showed little taste for running a gauntlet of photographers to take her by force.

The facts are these: Amanda Petock had spent the summer with her mother and her mother's new husband. During her visit, the couple asserted, the child had told them that her father, Eddie Petock, had abused her and that she did not want to return to his custody at summer's end. The couple violated the visitation agreement by keeping Amanda longer than they should have and answered a court order to appear before the judge to argue that she should not go back to her father. The judge refused to hear their arguments and ordered Amanda returned to her father. That's when her mother, Anita Walewski, and her new husband, Stanley, along with Rita and Buddy Lutsky, her grandparents, grabbed Amanda and fled. Police followed Anita and Stanley. The Lutskys brought Amanda to the Bloomsburg, Pa., Press-Enterprise, where I was a reporter.

I spoke to the girl's grandparents and then, accompanied by a female office worker, with the little girl. Their stories matched. Eddie Petock, at the very least, had beaten the child. Dark hints of sexual abuse also arose from our conversations.

Eventually, the Walewskis called the newspaper, and I persuaded them to join their daughter. After receiving assurances that social workers would investigate the abuse allegations, the Walewskis surrendered to police. Amanda was taken to the Child Protective Services headquarters and later, because the child would not

---

* Written for this volume by Michael Dillon.

repeat the abuse allegations she had made at the newspaper, was returned to her father.

The story seemed clear: Desperate mom and heroic grandparents defy an uncaring judge and rescue child from abusive dad.

It did not turn out to be quite that simple.

By the time Amanda had been carried, screaming, from the newspaper by a sheriff's deputy, and Rita Walewski had been helped from the sidewalk where she had collapsed in tears as the child went away, it was almost 7 p.m. I had done most of the negotiating with the police, the parents and the social workers. Another reporter suggested that perhaps he should write the story since I had become so enmeshed in it. I snarled and told him to put his notebook away.

I refused to give the story up. In doing so, I suppose I violated textbook canons concerning conflict of interest or interference in the course of a story. But this wasn't a textbook. It was a little girl. Journalists should not rush about trying to shape or direct the news, and they should resist getting emotionally embroiled in the stories they cover. But this story was unique. The Lutskys brought Amanda to the paper because they saw us as a sanctuary, a court of last resort. I was part of the story whether I liked it or not.

To me, at least, there was a more important issue involved: right and wrong. Not just what's right for journalists, but what's right or wrong for people. My personal values would not allow me to walk away from the story, but my professional values would not allow me to cross the line to unquestioning advocate for either set of adults or officials fighting over the child's fate. The kid was a different story. I was on her side.

But the clock was ticking, and I was nervous. Ethically and legally, I had a problem with running a story containing vivid abuse allegations without giving Eddie Petock, the father, his say. But Eddie was nowhere to be found. He had left the courthouse. He had not gone home. His relatives and lawyer claimed not to know where he was. Darkness was falling when I drove to his parents' rural home to ask their help in finding him. No need. He was there. And so was Amanda.

The little girl clung devotedly to her father. She smiled as he tousled her hair. Her mother, Eddie told me, had "brainwashed" the girl to make allegations against him. "I'm going in the paper as an abuser no matter what happens now, aren't I?" he asked sardonically. He let me speak to Amanda alone. She told me she had not lied when she made the allegations at the newspaper and pleaded with me to "not tell Daddy what I said." She added that her father was not cruel and that she did not object to living with him. She protested going back to him "because I didn't want to hurt Mommy's feelings."

The story I wrote for the next day's newspaper was circumspect. Every paragraph that contained an allegation of abuse was followed by one that mitigated that claim. Stylistically, it was no masterpiece. In the end, attention was drawn to the practices of the judge who had handled the case, but Amanda remained with her father.

I learned three things that day. One I already knew: that when moral right or wrong comes into conflict with journalistic right or wrong, I will base my actions on the former.

I also was reminded of the power of newspapers to serve as a court of last appeal—without the glare of publicity, no investigation of the girl's claims would have been conducted. We should not shrink from this power. It is worth more to the integrity and future of journalism than all of the marketing surveys we endlessly ponder.

Finally, more than any other, Amanda's story made me feel the full weight of the responsibility reporters assume in depicting those they write about. Eddie Petock had never been in the newspaper before Amanda's abduction. What I wrote about him—for better or worse, fairly or unfairly—will forever define him in the rural community in which he lives.

How will his neighbors judge him? Those who read closely will judge him on the facts. Those who didn't will see him and instantly think of the words "Child Abuser." No matter how fairly I wrote the story, he will have to live with that. And so will I.

. . .

Dillon's first concern, what he describes as the conflict of personal morality and journalistic morality, is not so serious as it may first appear. The conflict is not really between competing moral standards, but between a deeply held moral sense on the one hand and an item on the checklist of appropriate journalistic behavior on the other. The underlying principles are not really in conflict. He is quite right in noting that many ethics codes caution against reporters writing about things if they are "too close" to them. The reason for this sanction is to preserve the honesty and integrity of the story. Many competent professionals would recommend just what Dillon's colleague at the paper suggested: that someone else write the story of the bizarre custody fight. But Dillon chose to write the story himself and took great pains to be fair to all sides. In a sense, he was choosing to remain on the beat on the grounds that he understood the story's complexities rather than hand it off to another reporter in order to maximize impartiality. That is not a question of right and wrong, either in the sense of correct and incorrect or in the sense of moral and immoral. Instead, it is a case of different people with the same fundamental principles assigning different weights to the different parts of the question.

His second lesson, the reminder that people turn to their news organizations in times of need, is an important counterargument to periodic poll data showing a decline in public confidence in the news media. There is no doubt that it has become fashionable to decry sensationalism and privacy invasions. Responsible journalists decry those things as well, maybe more so than the general public. Yet in such major disasters as the Oklahoma City bombing and the Challenger shuttle explosion, through such armed conflicts as the Gulf War, to such private tragedies as the custody fight Dillon discusses here, people frequently turn to news organizations for help and information when there is nowhere else to turn. Dillon's story is unusual in that the fugitives actually came to the newspaper office, but the principle is commonplace: Citizens generally expect their news media to hear them out, to make bureaucracies work and to make right the wrongs done to them. Any telephone operator or receptionist at almost any news organization will say the same thing: Whatever people say in the polls, large numbers of them have a strong sense of the news media's public service obligations. It is a good thing that they do; it makes the journalist's job a great deal easier.

The third lesson Dillon writes of is also important to remember: Most citizens who do not have public relations professionals on the payroll are largely at the mercy of journalists. What journalists do and do not write about people makes an enormous difference in their lives, a difference that in many cases will linger long after the reporter has moved on to other stories. Recognition of the lasting impact of our work does not necessarily mean that we should weigh things differently, but it is a caution against weighing them haphazardly or considering the outcome trivial. Real human beings occasionally suffer real harm in the course of much public work. A judicial decision to jail a felon nearly always causes harm to relatives. Failing to incarcerate him or her may cause more harm to future victims. An executive decision to cut off or reduce social services in tight times causes harm to the poor who most need the help. Refusing to curb spending may cause harm to all taxpayers. Rarely is the question of avoiding harm simple.

In this case, there might have been some harm done to the child's father by putting the story in the paper at all. But the greatest harm to the public would have occurred if the paper had lost credibility by not covering the story. Readers trust the news media to inform them about issues of public interest and importance. This story surely qualifies. Failing to report it would have been an abdication of duty. Some readers would have never known about the case. That is the lesser problem. The more serious problem is that some readers would have known of the incident and looked to the paper to provide a full and impartial report of the day's events. Not finding it, they would have been entitled to conclude that, through ignorance or design, the newspaper was not telling them of important events around them.

On the narrow question of whether to cover the story, then, the issue is whether to do some harm to Eddie Petock by publishing or to harm the general populace by causing an unknown number of readers to lose just a little bit of confidence in the newspaper. Dillon's solution—a course of action that most responsible reporters would choose as well—was to write the story and use extreme care to be as fair as possible.

Questions to Consider

1. Would you have published the story? If you had been in Dillon's position, would you have written the story or would you have handed it off to another reporter?

2. Dillon was certainly involved in the story. Does that mean that he was not objective?

3. What should Dillon have done if he had not been able to track down Eddie Petock? Should he have written the piece and said Petock was not available for comment?

4. You probably came away from Dillon's account unsure about whether the girl had been abused or not, and he had had an unusual amount of access to the girl—two face-to-face interviews. In many, maybe most, cases, reporters feel that they do not have all the information they would like to have about an issue—information that would enable them to make a definitive case instead of writing an article that reads like a debate. Those kinds of stories often irritate readers and listeners, who would like to know if something is right or wrong, safe or unsafe. Would it be better if reporters waited until definitive answers were available before reporting on such issues?

5. If the girl had told Dillon in the second interview that she was afraid of her father and wanted to go back to her mother, what should he have done?

6. Assume the case wound up in court and Dillon was subpoenaed to testify about what the girl and the adults in the case had told him—all of it, not just what had appeared in the newspaper article. What would be the ethical response to such a subpoena? Would his obligations as a journalist point him toward the same decision as his feelings as a person, or would they be in conflict?

24

The Exploding Truck: If It Doesn't Have Pictures, It's Not Good TV

One of the significant developments in the last decade of television news is the proliferation of newsmagazines. For years, CBS's "60 Minutes" had the field largely to itself, and the show has been a huge success, both with viewers, who have consistently made the program among the top-rated shows, and with critics, who have praised its solid investigations and dedication to accuracy and journalistic integrity.

Then came cable and a proliferation of news shows like *Inside Edition* and *Hard Copy*, which are electronic versions of the tabloids—not the mostly fiction tabloids, such as the *Weekly World News,* with its stories of alien abductions and Elvis sightings, but the modern yellow journals, such as the *National Star* and the *National Enquirer*, with their emphasis on sex and violence and celebrity gossip. The response from the networks was roughly this: If (relatively) staid old *60 Minutes* worked, that is, drew enough readers to draw enough advertisers to make a good profit, and if the television tabloids worked, then there must be room for more newsmagazines with lighter formats than *60 Minutes*. CBS added *Eye to Eye* and *48 Hours*, ABC had *20/20* and *Prime Time Live*. NBC's entry was called *Dateline: NBC*. It was broadcast for the first time on March 31, 1992. The aim was to produce a show to rival *20/20*, but for a younger audience.

For six months, the show went well. But in November 1992, *Dateline* broadcast a segment on pickup-truck safety that cast a pall over the whole industry. Producers and executives involved with the segment were fired outright, and Michael Gartner, president of NBC News, resigned over it. In the furor that erupted after the broadcast, the events themselves tended to get lost. Here is what happened, based on interviews with Gartner and the segment's producer, Robert B. Read, and on a report from an internal investigation at NBC following the uproar over the broadcast.

In the late 1980s and early 1990s, more than a hundred people had sued General Motors, alleging that GM pickup trucks built between 1973 and 1987 had a serious design flaw that made them prone to burst into flames when they were hit from the side in an accident. The allegations centered on the truck's two gas tanks, which were mounted behind the cab outside the truck's frame like saddlebags, making them vulnerable to rupture.

The *Dateline* story was a fifteen-minute segment on the case against GM, based on interviews and industry documents that appeared to indicate that GM had continued to build the trucks with the safety flaw even though it was aware of the dangers the sidesaddle fuel tanks posed.

The show interviewed a wide range of people in preparing the segment: families involved in lawsuits against the giant automaker, auto safety experts —some neutral and others who regularly side with plaintiffs in lawsuits against the industry—as well as current and former GM employees. A GM senior executive, Robert Sinke, the company's director of engineering analysis, was allowed to make the company's defense.

But then came the last fifty-five seconds. In that final minute, NBC ran a tape of what it called two "unscientific crash demonstrations" the trucks' susceptibility to fire in the event of a side impact. On the tape, which was made at NBC's request, an unoccupied car was sent hurtling into the side of an unoccupied GM pickup truck. In one collision, nothing happened. Then a second car was sent into the side of a second pickup. In that second crash, both car and truck erupted into a spectacular ball of fire. The explosion is repeated in slow motion and then again from a camera mounted inside the car, approximating the view from the driver's seat.

GM complained to NBC that the piece was not fair, and it asked for NBC's evidence, including access to the trucks. NBC refused, and GM called a news conference to announce that it was suing the network for the *Dateline* segment, charging, among other things, that *Dateline* had committed one of the most serious sins in journalism: it had made up part of its story. A senior GM executive decried NBC for "cheap, dishonest sensationalism."

There were several problems with the *Dateline* setup of the crash, but the most serious was that devices—variously called "igniters" or "sparking devices" or even (by GM) "rocket engines"—were hidden on the truck body.

Read, the producer of the segment, wanted footage to illustrate the fundamental contention of the show: the danger of fire from a side-impact collision. The *Dateline* segment featured family members of people who burned to death in two different side-impact collisions, and said there had been more than three hundred other fatal pickup-truck fires over the many years the popular truck was in production.

To ensure that a ruptured gas tank would have a spark to ignite the spilling fuel, the company that ran the crash demonstration for NBC secreted sparkers, or igniters, under the fuel tank on the side designated to be hit in the demonstration crash. On the first crash shown in the segment, the fuel tank did not rupture and there was no fire. But on the second, the tank did rupture and the gasoline burst into flames.

Read later explained to a skeptical audience at the Poynter Institute for Media Studies in St. Petersburg, Florida, that he had initially intended to include in the televised story information about the presence of the igniters as well as the fact that the spark, though a common occurrence in real accidents, had been set up for the taped demonstration. However, Read said, a close examination of the tape of the fire showed that the fire had been started, not by the igniters hidden in the truck, but by the headlight of the crash car as it plowed into the side of the truck. Thus, he explained, the fire started without the igniters at all. He said that he thought it would be confusing to the audience to include the information that there had been hidden spark generators but that those igniters had not started the fire after all. So the piece ran without any mention of the igniters. It is important to note that the NBC report on the whole incident, which is otherwise quite critical of Read, states clearly, "There is no evidence that anyone at 'Dateline,' including Read, conceived of the idea to use igniters as a means of rigging the test results. They did not, in our view, deliberately set out to falsify the 'test.'"

But what the report did accuse Read of was fuzzing up the distinction between a "test" and a "demonstration." The difference is crucial. As the lawyers who prepared the internal report for NBC put it, the journalists doing the *Dateline* segment set up the fifty-five-second controversial scene because they wanted "to tape a crash fire—and that this was as important to the decision to do the test as was the desire to determine whether the trucks were unsafe."

Although the piece was titled, "Waiting to Explode?"—with the question mark—the thrust of the piece was not equivocal at all. The segment clearly depicted the trucks as unsafe, and it presented evidence that appeared to indicate that all three major manufacturers—GM, Ford, and Chrysler—knew that fuel tanks located outside the truck frame next to the sheet-metal skin were more vulnerable in a side-impact crash than were tanks located inside the heavy steel frame. The *Dateline* segment even included GM documents indicating that increased safety was one of the arguments made for moving the tanks inside the frame.

So the show was not really asking the question: Are these trucks dangerous? The show was saying, in effect, "Warning! These trucks are dangerous." So Read, the show's producer, set up the two crashes to "illustrate" that danger, not to "test" whether the danger was there. The point, he said, was to illustrate a danger that other evidence had proved to be there. Therefore, he argued, the igniters were not a serious intrusion.

What was gained by the use of that last fifty-five-second clip of the "unscientific crash demonstration"? Wonderful tape, a strong visual record of what the show was trying to show. And that, of course, goes to the heart of what television does better than any of its rival media: showing what things look like. By nearly all measures, the fundamental strength of print is its ability to deal with complexity and with nuance, to provide intellectual and historical context. And the fundamental strength of television, aside from its speed of delivery, is its ability to provide the visual dimension of a story.

In a later interview, Read stressed "something that print reporters sometimes do not understand, and that is the need for strong visuals, especially on a newsmagazine, but even on the nightly news as well."

Interestingly, Gartner, a former top editor at the *Louisville Courier-Journal* and the *Des Moines Register*, two of the nation's most highly respected papers, disagreed and argued that television was sometimes at its best when it ignored pictures altogether. "There are some things you can't tell with pictures, but that doesn't mean you can't do them on television," Gartner said in an interview. By way of example, he cited a conversation he had with John Chancellor, the longtime NBC correspondent and commentator, toward the end of Chancellor's career. Gartner recalled that he had expressed amazement to his old friend Chancellor about how much information Chancellor could pack into a ninety-second commentary. Chancellor reminded Gartner that the visual dimension of the spot was "just my face," no other pictures at all. Television is a visual medium, Gartner and Chancellor agreed, "but that doesn't mean you can't tell a story without pictures," Gartner said. "There is news that doesn't have pictures."

If it may fairly be said that *Dateline* reached too hard for a visual element for the GM truck story, what was lost by doing so? Several things. Several NBC employees were fired over the incident, and Gartner resigned in an effort to quell the firestorm of criticism. (Gartner said in an interview that he had long planned to leave NBC later in 1992 and had merely accelerated his departure by a number of months. He is now the editor and part-owner of the *Daily Tribune* in the college town of Ames, Iowa.)

Far more important, NBC lost the story it was trying to present to the public. Once the bogus details of the "unscientific demonstration"—essentially an event staged for its visual appeal—became public, the attention shifted immediately to the serious challenge to the network's integrity and away from the contention of *Dateline* that GM had built dangerous trucks for more than a decade and did not do anything about it. Except for the last fifty-five seconds, the program was legitimate journalism, which took on a problem that needed addressing. In early April, the federal government asked GM to recall voluntarily the million-plus trucks at issue in the *Dateline* segment.

The revelations about the *Dateline* show gave the whole journalism profession a major black eye. When all is said and done, the most important dimension to journalism is its integrity. Anything that damages the trust between the journalists and their readers and viewers lessens the chances that the citizen-governors will be able to make the rational decisions necessary to manage their own affairs.

Gartner saw another major problem with the segment; he said that the show's staff had become too enthusiastic about making their point because they had gotten too close to a major source for the piece, in this case, the Institute for Safety Analysis, which regularly helps plaintiffs in suits against the auto industry. Gartner was quick to add, however, that he was not trying to say that reporters should never take information and ideas from people or institutions with their own agendas to advance. On the contrary, journalists do that all the time, and legitimately so.

Routinely, Gartner said, "They are using you and you are using them. That's OK." But journalists need to keep their sense of balance. The significance of using igniters in the crash sequence is open to debate. But the appearance of deception in journalism will always be a problem.

Questions to Consider

1. *Dateline* labelled the crash tests "unscientific crash demonstrations." Should that have let *Dateline* off the hook? (After all, newspapers and magazines run "photo-illustrations" with feature stories all the time.) Was there any way *Dateline* could have used the igniters in the crash demonstrations without being accused of deception?

2. If the igniters were clearly shown not to be the cause of the fire in the crash demonstrations, why was their presence relevant to the story?

3. Were there any other ways to illustrate the story that would have been just as good without getting into the crash-demonstration issue at all?

4. NBC, which is owned by General Electric, quickly backed away from the *Dateline* story when GM complained and had an apology to GM read on the program. Was NBC being responsible in doing this, or was it a case of one big corporation inappropriately caving in to the demands of another big corporation (and advertiser)?

5. When you are handling a consumer safety issue and you are trying to cover the issue fairly, what problems with sources do you need to anticipate and handle?

25

Should TV Cameras
Record an Execution?

arly in 1990, as the date drew nigh for California's first execution in more than 15 years, Michael Schwarz, a senior news executive at public station KQED-TV, had an idea: Get television cameras into the witness room to record the execution—not to broadcast live, nor even to use as breaking news that night, but to get the state-ordered death on tape nonetheless for possible inclusion in a planned documentary on the man being executed.

In the months that followed, Schwarz, then director of news and current affairs at the San Francisco station, sought permission to tape the execution, but permission was denied. Then his station sued for access, which was denied again. Eventually, the condemned man, Robert Alton Harris, who had shot dead two San Diego teen-agers in 1978, was executed on April 21, 1992. Schwarz's news cameras were not present. It was a case that drew enormous attention. Initially, the case was highly newsworthy because it was the first execution in California since the death penalty was reinstated by the Supreme Court in 1976. The Harris case drew further interest because the American Civil Liberties Union sued to prevent the execution, arguing that the gas chamber was a violation of the United States Constitution's Eighth Amendment ban on cruel and unusual punishment.[1]

Schwarz, now president of an independent production studio called Kikim Media, says he was not being ghoulish or macabre, and was not pandering, when he considered using footage from an execution as part of a documentary he was planning on the death penalty. He is not even sure he would have used the tape had

---

[1] The execution was taped after all, although not in connection with Schwarz's planned documentary, but as part of the lawsuit from the ACLU and others who wanted to use the tape as part of their case that the gas chamber causes excruciating pain and thus could be challenged on Eighth Amendment grounds. The tape was sealed under court order and never shown. The tape was eventually ordered destroyed.

his camera been allowed in. But he said that "as a journalist and as a filmmaker," he was entitled to record the event. "Executions have always been open to the public," Schwarz said. "Why not television cameras?" He said the issue was surely one of consequence and public importance. "There is nothing more serious that the state can do than to deny one of its citizens the right to life," he said. As Tunis Wortman would have it, in the first generation after the American Revolution, things done in the people's name by the people's servants are properly the people's business.

Schwarz noted that both supporters and opponents of the death penalty had taken stands on the question of televising the execution, some arguing that the gory scenes would deter would-be criminals while others speculated that a citizenry that truly knew what went on during an execution would demand an end to the practice.

Schwarz said he was "personally ambivalent" about the death penalty. "I question whether the state ought to be in that business at all," he said, but he added that he had once been tied up and threatened with murder by intruders, "so I understand viscerally" the demand for retribution. However, Schwarz then made an important journalistic point, one that eludes many who would use journalism's astonishing power for particular ends. "Changing minds about the death penalty is not my business," Schwarz said. "That's the propaganda business. My business is to present things in a way that will help raise the level of public debate about important questions of public policy."

He noted that "we have death scenes we have seen on TV all the time—Jack Ruby executing Lee Harvey Oswald" in Dallas in November 1963, the point-blank execution of a Vietcong suspect in South Vietnam and others. Schwarz wondered if the visceral objection to seeing an execution on television might be "because we don't want to think about the state doing this in our name and on our behalf? Perhaps, and if so, is that then an even greater reason to show the film?"

Schwarz said his intent had been to film the execution and perhaps use some of the footage, tastefully edited, as part of the planned documentary on the death penalty. Yet what comes most quickly to mind when considering a televised execution is a brassy, tabloid-television approach. Schwarz rejected that line of reasoning, saying, "You can't use an argument not to allow television to be present because Geraldo may sensationalize it. You don't keep The *New York Times* from covering the William Kennedy Smith trial because the *National Enquirer* might sensationalize it."

There are ways to deal with sensationalism other than to impose censorship, Schwarz said. "Viewers can choose not to watch. Advertisers can choose not to advertise. The public has ways to encourage journalists to do their jobs well."

At first, Schwarz's request to televise an execution seems ghoulishly grotesque and brings to mind a made-for-TV movie called "Witness," in which a cable channel puts an execution on pay-per-view. It also recalls Geraldo Rivera in January 1977, standing outside the spot where Gary Gilmore was about to be executed by firing squad, shouting to his producers to get him live, promising that the microphones would pick up the sounds of the shots.

Why is this so troubling? In trying to sort out the journalistic question about televising an execution, it is crucially important to keep Schwarz's admonition in mind that the journalist's job is to inform the public about matters of public interest and importance, not to further the cause of those for or against the death penalty. The question of televising executions has raised a good deal of interest, but much of that debate has dealt with whether such coverage is likely to work for or against public support for the death penalty. Proponents have generally argued that such coverage should increase the death penalty's potential for deterrence, while opponents have argued that such coverage would further cheapen life and coarsen American culture.

Executions were generally held in public squares and other public places until the 1830s, when one state after another moved them behind prison walls, generally on grounds of taste.[2] Since then, reporters in most states have been allowed among the witnesses to executions, but, with the advent of broadcast media in this century, radio and television reporters have had to leave their equipment outside. Electronic journalists have sued for access to execution scenes, but they have never prevailed. In an important Texas case in 1977, the station won in district court when the court held that the television reporter must be allowed to record the execution. Although the station lost on appeal, the lower court's argument is worth quoting because it has a great bearing on the central question of how much public scrutiny of government is appropriate:

"It is argued," the district court held, "that such broadcasts would be an 'offense to human dignity,' 'distasteful,' or 'shocking.' This may well be true, but the question here is whether such decisions are to be made by government officials or by television news directors. The state says, in effect, that 'We, the government, have determined that the governmental activity in this instance is not fit to be seen by the people on television news.' In addition to being ironic, such a position is dangerous. If government officials can prevent the public from witnessing films of governmental proceedings solely because the government subjectively decides that it is not fit for public viewing, then news cameras might be barred from other public facilities where public officials are involved in illegal, immoral, or other improper activities that might be 'offensive,' 'shocking,' 'distasteful' or otherwise disturbing to viewers of television news."

The court concluded by saying the viewing public already had a way to avoid a show it considered to be in poor taste: people do not have to watch. On appeal, the higher court overturned this ruling, declaring that the television station could report on the execution but that there was no reason to allow television cameras into the viewing room if the prison authorities did not want them there.

In Schwarz's case at KQED-TV, the station sued for the right to videotape the execution, but the court held that the station could not do so without the prison

---

[2] Much of the historical and legal argument in this matter comes from John D. Bessler, "Televised Executions and the Constitution: Recognizing a First Amendment Right of Access to State Executions," *Federal Communications Law Journal* (45:3) 355-435.

warden's permission. The warden argued that a television account of the execution might make other prisoners unruly, that guards involved in the execution might be singled out for retribution by other inmates and, bizarrely, that the camera operator might hurl the videocamera against the glass partition between the gas chamber and the witness room, breaking the glass and ruining the execution. To the station's argument that such an action would cause poison gas to spill into the witness room, endangering the life of the camera operator, the judge replied, "The warden is not required to trust anybody. It is no answer to say the press are all nice people and would never do anything irrational."

The station lost and eventually Harris was executed, but the question will doubtless arise again. The problem contains at least three problem areas for ethical journalists.

One is a question of privacy. Would televising an execution improperly invade the prisoner's privacy? If the condemned prisoner refused permission, that would be an argument against televising it, but not a weighty one. Schwarz said in the station's lawsuit, it tried hard "to keep privacy out of the equation." He argued that journalists "do not give other people, who have done far less serious things than Harris had done, the veto." He also said it was "not logically consistent to argue that government can't tell journalists how to cover a story and then turn around and give the veto to Harris." So other considerations could outweigh the privacy concern.

A second is a question of taste: What harm could gory or gruesome footage do? A visual image of someone being put to death is much more powerful than a written account could ever be. Schwarz acknowledged as much in saying that he would not consider broadcasting such footage live or during the hours that children are most likely to watch. He also said such footage would need discreet and tasteful editing. His interest was in doing a documentary, not in breaking news. Would he use it—or allow others to use it—as breaking news? "That would be harder," Schwarz said. "I'd still try to get it in context."

Some critics of the idea of televised executions argue that doing so would cheapen our notion of life and coarsen the culture. While this probably gets extremely close to an argument about the merits or the death penalty itself, this argument has some validity. Several judges, in ruling against television stations seeking to record executions, have excoriated the stations, accusing them of ghoulishly bad taste in proposing to sell (for advertising dollars and ratings points) pictures of people dying.

Cumulatively, these objections carry considerable weight. So what are the arguments for televised coverage of executions?

There are at least two, one having to do with television's pervasiveness as an information medium and the second based upon the unique values of the visual medium of television. First, since it is undeniable that television is the primary source of news for most people and has been so for a generation, it is a significant obstacle to a fully informed citizenry to bar that medium from coverage of any sort of news.

That executions are fundamentally newsworthy is not difficult to argue. An execution involves the most extreme action a state can take, short of war. It is undertaken in the name of the sovereign people, with their money and for their benefit, whether one sees "benefit" as deterrence, real or imagined, or retribution. An execution is of consequence, it has impact, it is of interest, and so on. The only argument against the newsworthiness is the suspicion that the interest shown in an execution might be morbid rather than wholesome, and, in truth, it is almost certainly a combination of the two. That is a real fear, but the moral, as opposed to the legal, way to deal with that concern is to seek to avoid pandering and titillation. As Schwarz put it, the fact that information may be used irresponsibly is not a convincing argument for prohibiting its responsible use.

Second, the medium of television can provide information that print cannot in the important debate about the death penalty and how the condemned are killed. That is where the press can play an important role in upholding the Eighth Amendment, which bars cruel and unusual punishment, just as it already does in the upholding the Fifth's guarantee of a public trial and the right to face one's accusers.

It up to the courts to decide whether the death penalty is, under current standards, cruel and unusual punishment. Those standards change over time with the evolution of society. The citizens of that society set those standards, either directly, through referendums, or indirectly, through the electoral process. If the public is to make a reasonable choice concerning a question as important as life or death, it needs sound information upon which to make the decision. To argue otherwise is to argue the virtue of ignorance over knowledge, a difficult case to make.

There is a corollary as well. The public not only decides whether to execute, but how: whether to use hanging, firing squad, gas chamber, or lethal injection. The ACLU's suit in the Harris case was based in part upon the argument that the gas chamber was "cruel and unusual" because of the great pain felt by the condemned. Scientists were split on the issue. Surely, direct observation would contribute valuable information on the question.

Questions to Consider

1. If you were the judge and a television station was seeking to videotape an execution, what points would you consider and how would you rule? Would it make any difference to you if the footage was to become part of a documentary, if it was to be shown on the evening news, or if it was to be shown live? Would it make any difference if the station was known for serious professional work or if it was known for tabloid-type coverage?

2. All of the penal system, not just the apparatus for executions, is the people's work done by the people's employees (or, given the trend for prisons to be run by private companies, by employees being paid out of government contracts.)

How much right does that give journalists to do independent reporting inside jails and prisons? What are the arguments for restricting such coverage?

3. Assume that television stations win the right to televise executions. Should they screen the reporters covering the executions to exclude any who are part of any group, that has taken a stand on the death penalty? Bear in mind that even such a broad-based group as the Roman Catholic Church has taken a public stand against executions.

26

Tears on Tape:
Why Must We Film Grief?

When he was just getting into journalism, Marty Gonzalez, a former television reporter who now teaches journalism at San Francisco State University, was unforgettably introduced to what he calls "the crying game"—television's peculiar penchant for getting grieving relatives to break down on camera. Years later, it still bothers him.

Gonzalez was a young reporter with KCRA-TV, the NBC affiliate in Sacramento, California, when the assignment editor at the station handed him a newspaper clipping about a horrific accident in a small town half an hour north of the city.

Seven teenagers on their way home from a high school football game had collided head-on with a drunk driver. All seven were killed and, Gonzalez recalled later, "as so often happens in accidents of this type, the wrong-way drunk survived with just a few scratches."

The second-day story for a station playing catch-up was obvious. "Go see if you can talk to the parents of one of these kids," the assignment editor said. Gonzalez recalled, "I was the rookie reporter who didn't know any better, the rookie who took directions from the desk as if they had been carved on stone tablets."

So out he went, he and a cameraman, out searching for reaction from the grief-stricken town. "Driving through the one street downtown, we could feel the stares and read the lips of residents as we passed in our garishly marked news car," he said later. The pair of them collected bits of the story: an interview with the highway patrol, film of the high school, shots of the accident scene. Everything but the reaction of the parents.

Gonzalez had tried to telephone the families, but the phone lines had been busy. Then the car's two-way radio crackled ". . . to unit 7. Have you got the family yet?" "No, not yet," Gonzalez answered. "I haven't been able to get them on the phone." The assignment editor told him that the station's news management team had just completed the customary morning meeting, in which the upcoming newscast is discussed and scheduled stories are put in rank order. "This is the lead at five," the assignment editor told Gonzalez, then signed off.

The lead story for the five o'clock newscast! It is an adrenaline rush for any reporter, but especially for a rookie. "I felt exhilarated and anxious at the same time," Gonzalez recalled. After several wrong turns in the unfamiliar town, and after coming close to turning back rather than seeking out an interview neither of them relished, the pair found the house. Gonzalez asked his cameraman to unload the gear as Gonzalez headed up the walk and knocked at the door. "A man of about fifty-five answered the door. His eyes were rimmed in red, his nose was runny. Behind him I could see about ten other people looking toward the door."

Gonzalez began, "Hello, sir. I'm Marty Gonzalez with Channel Three. I'm sorry to intrude. . . ." That was as far as the young reporter got. "The man leaped at me, grabbing my tie, trying to hit me," Gonzalez said. "I bent over and began backing up as he pounded on my back. Time moved in slow motion. I was thinking that I couldn't hit back, that he was an old man." Other people pulled the distraught man off the young reporter, who apologized again and retreated to his car.

On the way back to the station, the cameraman asked, "Are you O.K.?" Gonzalez answered, "Yeah, he didn't hurt me." But he was lying. "The old man had hurt me," the reporter recalled later, "not physically, but emotionally and morally. I considered myself one of the reporters with a heart, one who went out of his way to consider the feelings of the people I came in contact with during the course of a story. Yet I had ignored my better judgment and tried to get a family member so we would have 'tears on camera.'"

Gonzalez went back to the station with his story, but without the film of the grieving relatives. The assignment editor listened to the story of Gonzalez's confrontation with the relative. "He sort of laughed it off and said, 'Well, you know. That's the way it goes.'"

Gonzalez said, "One thing I have learned about a lot of desk people—once they fill up the board and get their newscast filled, they don't really care what you come back with as long as you come back with something. Because by 11 A.M., most of their job is done for the day. They've filled the board, they've got everybody out and scheduled for stories and can pretty much just wait for a breaking story and plan for the next day.

"So by the time we got back, it was several hours later, and he was in a whole other mode." The pieces of the story that Gonzalez and his cameraman had shot were assembled and the story was broadcast without the grief-stricken relatives. Nobody at the station minded, as Gonzalez recalled it later, so the story had something of a happy ending.

At an emotional level, the question of talking to grieving relatives is one of the toughest questions journalists face. Sometimes people react as the man in Gonzalez's story did: they explode in anger, venting some of the grief and rage they feel on an intrusive reporter. Other times, people will pour out their hearts and souls. Gonzalez said, "I am amazed at the things people tell us. To this day I don't understand why, whether they feel that they know you or feel that they have to unload on somebody. But it is still an amazing fact of this business that people will tell you things that you have no business knowing."

Reporters trained to get all the information they can from everybody they interview sometimes find they can get too much. Just as reporters must learn to ask themselves if information is newsworthy even if a whistle-blower or a politician has an ulterior motive in passing it along, so, too, a reporter should ask if information is in the public interest even if a distraught relative blurts it out, or, even lays it all out in what seems a calm and rational manner.

Sometimes what the relatives have to say is newsworthy, and a grieving relative often finds it cathartic to talk, Gonzalez said, a conclusion based on his many years in the news business. "There have been families that have come forward and they want to say something that is educational," he said, something that will serve as an object lesson or a warning to others. When a family has lost a child in a traffic accident, for example, "a lot of times the parents want to come forward and say, 'Look, we just lost our pride and joy. This was our future. And it was for no good reason,'" Gonzalez said. But out of that grief, to get some small good from the tragedy, parents want their loss to serve as a warning for others to drive with care, to not drink and drive, or to stay away from certain dangerous places or activities. Gonzalez sees that sort of interview "as really useful and informative."

But many such interviews add little to a story. Gonzalez said, "I don't see the point of having somebody break down and mutter incoherently just for the sake of having a picture on television. I really don't see how that advances anything, and it perpetuates the stereotype that we're ghouls jumping in on these people in their time of tragedy."

Note that in Gonzalez's comments, the journalist can commit an error in either of two directions, that is, he or she can put a thumb on the scale of either pan in weighing whether or not to go after an interview or use it once it has been obtained. A family's grief is at once intensely private and potentially newsworthy. The right to be left alone, to grieve in one's own fashion without reporters taking it all down, seems clear enough. On the other hand, the reporter's obligation is to explain the outside world so people can understand. The goal of almost every photographic and literary technique in journalism is to make stories more comprehensible, more memorable, and more meaningful. A vision of a family sharing its grief certainly does all those things, which is a reason to go ahead. What varies is the reaction of those grieving. If they see the journalist as a genuinely compassionate and sympathetic listener, then great good can come of hearing them out and including them in the story. On the other hand, if those in grief react as the parent did in Gonzalez's story, then the balance may well tip the other way, against trying to use such material.

But journalists must be cautious in making such decisions. News judgment needs to be made independently of the whims and wishes of individuals. Journalists do not give the subjects of their stories veto power over the running of a story, nor do they allow the subjects to shape the story to their liking. That is one of the fundamental differences between journalism and public relations. And that means that the journalist should not provide a soapbox of infinite size for anyone with a cause, even if that cause has its origins in legitimate sorrow. Just as people do not cease to be newsworthy just because they do not want to talk to a reporter, they do not become endlessly newsworthy just because they do.

Gonzalez's story is a prime example of print reporters having a much easier time doing their job than television journalists. A print reporter is equipped with little more than a small notebook and a pen—and those can be left out of sight in a pocket if need be—while a television reporter is encumbered with much more: a camera and a microphone and usually a crew to handle the equipment.

A cautionary note: As Gonzalez pointed out, people in grief are sometimes willing and even eager to talk, sometimes at great length. Often, what people say at such times can legitimately be used as part of a sensitive and valuable story. But in talking to people at such times, reporters must recognize that they are dealing with extremely sensitive material and must handle what they learn with extraordinary care and compassion. If a story about a tragedy is reported and written with care and grace it can become a precious remembrance and is often one of those documents that is clipped and saved in a scrapbook or a family Bible. This does not mean the reporter should lie or make things up, but it does mean the reporter must be extremely aware of the vulnerabilities of the people interviewed for the story and be extra careful that everything that winds up in the story is accurate. The family that trusted the reporter during their most fragile moments will almost certainly never forgive a factual error, a misquote, or a misinterpretation. Nor should they.

Questions to Consider

1. Why do journalists interview grieving relatives and friends after tragedies? Does it fulfill any fundamental journalistic responsibilities? Does journalistic responsibility extend beyond the Lockean duty, recognized in the Constitution, to keep citizens informed about their government?

2. If the cameraman had managed to film the attack on Gonzalez, would that have had any legitimate use on the air?

3. Sometimes the relatives of victims are involved in lawsuits after accidents, and sometimes they turn out to be suspects in homicides and other criminal acts. How should knowing that affect the way journalists use the interviews they get with victims' relatives?

27

How Real Is the Wall between Advertising and the News Side?

One of the most common accusations made against the news media, both by media scholars and by ordinary viewers and readers, is that news content is dishonestly influenced by advertisers. Conspiracy buffs suspect outright control, while more sophisticated critics see more indirect influences. The criticism does not usually involve accusations that individual reporters are personally corrupt, that they take envelopes full of cash as payment for including or omitting particular material in articles. More often, the charges involve more subtle influences and are based on the undeniable truth that newspapers, magazines, and broadcast stations get the great bulk of their income from advertising revenue. Therefore, it stands to reason that advertisers exert enormous, even if indirect, pressure to color the news.

The potentially corrupting influence of money has been noted and lamented almost from the moment the news business began to make money. In the middle of the nineteenth century, Horace Greeley, the great editor of the *New York Tribune*, believed, probably rightly, that money had profoundly corrupted his powerful rival, James Gordon Bennett, whose *New York Herald* made Bennett enormously wealthy. By the time of the great newspaper barons early in this century—Pulitzer, Hearst, Scripps, and Newhouse—it was commonplace to believe that money corrupted not only government and industry, but journalism itself. Later in this century, Upton Sinclair's *The Brass Check*, written in the 1920s, and A. J. Liebling's acerbic "Wayward Press" columns in the *New Yorker* a generation later are but two of a host of criticisms in this vein.

The accusation is one of the most important in all of journalism criticism, for it implies a fundamental breach of the trust that binds journalists to their readers and justifies journalism's very existence. If journalism is not honest, it loses much of the moral weight behind the sweeping protections of the First Amendment. It is important, therefore, to try to ascertain how valid the claim is that advertisements corrupt news.

Journalists certainly know how powerful money can be in the areas that they cover, if not in the places where they work. Serious campaign finance reform is almost certainly essential before anything resembling an honest, that is, unbought, Congress can ever be elected. Beginning investigative reporters are regularly reminded by veterans of the first rule of investigative work: Follow the dollar.

Because journalists are more keenly aware than many other people of the corrupting power of money, it is common for the news side of a paper or station to erect walls between it and the business side. Many reporters and editors take it as a matter of course, and of pride, that they do not know or care about the woes and successes of the advertising staff. In a great many papers, business-side people are literally forbidden to enter the newsroom at all, lest they taint the copy.

Warren Breed and other mass-media scholars argue that socialization occurs in the newsroom—that new reporters learn from more senior colleagues the unwritten rules that color and shape the news product. That mentoring can, though, work two ways. It can provide the rookies with a list of the subtle or blatant forms of tainted news judgment in the newsroom: This charity is a pet project of the publisher, that auto dealership is a sacred cow and must not be criticized in news copy. But the grapevine can just as easily and just as plausibly work the other way, too. The newcomer can learn: Don't talk to the ad staff, and never, ever trim your sails to try to curry favor with the rich or powerful.

The next line of argument from the "money corrupts" side is that, while reporters and editors may shy away from the business folks, it hardly matters because publishers, who oversee both news and business staffs, can make sure, with the power of the paycheck, that important advertisers are not offended.

It is a powerful argument, but is it true? Certainly not always. A case in point is a front-page article in the *New York Times* that appeared on January 21, 1995, discussing long-distance telephone services. The *Times* hired a New Jersey consulting firm to analyze claims made in a flurry of print and broadcast ads by long-distance telephone companies. Many of those ads had appeared in the *Times* itself. The result? AT&T, the industry leader and a huge advertiser in the *Times*, was "almost certainly more expensive for most customers." But the two other companies in telephone's Big Three—MCI and Sprint—fared not much better. "If you are among the tens of millions of people whose long-distance bills are typically less than $10 a month, you can probably get a better break on the few calls you do make by switching to one of the smaller cut-rate carriers that compete with AT&T, MCI and Sprint." It is worth noting that those "smaller cut-rate carriers" the *Times* news story recommended are not significant advertisers in the newspaper.

Here is as clear a case as one could want of a negative story about a major advertiser—in this case, three major advertisers. The story was played prominently, beginning at the top of the front page and jumping inside with another thirty inches of type, plus two charts comparing the cost of the services. On the jump page was a substantial how-to sidebar on how consumers can figure out which long-distance company would be the cheapest for them.

Is this proof that advertisers do not influence news copy? No. And it is no doubt naive to believe that advertisers never influence news content. But it is strong evidence that they do not always do so. Beyond the questions of personal and institutional integrity, there are at least two reasons for this.

The first is that it is in a paper's or station's own best interests, in the long run, to put out a high-quality, high-integrity product. As Philip Meyer, a journalism professor at the University of North Carolina at Chapel Hill, has noted, there is significant financial value in being a paper of integrity. To see that this is so, merely look at any copy of the *New York Times* and an issue of one of the supermarket tabloids, such as the *National Star*. The *Times* is full of ads from upscale clothing stores, jewelers, and impresarios of the arts—people with goods and services to offer discriminating, cultivated, high-income *Times* readers, with their large amounts of disposable income. Now look at the tabloid. First, the advertisers are few and their ads small. Second, what have offer for sale is often little more than quack medicines, ersatz enchancers of memory, breast, or penis and similar claptrap, items pitched to gullible tabloid readers willing to believe that Elvis and John F. Kennedy are still alive, that space aliens are taking over, or that Bigfoot and the Loch Ness monster have been secretly captured.

The second reason is that the advertiser's biggest threat—to withhold advertising—is, at least in part, hollow. Advertisers pick the media outlets in which to advertise their products on the basis of their own self-interest. AT&T does not advertise in the *New York Times* because the phone company likes the newspaper. AT&T advertises in the *Times* because its marketing people are convinced that buying space in the *Times* is the most cost-effective way to do what it wants, whether it is to improve its corporate image, sell particular goods or services, or whatever. There are many horror stories of advertisers in some papers or on some stations successfully bullying their way into more-than-fair coverage for the short term, but in the long run, the advertiser needs the papers or stations as much as the news outlet needs the advertiser. And at news organizations, like the *Times*, with broad advertising bases, a single advertiser, or even a few advertisers, who pulled ads would not have a major effect.

Nonetheless, advertising doubtless does have some influence, mosly indirect, on editorial copy, especially on papers and stations surviving on the margin. But consider the alternatives to an advertising-based news industry. Who else would pay? There are only two other choices: Government could pay, or the reader or listener could pay.

The problems with government subsidies for news outlets are obvious and legion. Most important, the same potential for corruption that now comes from advertisers would come from government, only it would be worse. There are far more potential replacement advertisers than replacement governments. No one advertiser, or even one industry, can make or break a news organization, especially at successful operations. If news were publicly supported, that would not be so. Further, while it is doubtless true that the business world has an enormous influence on all our lives, the primary purpose of journalism in the American system is to be a watchdog for political malefactors, not economic ones.

That leaves asking the reading and viewing public to pay the full freight for their news. Ad-free publications have been tried many times in the nation's history and have never succeeded as general-circulation newspapers (A tiny number of specialty magazines such as *Consumer Reports* survive without ads.) Trying to publish a general newspaper or magazine without advertising would mean that only those people who value news highly and who have the disposable income to pay for it would be informed. News organizations, especially serious newspapers, already have serious problems attracting and retaining low-income readers. Doubling and trebling the cover price of the paper would either make serious news even more elitist than it is already or else would increase the pressures to pander and titillate to scrape up a few more readers. Either way, the notion of a broad-based democracy would suffer a serious blow. One could argue that cable television customers already pay part of the cost of their news, but few would want to pay the entire bill, as they would have to do if advertisers disappeared.

In the end, a system in which journalism is largely financed by advertising is far from perfect, but it has fewer drawbacks than any of the alternatives.

28

The 'Revisionist' Ads on the Holocaust: What Should Student Editors Do?

Not all ethical problems concern editorial matter. One of the more troubling dilemmas many college newspaper editors face concerns advertising, particularly ads from people like Bradley Smith and other so-called Holocaust "revisionists." Smith buys advertisements in college newspapers across the country, seeking to spread his claim that the Holocaust either never happened or was much less widespread than historical records clearly show it to have been. When the ads are run, they almost invariably generate widespread protests, especially from Jewish groups, which maintain that Smith's message does not deserve even the hint of legitimacy conferred by the publication of his ads. While some college editors turn down the ads, others run them, seeing the ads as a powerful First Amendment, free-speech issue.

Perhaps the best argument against running anti-Holocaust ads has been made by Stephen Klaidman, a distinguished journalist and ethicist who has been a reporter for the *New York Times* and the *Washington Post* and a Senior Research Fellow at Georgetown University's Kennedy Institute of Ethics. He is the coauthor of an excellent book on journalistic ethics, *The Virtuous Journalist* (Oxford, 1987). In a sense, Klaidman's argument against running Smith's ads looks at the quotation marks around the word "revisionists" in the preceding paragraph. Historical revisionists are those scholars who legitimately take a fresh look at a historical period, person, or movement and often reach new conclusions. They frequently rely on new evidence or new methodology, such as the quantitative methods of the social scientists, in arriving at their conclusions. Klaidman argues that Smith's ads are not revisionism at all, but hate-filled rubbish, and they should be treated as such.

Here is his argument:

WHY WE SHOULD NOT DIGNIFY HATE
WITH REASONED DISCOURSE*

American journalism has spawned a host of hallowed aphorisms, many of which derive from the well-grounded, right-sounding, but inadequate principle that the public has a right to know. The notion of a sweeping right to know is well grounded in democratic political theory and the ethical principle of respect for persons, and it is right-sounding because it expresses an intuitively appealing liberal democratic sentiment. It is inadequate, however, because it implies a morally indefensible right to know everything.

Two corollaries to the public's right to know are the concepts that a commitment to free speech is necessary to protect the speech we hate and that the best antidote to hateful speech is more speech. The first of these corollaries is correct for liberal democracies where a commitment to free speech does serve mainly to protect unpopular speech. More to the point here, however, is that enlightened speech as an intellectual antidote to hateful speech requires a comprehending audience; it ought to work best in an environment where informed debate thrives—a university, for example.

That sounds right. But disappointingly, a late 20th-century American university can be precisely the kind of environment in which ignorance of history and unexamined ideas doom this generally desirable response. I watched this happen at two very different universities, Georgetown and Penn State. The relevant example at both universities was a heated debate over whether student newspapers should publish an advertisement submitted by a California-based organization called the Committee for Open Debate on the Holocaust, one of the number of revisionist fringe groups that seek to cast doubt on the existence of death camps, gas chambers and a systematic Nazi policy of genocide against the world's Jews.

At Georgetown, one of the two student weeklies published the ad, and the other rejected it. At Penn State, the student daily published the ad. When the debate took place at Georgetown, I was the adviser to both papers. When it took place at Penn State, I was teaching journalism there. At both universities, I tried to clarify the issues for the students—most of whom knew a little bit about First Amendment theory and almost nothing about the Holocaust—and to explain why I opposed publishing the ad.

To begin with, there is no legal obligation to accept the ad. The Supreme Court's 1974 decision in *Miami Herald Publishing Co. v. Tornillo* makes this clear. Chief Justice Warren Burger wrote for the court: "A newspaper is more than a passive receptacle for news, comment and advertising. The choice of material to go into a newspaper, and the decisions made as to limitations on the size and content of the paper, and treatment of public issues and public officials—whether fair or unfair—constitute the exercise of editorial control and judgment. It has yet to be demonstrated how governmental regulation of this crucial process can be exercised

---

* Written for this volume by Stephen Klaidman

consistent with First Amendment guarantees of a free press as they have evolved to this time."

Since the student papers are legally free to publish or reject the ad, the problem is appropriately analyzed in terms of an individual's right to free expression and the public interest, in other words, the moral responsibility of journalists to provide citizens with the information they need to function adequately in a democratic political system.

I know of no theory of freedom of expression that imposes a moral obligation on a particular media organization to publish or broadcast any and every opinion on a matter of public concern that is submitted to it. And I know of no moral criterion by which this specific example of political-commercial speech would have a moral claim to bypassing the normal judgment criteria a media organization uses to decide whether to publish or broadcast opinion. The Committee for Open Debate on the Holocaust was and is free to seek to distribute its ideas among the myriad print and electronic communication outlets available. As a practical matter, it has had enough success in circulating its views to defeat any argument that they have been stifled.

Since there are no legal or moral obligations to disseminate the committee's material, a decision to do so should depend on whether such dissemination is likely to undermine the public interest. Here, the ad's content—specifically, any tendency it might have to mislead and the importance of the matter about which it might be misleading—is central to the argument, along with the intellectual preparedness of the audience to grapple with the issues raised. The ad under discussion attempts to cast doubt on the Holocaust by arguing that the U.S. Holocaust Memorial Museum contains "no proof that even one individual was 'gassed' in a German program of 'genocide.'" The argument can be dismissed in a phrase by noting that the museum does not exist to provide such proof, which is available in overwhelming quantity elsewhere.[1]

Why publish it, then? How does it serve the public interest? Since most students are demonstrably ignorant about the Holocaust, is running the ad not likely to mislead them about the meaning of one of the most morally relevant events of recorded history? The only serious argument advanced for running the ad at either Georgetown or Penn State was that its publication would stimulate debate and thereby promote learning. It did provoke a few weeks of scattered discussion on both campuses, but for the most part, the only sustained interest was among Jews and a few faculty members—i.e., those who already know something and therefore were least likely to be misled. A good alternative to running the ad, which would have been less inflammatory and more informative, would have been to publish a news story about it in which the text was quoted in the context of indisputable facts

---

[1] To name just two exceptionally well-documented examples from a wealth of materials, see Hilberg, Raul, *The Destruction of the European Jews*, (Chicago, 1961) and Kogon, Eugen, Langbein, Hermann and Ruckerl, Adalbert, eds., *Nazi Mass Murder, A Documentary History of the Use of Poison Gas*, (Yale, 1993).

about 'gassing' and 'genocide' and in which revisionist organizations such as the Committee for Open Debate on the Holocaust were exposed in the spirit of true public-service journalism.

More speech was generated in response to the ad, but my experience at both Georgetown and Penn State was that its most notable effect was to create an appearance of debate on an issue about which no legitimate ground for debate exists.

. . .

In Klaidman's eloquent argument, he brings up and rejects several unsatisfactory reasons for running the ad, then raises what he considers the "only serious argument" for accepting the ad—that its publication would stimulate debate and thus promote learning. That could be considered a weighty argument for publication. It is an argument that has been made for centuries, at least from the time of John Milton to that of John Stuart Mill. On the other side of the scales, Klaidman puts the possibility of misleading the ill-informed into believing that accounts of the Holocaust are grossly exaggerated by giving the "appearance of debate on an issue about which no legitimate ground for debate exists." The determining factor, to Klaidman, is the likelihood that learning will take place versus the likelihood that a totally specious argument will be given credence and thus falsehoods—extremely dangerous falsehoods, at that—will be spread.

That is where the judgment comes in, and why there are rarely any absolutely right and wrong answers in moral reasoning. It should be noted that in trying to weigh how well prepared students are to assess the ads in question, Klaidman was not merely guessing or hypothesizing. He relied on empirical evidence from personal observation on two well-regarded but quite different university campuses. Further, when the issue came up at Penn State, he explored the possibility of doing serious scientific polling of student opinion, only to discover that it was more costly and more time-consuming than circumstances allowed. But the principle is a sound one, one of the most fundamental in journalistic decision making, or, indeed, any high-level decision making: Do all the reporting you can before coming to any conclusion.

Klaidman has successfully demolished the argument that there is some people's right to know that mandates the running of Smith's ad. While the First Amendment surely guarantees Smith the right to make his case, however hateful or wrong, nothing obliges anyone to help him make it. What is left of the argument to publish is some variation of Milton's belief that truth will always win out over falsehood, perhaps coupled with Mill's belief that successfully refuting a bad idea inevitably strengthens the good one, that, indeed, without the exercise of argumentation from time to time, even the best ideas and concepts degenerate into what Mill called "dead dogma."

If a student newspaper refuses the ad, then that paper's readers will not hear Smith's argument, at least not from that particular ad. In an immediate sense, then, what happens if the ad is declined is that nothing happens. Students do not hear a sham debate where no true debate exists. That is good grounds to refuse to publish.

But what if the ad is accepted? If the past is any guide, we can expect at least some discussion on the campus over Smith's ad, a perfect example, in Milton's phrasing, of truth and falsehood grappling in free and open encounter. If we trust that truth will out, Smith's ad should be discredited and the running of it will have contributed to a greater, not lesser, understanding of the horrors of the Holocaust. If we do not trust truth to be more powerful than lies—if we do not, at bottom, believe in the power of the rational mind—then a great deal more than Smith's ad is at stake. If students are so woefully ignorant of the Holocaust that they cannot be taught by debate, then is there any hope at all for the future of popular sovereignty and democratic self-government?

It should be kept in mind that Smith and others like him are making their case wherever and however they can; their arguments are in the marketplace of ideas. It is fatuous to hope that students will never hear the claim that the Holocaust was a hoax. If the Smith position, however hateful and wrong, is being made, it seems reasonable that it would most effectively be demolished on a college campus, where there are historians and other scholars ably equipped to counter it. If Smith's argument cannot be refuted on a college campus, then it seems unlikely that it could be successfully refuted anywhere.

Klaidman's alternative—that of running a news story about the speciousness of the argument denying the Holocaust—has merit, but it, too, assumes that the student audience is not hopelessly ineducable about history. It merely shifts onto the journalist the job of providing the education, rather than providing a forum for others to undertake the lesson. If the audience is so ill-informed that it cannot benefit from the ad and the response it is likely to engender, it does not stand to reason that a student-written story in the campus paper could provide the needed lessons better than could professional educators knowledgeable in the field.

Questions to Consider

1. The above discussion mentions several possibilities: running the Smith ad, rejecting the ad, or rejecting the ad and running a news story on the Holocaust revisionism issue. What other possibilities can you envision for handling this question? What are the pluses and minuses in each case? What do you consider to be the best course of action?

2. Does the issue change if the newspaper asked to run the Smith ad is a general-circulation paper instead of a student newspaper? What about if the question is whether to run such an ad on a student broadcasting station or on a nonstudent radio or television station?

3. How much responsibility—in an ethical, not a legal sense—does a newspaper or broadcast station have for the accuracy and fairness of the advertisements it carries? Does that ethical responsibility vary according to whether the ads are commercial or political?

4. This book talks a great deal about the responsibility journalists have under the Lockean contract recognized by the framers of the Constitution. But what about the citizenry—what kind of responsibility does it have under the Lockean contract, and how well is it fulfilling that responsibility? How do you think Klaidman would answer that question? Is it necessary that all of the nation's citizens, or even most of them, fulfill their Lockean responsibilities in order for journalism to be practiced in a meaningful way? Why or why not?

29

Speaking Fees: Honest Moonlighting or an Invitation to Corruption?

Journalists often talk about their only loyalty being to the commonweal, the public good, the truth that allows a democracy to work. But as the skeptical reader or viewer knows, journalists are susceptible to all sorts of corrupting pressures that push and pull them away from the path of honest hunter-gatherer of the people's information.

Little seems more obviously corrupting than taking money or other things of value from a news source. Its most blatant form, outright bribery— *film noir's* classic envelope full of cash—is both extremely rare and is so obviously dishonest it can be dismissed with a word: Don't. But there are other, much more subtle ways to influence news coverage.

Many journalists argue that one such potential for a conflict of interest comes from speaker's fees, the money an organization pays to a guest speaker. On any given night, dozens, perhaps hundreds, of lecturers, thinkers and writers all over the country are dispensing wisdom and insight, inspiration and palaver, to banquet-rooms full of people working on their dessert. Among them are dozens of big-name journalists who are also celebrities and who thus can command ten thousand dollars and up for an after-dinner speech.

Is there anything wrong with this? The reporters' primary trade association, the Society of Professional Journalists, cautions against journalists accepting "gifts, favors, fees, free travel" and other perquisites "if they compromise journalistic integrity." While the code is non-binding, it can be considered something of an industry standard. However, it is important to note that not everyone in journalism tries to follow the code or even believes the code should exist. Some of the most important players in journalism argue that any written code is a limitation on important free speech principles and as such must be resisted. But code or no code, no serious journalist will countenance the compromise of journalistic integrity, which is, after all, the most valuable asset a journalist has.

But there is a second issue: Does the reading and viewing public perceive the big fees to be corrupting, or potentially corrupting? At a time when journalism is held in perilously low esteem among the public, the appearance of corruption is a serious matter. The SPJ code is clear on this point as well: "Journalists should," is says, "avoid conflicts of interest, real or perceived." The profession is split on the question of whether speaker's fees are appropriate, sometimes strikingly so. For example, Jim Lehrer, the anchor of the highly regarded *News Hour* on public televison, accepts speaking fees, according to a cover story on the phenomenon in the trade journal, the *American Journalism Review*. Lehrer's co-anchor for many years, Robert MacNeil, did not. Former CBS anchor Walter Cronkite, often regarded as the conscience of journalism, used to accept such fees, but in recent years has had second thoughts.

One outspoken defender of the practice is ABC News's Sam Donaldson, coanchor of *Prime Time Live* and one of the biggest draws on the after-dinner circuit. Donaldson is among many journalists who are paid many thousands of dollars at a time to speak before various groups, and he sometimes covers those groups and their issues.

Donaldson became the focus of a debate on speaking fees early in 1994 when *Prime Time Live* broadcast an investigative piece by the reporter Chris Wallace, charging an insurance trade group, the American Insurance Association, with trying to buy influence with Congressional staff members with a junket to Key West, Florida. The show noted that the year before Wallace's story ran, Donaldson had accepted a speaking fee to address many of the same insurance companies that had sponsored the Key West trip. Paul Equale, senior vice president of the Independent Insurance Agents of America, complained of what he called a "cynical double standard," demanding to know why ABC assumed that Congressional staff members could be bought with a junket while maintaining that Donaldson could not.

Donaldson is happy to discuss the insurance story and speech, and a similar situation the year before, in which *Prime Time Live* did a story on a Congressional island junket paid for by an electronics trade group that Donaldson had also been paid to address. ABC also noted at that time that Donaldson had been paid by the group targeted by the investigation. In a telephone interview, Donaldson argued that the stories had been hard-hitting, solid evidence, he said, that he has not been influenced by the fees he was paid.

At the heart of Donaldson's argument is the assertion that the groups that pay him to speak are not seeking to buy influence, but rather to rub shoulders with a star. When he first started speaking for money, Donaldson said he was shocked to discover that people hire high-profile journalists for their celebrity status. He considers himself first and foremost a reporter. "I carry my own bags, I drive my own car and do my own work," Donaldson said.

Donaldson said that in the nearly three decades that he had been on the lecture circuit, never has any organization that had paid him to speak ever asked him in the way of coverage or noncoverage. If these groups were trying to buy influence, he said, "You would think that at some point, one of these groups—that *somebody*—would say, 'Sam, we've got a problem.'"

Donaldson said he understood that many of his critics saw the speaking fees as an attempt to buy influence, but he considers himself to be just another part of a hired banquet, like the caterer or the band. Does he consider himself worth what he charges? As a journalist, he said, he does bring some perspective, but not "twenty-five thousand dollars worth." It has to do with his being a recognizable face from television, he said, a media star.

Donaldson anticipated the next objection from skeptics—that the influence organizations were trying to buy might show up, not in blatantly favorable coverage, but in pulled punches, something that either was toned down or did not get covered at all. Donaldson discounted this argument unless critics of this can point to specific examples where clearly there has been a distortion or a suspected distortion. Without that, he said, the argument is specious. And, as negative evidence, it is absolutely impossible to refute.

How much money is at stake here, and does it matter in terms of whether there is an appearance of a conflict of interest? In Donaldson's case, he has consistently declined to provide figures, but published reports say Donaldson gets up to thirty to thirty-five thousand dollars a speech, a little less than a week's pay for him. Is either the dollar figure or the fact that Donaldson makes that much in a week germane to the case?

The amount of money involved in this case—both in absolute terms, that is, the dollar figure itself, and in relative terms, that is, how many days' or hours' work that money represents—is important for the same reason that such details are important in other news stories: They help the reader make an informed judgment. More people will allow themselves to be corrupted for a year's salary than for a day's. The figure of thirty thousand dollars that has been cited as Donaldson's fee represents more than a year's pay to many rookie journalists; but it is only a few days' pay to a major network star. It is also important to note that Donaldson, and most other celebrity speakers, make many speeches to civic, educational, and other nonprofit groups either for no fee at all, or for far less than they charge, for example, insurance executives.

Whatever his protestations that the groups he addresses are renting a star, not trying to buy influence with a journalist, Donaldson said it was his audience that would eventually decide whether he continued to speak to groups for money. If the network is someday convinced that he is losing his credibility, he will reconsider, he said, but so far he does not think that is the case. From reading his mail, from the reactions of people he calls on for interviews, from the news stories about him, Donald said he has considerable insight into the way people perceive him, and "the viewers do not believe that somehow I've gone bad."

The question of whether to accept or decline thirty thousand dollars to spend an hour speaking to insurance executives is not a problem that is likely to arise for a reporter in the early years of a career. In fact, most of the celebrity journalists who command thousands for speaking fees are the Washington stars: Donaldson, Cokie Roberts, Eleanor Clift, Fred Barnes, George Will, etc., who regularly appear on television. Most of the rest of the big-money speakers are in New

York—network celebrities or stars from the major news organizations, such as columnist William Safire of the *New York Times*. Far more likely for a journalist in the early stages of a career is an offer of perhaps one hundred dollars or so from the local chamber of commerce or a local trade group. Ironically, this small amount of money is potentially more corrupting than the thousands offered to Cokie Roberts or Tom Brokaw (who commands top dollar but donates his speaking fees to charity).

A hundred dollars or so may seem like a lot to a reporter trying to pay the rent, and it is difficult for that reporter to say that the group paying the fee is just trying to hang out with a celebrity. While many journalists decry the practice of accepting large fees on the grounds that those fees appear to be an attempt to buy influence, Donaldson and those who do speak for money do make a strong case. However, unless you accept the star defense, there is little other justification for a journalist to accept speaking fees because there seems to be no other reason for anybody to rent some of a reporter's time except to buy influence.

Questions to Consider

1. Do you agree or disagree with Donaldson's position on speaking fees? Why or why not?

2. Have the journalists who have become celebrities lost some of their ability to be good journalists? Or does that status help them do their jobs? Should a journalist try to become a celebrity? Explain your answers.

3. Why would the organizations that employ journalists like them to get out and talk to trade and civic groups?

4. How much difference does the amount of money involved make? If you are invited to cover the local Rotary meeting and you are given a free lunch worth less than ten dollars, is that corrupting? What about if you take a source out for coffee, or a full-course meal, and the source wants to pay the tab?

5. Why might the appearance of a conflict of interest really be a conflict of interest for a journalist?

30

Celebrity Interviews: Is There Real News amidst the Puff?

Ben Bagdikian, a veteran journalist and one of the nation's most thoughtful media critics, makes a powerful case that the number of independent voices in contemporary America is dwindling precipitously and this decline is bad for journalism and thus bad for a democracy of sovereign citizens. Westinghouse buys CBS, Disney buys Capital Cities/ABC, and so on.

There are many signs that Bagdikian's fears about gigantism in the news and entertainment industries have considerable merit. As independent outlets are merged into communications conglomerates, the distinctions between their news and entertainment divisions tend to blur, creating a considerable danger that important journalistic principles may lose out to entertainment value. This is a particular danger in television, where the costs, and thus the stakes, are much higher than in print and where production values are considered to be more important they than in print.

A case in point arose from the June 1995 release of a new album by the pop singer Michael Jackson, his first since his career had been sidetracked for several years following allegations that he had molested a twelve-year-old boy. (A civil suit was eventually settled out of court for an undisclosed sum and no criminal charges were filed.)

The new recording, "HIStory: Past, Present and Future, Book 1," generated a good deal of interest, in part because of the recent scandal, but mostly because of Jackson's enormous popularity. Major newspapers and magazines had section-leading stories on the album's release, most mentioning lyrics in a song titled "They Don't Care about Us," that certainly seemed anti-Semitic, Jackson's denial notwithstanding. (The original lyrics were, "Jew me, sue me, everybody do me/Kick me, kike me, don't you black or white me." After much furor over the words, Jackson rerecorded the song and toned down the anti-Semitism in the lyrics.)

ABC's *Prime Time Live*, one of a spate of newsmagazines that arose in the late 1980s and early 1990s, secured a joint interview with Jackson and his wife, Lisa Marie Presley, daughter of Elvis Presley.

The show was an enormous success from one perspective but an embarrassment from another. Ratings showed that it had been a big hit for ABC, as Jackson's new CD quickly became for Sony, even if not as big a hit as Sony had hoped. More than 60 million people watched the show, giving the program a rating of 25.9, tops for the week by a wide margin.

But from a journalistic perspective, the show was embarrassing. The interviewer, Diane Sawyer, a veteran television reporter, asked predominantly softball questions of pop music's most famous couple—such as which of them had first mentioned the word "marriage" to the other, and similar dreck. Fans appeared on screen to ask if the couple had a normal sex life, with Ms. Sawyer demurring, "I didn't spend my life as a journalist to ask this sort of question." Yet for an hour, she did ask just that sort of question, treating the audience to a celebrity interview that bordered on fawning. While Sawyer asked about the questionable lyrics and the accusation of molestation, she did so gently, never challenging the answers. The interview represents an increasing trend toward what can charitably be called "soft news" in both print and broadcasting. *Us*, a popular magazine about the entertainment industry, has run full-page promotional ads that feature a picture of two stars and the copy: "They say it's getting hard to draw the line between news and entertainment. So what?"

So what, indeed? Does it matter? There is nothing new with celebrity interviews, of course. James Gordon Bennett made history and a fortune when he invented the genre in the 1830s. In the 1890s and beyond, such fare was a staple of many a major daily, including William Randolph Hearst's and Joseph Pulitzer's papers and their many imitators. And on the broadcast side, Edward R. Murrow, a broadcast pioneer revered as perhaps no other broadcast journalist in history, had, toward the end of his career an extremely popular television interview show called *Person to Person*, which was filled with the same sort of softball questions that Sawyer asked Jac kson and Presley.

Not all television newsmagazines are endless fluff, of course. CBS's *60 Minutes* has a long history of serious journalism, and television reporters like ABC's Sam Donaldson, who also appears on *Prime Time Live*, pride themselves, and rightly so, on being serious journalists. Yet it is undeniable that the television magazine has deliberately comingled news and entertainment, even coining such new terms as *infotainment*.

The archetype of the talk show that is not really news is *Larry King Live*, whose host does not even pretend to be a journalist and almost never does his homework before interviewing his guests. He makes a virtue of his ignorance, saying that the questions he winds up asking are the sorts of questions that ordinary citizens would probably ask, given the chance.

While this argument seems to have a certain democratic charm, in point of fact King's show is dedicatedly banal. Newsmakers love to go on the show because they can make their pitch to the viewers with little chance that King will remind them of their earlier statements to the contrary or note the fiscal or logical fallacies of their arguments. It may be amusing to watch, but it is not news because it does not provide citizens with the useful information needed to make representative government work.

Walter Goodman, television critic for the *New York Times*, wrote of the Sawyer interview with Jackson: "it was an expertly modulated hour of synthetic collision and wholehearted collusion" between two media giants, Capital Cities/ABC and Sony. ABC wanted the huge ratings that an interview with Jackson would deliver, and Sony wanted publicity for Jackson's new album.

Pop music is a multibillion-dollar industry, and a new album by the so-called king of pop certainly generates enough fan interest to go around. ABC gets its ratings, which makes it happy; Sony sells CDs, which makes Sony happy; pop music fans are presumably wildly happy. This seems to be a win-win-win situation—the communications giants get what they want, and the audience does as well. And doubtless the advertisers who bought time during the show were tickled as well. All of this seems to say that the interview was a good, or at least innocuous, thing.

But on the minus side, fluffy celebrity interviews are simply not news. They are pure entertainment. There is nothing wrong with entertaining news. For more than 150 years, journalists have been trying to make the news entertaining to attract and hold readers' attention (and, for 50 years, their viewers' attention). Virtually all recent innovations in newspaper page design, use of color, experiments in narrative and other writing styles, and many other expensive and time-consuming efforts have had the common goal of attracting and holding readers.

There is nothing wrong, morally or in any other sense, with entertainment. Most television programming is entertainment, the film industry is almost exclusively entertainment, books and magazines are mostly entertainment, and there are many purely entertaining elements of even the stodgiest newspaper.

The serious problems lie with presentations that purport to be news but are in truth almost wholly devoid of news. An analogy with food and diet is appropriate. Nearly all agree that it is healthier to eat nutritious food than to eat only empty calories. And most dieticians agree that, taken in moderation, snack foods, candies, and other empty calories are healthy as well. The problem arises when one eats empty calories, not in addition to nutritious food, but instead of it. And that is most likely to happen when the diner does not know, does not care, or cannot tell the difference between junk food and food with serious nutritional content. The same is true with information. In moderation, for most people there is probably nothing wrong with reading or viewing purely for relaxation, for entertainment, be it a baseball game, a sitcom, a murder mystery or almost anything else. The problem comes when the diet is overloaded with empty entertainment to the exclusion of the news and other information a citizen needs to understand and be able to act upon the world outside.

The fundamental problem with the Jackson interview was not that Sawyer did it, nor was it that the questions were easy, with responses ranging from banal to insipid. The real problem, as Goodman noted, was with the closing line of the show: "This has been a presentation of ABC News."

The reason many journalists are concerned about a decrease in the number of news voices available and the concentration of media power in fewer and fewer hands is that, especially in television, pure entertainment is far more profitable than serious news. Turning news into entertainment thus makes sense from a corporate perspective. When ABC News becomes, as it has, merely a division of the huge Disney entertainment empire, the pressures increase for the news division to turn a maximum profit for the parent company, just as the theme-park division and the animated-film division do. This robs viewers of the less amusing but more important information that they need. In the case of ersatz news, which ranges from celebrity fluff interviews to most of the coverage of the O. J. Simpson murder trial, it robs them again by allowing them to believe that they have taken in legitimate, if nicely garnished, morsels of news, when in truth those tidbits have just been empty information calories.

Questions to Consider

1. If you had been the *Prime Time Live* producer, would you have said yes to a chance to interview Jackson and Presley? Why or why not? If you had been calling the shots, how would you have handled the interview?

2. Are there circumstances in which a journalist could justify not being as hard hitting in an interview? Or should journalists always be aggressive?

3. The concentration of media ownership decried by Bagdikian involves more than just news and entertainment operations. It also involves music and book companies and other entertainment and communications enterprises, which are often international in scope. How might these business trends affect the practice of journalism and the availability of information in the future?

31

A Lorena Bobbitt Update: Paint My Nails, Answer My Questions

In January 1995, Michelle Meyers, a young reporter at the *Arlington (Va.) Journal*, a suburban daily just outside Washington, D.C., got a tip from a source that Lorena Bobbitt, notorious for having cut off her husband's penis, was working as a manicurist in an area beauty salon.

Bobbitt's trial the previous summer had been one of the most garish assault trials in American history. Meyers thought there might be an interesting feature updating readers on what such a famous person was doing, so she set out to find her. She began calling area salons, asking for "Lorena." In short order, Meyers located the shop where Bobbitt was working in a small shopping center in Shirlington, squarely within her paper's circulation area.

Meyers drove to the shop, parked, and went in. "I told her who I was and that I was a reporter and wanted to interview her," Meyers said later in an interview. "And she told me that she had been advised by her attorney not to talk to reporters. But she seemed very nice and eager to talk." So Meyers and Bobbitt agreed that it would be all right for Bobbitt to talk to Meyers if Meyers was a customer having her nails done. "She certainly knew I was a reporter and that I was doing a story on her," Meyers said, recalling that she had hoped that she would be able to remember quotations from the conversation with Bobbitt. "I kept looking at my notebook, but I couldn't get to it because Lorena had my hands in hers, doing my nails."

The two women talked, simultaneously manicurist to customer and news source to reporter. At the conclusion of the manicure, Meyers paid the fifteen-dollar fee, gave Bobbitt a three-dollar tip and went back to the office to write her story. The result was a pleasant, if not earth-shattering, feature, plus "questions from my editor and everybody else, 'Well, did she do your nails?'" The answer, of course, was yes, although the story did not say so. "It didn't seem to fit in anywhere," Meyers said.

Meyers worried about whether she had done the right thing, if hiring Bobbitt to do her nails had in some way compromised her neutrality and objectivity. She was also astonished by the journalistic frenzy that her story set off. "Camera crews and reporters were all over the shopping center for days," Meyers said. "Even the BBC [British Broadcasting Corporation]. Lorena wouldn't talk to them, so they interviewed me, live, asking me what it was like. The BBC," Meyers said again, with some wonderment in her voice.

Did Meyers act ethically in having Bobbitt do her nails so she could get an interview, or did she compromise her journalistic integrity by having some relationship other than that of a reporter and a news source?

There is a case to be made for declining to talk to Bobbitt unless it was strictly as a reporter talking to a news source, and that was Meyers's first choice. Indeed, she felt uneasy about talking to Bobbitt under any other circumstances. But Bobbitt made it clear that the interview could not take place under those circumstances, but that it could if Meyers was a client.

Meyers said she had made it very clear to Bobbitt that the conversation was on the record and that Meyers intended to write a story based on the conversation. In this regard, engaging Bobbitt's services as a manicurist seems to be comparable to buying a news source a meal, certainly a common occurrence in the journalistic world. Ideally, reporters would prefer to have their relationships perfectly clean, that is, unencumbered by any personal relationship beyond professional civility. In actual fact, as most beat reporters will acknowledge, a pure reporter-to-source relationship is almost impossible when the source is someone the reporter sees regularly. When two people encounter one another on a daily basis, even if it begins purely professionally, eventually the two will come to like or dislike each other. Moreover, a polite civil distance is not even desirable when a reporter is cultivating sources to provide tips, background information, reliable context, and so on. Such information comes only with trust, and trust must be mutual. Given the circumstances, it is hard to find fault with Meyers for getting a manicure in order to get a story. The alternative was to not get the story at all.

One problem was that Meyers was not able to take notes during the conversation because her hands were being worked on. There was a risk of inaccuracy, one of the most serious journalistic problems. But Meyers said she had written down some notes right after the manicure was finished and was confident that she had both quoted and paraphrased Bobbitt fairly and accurately in her story. Reporters frequently have to rely on memory for quotes for at least a short time for a broad range of reasons—usually because taking notes would be so obtrusive as to risk changing the story.

While having your nails done is rarely the reason for not taking notes, there is nothing inherently wrong with this reporting technique. Meyers was not attempting to deceive Bobbitt. In fact, she provided fuller disclosure than is often the case when a reporter puts the notebook away and takes mental notes. Often in such circumstances, the reporter is, while not denying her or his status as a journalist, deliberately not calling attention to the fact. There is ethical value in avoiding any sort of deceit, even the deceit of pocketing a reporter's notebook, but most reporters consider that the benefits from such modest deception outweigh either of the alternatives: altering the story by obviously taking notes or not getting the story at all.

Should Meyers have noted in her story that she had engaged Bobbitt professionally? Most reporters leave themselves out of their copy for very good reason. Journalists try hard to report the news, not make it. In this case, involving a light feature, Meyers could probably have worked the manicure into the story.

Full disclosure is usually considered a major journalistic virtue. Since it is a foundational premise that knowledge is crucial to sound decision making, most journalists figure that the reader must be presented with all the salient facts of a story (although, of course, reasonable and honorable people may disagree as to which facts are salient). Many stories in which there is any hint of impropriety or irregularity—or even something unusual in the reporting—will carry an explanation, either in the story itself, or in an italicized "shirttail" at the end of the story. Some investigative stories carry small sidebars about how the reporting was done.

A common example of this sort of thing occurs in travel stories in which part or all of the writer's expenses were paid either by an airline or by the destination visited. Few papers, other than the largest and most well heeled, can afford to pay the full cost of a reporter's or freelancer's trip, and airlines and tourist spots are more than happy to help subsidize the travel. The principle of full disclosure suggests telling the readers that an article about a trip to France was paid for, in part, by the French tourism office. That gives the reader important information about how credible the story is. The alternative would be to not include travel articles unless the news organization could pay the entire cost to get them.

It certainly would not have hurt to apply this principle to the Bobbitt story by telling the readers that the interview had taken place while Meyers was having a manicure, and it might even have added more color to the feature story, but it was probably not necessary. Paying the standard fee and giving the standard tip does not seem likely to have interfered with the essential integrity of the story.

The larger question about Meyers's Lorena Bobbitt story is: Was the story news at all? Although this story is not profoundly important one way or the other, its publication did have immediate and identifiable consequences, primarily a new flurry of journalistic attention focused on a woman who was famous in the first place only because of the extraordinary nature of her assault on her husband. It is doubtless true that when the Bobbitt story broke, it was legitimate medical news, in the surgical reattachment of her husband's severed penis, and legal news, as a compelling case calling attention to questions of spousal abuse. These elements were arguments for playing the story prominently in the summer of 1994, outweighing in the minds of serious editors the knowledge that the story was being overplayed because it had a strong sex angle. Those elements of legitimacy were missing from the follow-up story.

So why was the story interesting? The "whatever happened to . . ." story has been a staple of American journalism for generations. When a story has had legitimate news value, a follow-up on an anniversary generates interest, even if it has less news value. It is perfectly reasonable—indeed, one can argue that there is a positive obligation—to provide readers and viewers with stories they were not consciously seeking. Most enterprise reporting is of this type.

Meyers avoided privacy problems with this story. She was fully candid with her subject about her intention to write a story, and certainly Bobbitt had, by that time, become fully aware of what journalists do. And, as a beginning journalist, Meyers showed commendable initiative in tracking down Bobbitt. But should she have done the article?

Probably few journalists could resist tracking down a Lorena Bobbitt if they found out that she was working in the area, and Meyers's story was certainly not particularly salacious. But just as most of the original Bobbitt story involved more pandering than information, this follow-up seemed to add little of value to the readers' storehouse of important or useful information.

Questions to Consider

1. How do you weigh the arguments for and against publishing the Bobbitt article? What would you have done?

2. If Bobbitt had refused to cooperate, would Meyers have been justified in posing as a customer, not a journalist, and getting an interview that way? Some news organizations say their reporters must identify themselves as such to everyone they interview. Others allow "undercover" reporting if the story is an important one and there seems to be no other way to get the information. How much deception would have been justified in obtaining the Bobbitt story?

3. Reporters and sources often develop personal relationships. What should be the rules for such relationships? Should reporters encourage friendly relationships with sources? Should reporters be allowed to socialize with sources in settings unrelated to their business relationships? Should they be allowed to have romantic relationships, perhaps including live-in relationships or marriage? What about editors who have almost no direct business contacts with sources? What about journalists who have personal relationships with sources but no professional relationships with them because they do not work on that particular beat?

4. What should Meyers have done if Bobbitt had refused payment for the manicure? Should reporters ever accept gifts from sources? Are small gifts, like a souvenir pen or box of candy, acceptable? What about larger gifts, like tickets to sports or entertainment events?

5. At some point in her life, will Bobbitt have the same right to privacy enjoyed by someone who has not been in the public eye?

32

Ruth Snyder: Still Dead but Now Her Picture Is Mainstream

For more than sixty years, a slightly blurry photograph of a blindfolded woman strapped into an electric chair has served as the symbol of the wretched excess of tabloid journalism. Now the photo is back, minus its news value, as a photo-illustration in America's most sober-minded general circulation daily. The movement of the picture of the electrocution of Ruth Snyder from the New York *Daily News* to the *New York Times* says a great deal about the moving line of good taste, the line between the use of violent images to shock and titillate and the use of images to inform and illustrate. Has the photo of Ruth Snyder moved from one side of the line to the other?

The first use of the photograph of Snyder came in early 1928 as a climactic moment in one of New York City's tawdriest circulation wars among papers vying for the absolute lowest common denominator of public interest. The leading players were William Randolph Hearst and the *Daily Mirror*, Joseph Medill Patterson with the *Illustrated Daily News* (now just the *Daily News*), and Bernarr MacFadden with the *Evening Graphic*, which was quickly nicknamed the *Pornographic* for its lurid tales of sex and violence.

The papers vied with one another for the most sensational details of murder and mayhem for much of the 1920s, a period known in historical shorthand as the era of Jazz Journalism. In the spring of 1927, they latched onto a love triangle that ended in murder—a corset salesman named Judd Gray; his lover, Ruth Snyder; and her husband, Albert Snyder. It was the O. J. Simpson trial of its day, and the papers went all out. Damon Runyon, for example, covered the trial for Hearst's International News Service. Gray and Ruth Snyder were tried and convicted of a particularly brutal murder in which they beat Albert Snyder with a blunt instrument, chloroformed him, and then garrotted him with picture wire. By January 1928, on the eve of a grisly first—Snyder was the first woman to be electrocuted—the *Graphic* promised its readers:

"Don't fail to read tomorrow's *Graphic*. An installment that thrills and stuns! A story that fairly pierces the heart and reveals Ruth Snyder's last thoughts on earth; that pulses the blood as it discloses her final letters. Think of it! A woman's final thoughts just before she is clutched in the deadly snare that sears and burns and FRIES AND KILLS! Her very last words! Exclusively in tomorrow's *Graphic.*"

The counterpunch from the *Daily News*? The *Graphic* promised words, the *Daily News* provided a picture—a photograph that was at the time the most sensational photograph of the year, maybe ever. The *News* slipped a photographer into the reporters' witness area at Sing Sing to get a picture of Snyder at the moment the executioner threw the switch. Photographers were banned in the area, and the *News,* fearing their staff photographers would be recognized and barred, brought in a Chicago photographer, Tom Howard, who strapped a miniature camera to his ankle, with a shutter cable running up his leg and ending in a shutter release inside his trousers pocket. At the moment of electrocution, he calmly tugged on his pants leg enough to expose the lens of the camera and tripped the shutter. The reason the famous picture is slightly blurred is that Howard, correctly gauging the light to be inadequate for proper exposure, took a second exposure on the same piece of film. He could not, of course, advance the film in his camera without being noticed, so the picture that covered the front of the *Daily News* is actually a double exposure.

The *Daily News* put out an extra that day, January 13, 1928, running Howard's photograph of Snyder's execution under the single-word headline "DEAD." They ran the picture again the next morning, again covering the whole front page, under the headline "FUNERALS HELD." The *News* enlarged its press run by 250,000 to accommodate increased sales, and it subsequently printed another 750,000 copies of the front page for souvenir hunters.

Generations of journalism history textbooks have reprinted the photograph, describing it as the archetype of sensationalism or its synonym, tabloid journalism, a reference to the propensity of half-size newspapers, such as the *Graphic* and the *Daily News,* to pander far more than the full-size papers, which are called broadsheets.

Yet more than sixty years later, the staid *New York Times,* the world's very definition of responsible journalism—the broadest of broadsheets—used the photograph again, even larger than the original in the *Daily News,* not quite on the front page, but on front of the news analysis section called the Week in Review. In its most recent incarnation, the photograph does not even have any news value, which it surely did have in 1928, whatever else may be said about the decision to use it. The *Times* used the picture to illustrate a story about a rise in the use of the death penalty and an analysis of whether the state's ultimate punishment deters crime. (The *Times* article concluded that it did not.) Most of the article itself was on the third page of the section because the picture of Snyder took up the bulk of the section's front page.

How did this happen? Carolyn Lee, assistant managing editor of the *Times* and a former picture editor at the paper, said there were so many more strong images around today—on television, but in other places, too—than there were at the time of the photograph's first publication that standards had changed. "We've been bombarded with images that make us far more tolerant of what would once have seemed excessive," she said, acknowledging that the picture probably still shocked some. But overall, she said, "society has become slightly less queasy than it once was about images of death and dying and destruction."

The Snyder picture moved from a *Daily News* lurid picture to a *New York Times* photo-illustration "because of its place in history," she said, both in American history and in the history of journalism. It has lost much of its power to shock precisely because it has been reproduced so many times, in journalism textbooks and elsewhere. "If the chance were there to photograph an execution today," she said, "I'm pretty sure we would not publish the actual execution."

Even though history may have inoculated the public against the photograph of Snyder in the throes of death, taking away much of its ability to shock, surely the *Times* would not have run it so large had it not still possessed some ability to startle.

News organizations are very much products of their times. In interview after interview, veteran editors all over the country have noted the changes that have occurred in public taste since they entered the news business a generation ago. It is debatable whether this is a good thing or not, whether such changes represent a coarsening of public sensibilities or a refreshing willingness to look honestly at issues too long dangerously hidden. And how one sees the shift may be reflected in how enthusiastically one embraces the new candor. But it will not, eventually, determine whether one adjusts to it. Whether try to accelerate the current or slow it down, eventually all go with it. It does not mean that everyone gives up on standards of good taste just because daytime talk shows and other phenomena have coarsened public discourse. But journalism, as something of a public trust, can never be too far distant from the tastes and desires of those ultimately in charge—the sovereign citizenry that relies on the output of journalists to give them the information they want in a form they want it in. Journalism may reflect society more than it shapes it.

Questions to Consider

1. If you had been the editor making the decision, would you have used a photograph of an execution as a photo-illustration? Why or why not? How else could a news analysis on the use of the death penalty have been illustrated?

2. Photo-illustrations are not news photographs. In what sections of the paper, if any, are photo-illustrations acceptable? Is there anything newspapers can do to reduce the chance of misleading readers into thinking that a photo-illustration is a news photo?

3. If Snyder's execution had in fact been filmed, do you think standards of public taste have changed so much that a mainstream television news program could run such footage to illustrate a piece on the death penalty? Why or why not?

4. How do we know when standards of public taste have changed? Who decides, and how? Should the news media reflect those changes as soon as they are perceived, or should there be a lag time?

5. Does journalism reflect society more than it shapes it?

33

Composite Pictures: New Possibilities or Just More Credibility Trouble?

In the months leading up to the 1994 Winter Olympics in Lillehammer, Norway, national attention was focused on a real-life soap opera of almost addictive fascination: the morality play on ice of Tonya Harding and Nancy Kerrigan.

Harding and Kerrigan were the nation's two best figure skaters and the two best hopes for the women's figure skating competition, the perennial centerpiece sport of the winter games.

During the pre-Olympic competition to determine the makeup of the United States team, a mysterious figure ran up to Kerrigan just as she was leaving the ice and viciously clubbed her just above the knee. At first, the injury seemed likely to keep her out of the Olympics or end her career. At stake was far more than glory; Olympic champions, especially in a glamour sport like figure skating, stand to make millions from product endorsements and a few years on the professional skating circuit.

Kerrigan, already an Olympic medal–winner from the previous games,[1] the working-class ice angel with a winning smile and a blind mother, became America's sweetheart. Harding was the tough bleached blonde who smoked cigarettes and did her own engine repairs. The normally breathless run-up to the Olympics became a tabloid frenzy when Harding's former husband was charged in the attack and Harding herself was suspected of involvement. The story then dashed off on two fronts: Would Kerrigan's injury heal enough for her to skate in Norway, and would Harding become an Olympian or a felon? (In which sense would Harding be on ice?) For months, the Nancy-and-Tonya story was

---

[1] Kerrigan won a bronze, or third-place, medal in the winter games in Albertville, France, in 1992. Through 1992, the quadrennial winter and summer Olympics were held during the same year, but the Olympic organizers decided to stagger the games so winter and summer games would be held on alternating even-numbered years. Thus, the Lillehammer games, the first on the new schedule, were held only two years later than the games in Albertville.

everywhere. Serious pundits lamented that greed had so corrupted the spirit of the games that they had come to this. The supermarket tabloids ran pictures—masked as a tease or for modesty—of Harding stripping for her husband. The talk shows were full of legal analysis of whether criminals could or should be Olympians; doctors endlessly discussed kneecap injuries.

As it turned out, Kerrigan healed and Harding stayed on the team, so the skating soap opera moved to Lillehammer, Norway. The final chapter of the Tonya-and-Nancy story would be played out on the skating rink in what had been covered as a morality play of epic proportions. As the games opened, *New York Newsday*, usually the most restrained of the New York tabloid papers, ignited a fleeting controversy in the journalism world that, for a moment or two, diverted a bit of attention away from Nancy and Tonya themselves.

On Wednesday, February 16, *New York Newsday* ran a full-page photograph on the paper's front page of what appeared to be the two women skating together on the same rink. The headline overlaid onto the picture read: "Fire on Ice." At the bottom of the picture, the bold type read: "Tonya, Nancy To Meet At Practice," and then, in smaller type, the caption read in part, "Tonya Harding, left, and Nancy Kerrigan appear to skate together in this New York Newsday composite." In the picture, there they were, at that moment the world's two most famous skaters, practicing away, each heading straight toward the camera, each on her left skate, their left legs and torsos almost perfectly parallel, their right legs raised high behind them. It was, all in all, a terrific news picture. Except it never happened. The picture of Harding had been one photograph, the picture of Kerrigan another, and the image on the printed page had been created on a computer screen, using the contemporary version of darkroom alchemy.

Newsday's editor, Anthony Marro, was quoted the next day as saying that he had believed that the paper's readers would realize full well that the picture was not really a news photograph, that readers would see the front page for what it was: an imagined scene, a representation of what was to happen, not a literal account of what had happened. The headline clue that this was illusion could be found in the infinitive form of the verb: "to meet" meaning "are to meet" or "will meet." Obviously, the thinking at *Newsday* ran, if they are merely "to meet," then they had not yet met and a picture of them together must be a rendering of what the paper thought might happen. The caption went further, explaining that the cover was "a composite" in which the two women "appear to skate together."

Marro told the *New York Times* that when he saw and approved the front page on Tuesday night, before publication, he thought it clear enough that the art was a modern version of the old photo-illustration. But he is quoted as adding, "When I picked up the paper on my front porch, I said, 'Uh-oh.' It looked very real."

At one level, this story is so easy to parse that it hardly warrants discussion. Journalists are supposed to tell the truth, the picture was not true, and thus it should never have been published. End of discussion.

But the *Newsday* picture is not just a case of journalistic technovillains cravenly trying to destroy the republic with pixels of propaganda. As Marro noted, he and his editors took great care to make readers aware that this was a photo-illustration, not a straightforward photograph. It wasn't until the cold light of day that Marro joined many other journalists, and, doubtless, the neighbors on his block, in agreeing that the warnings about the altered photograph had not been clear enough.

The photo-illustration, especially on the cover of a magazine—and since *New York Newsday* was a tabloid, its front page was its cover—is something of a special case in journalism (whether it should be is a different question.) Most of the notable recent examples of altered photographs have involved covers: *National Geographic* began the current wave in the early 1980s, when it digitally "moved" one of the Egyptian pyramids to make the picture fit the magazine's cover dimensions. *Scientific American* had a cover story on digital manipulation and illustrated it with a composite "photograph" of Abraham Lincoln walking in a garden arm-in-arm with Marilyn Monroe. At the time of O. J. Simpson's arrest, *Time* magazine darkened the skin tones of his police mug shot and slightly blurred the image, making him look vastly more sinister.

There is a reason that magazine and newspaper covers are considered legitimate subjects for manipulation while news pages are not, although, admittedly, there is an arbitrariness to the explanation. Editors argue that the primary purpose of the cover illustration is to attract readers by giving them a visual representation of what the story is about. From an editor's perspective, as opposed to a publisher's, this need not have anything to do with money. A cover story earns that spot in the publication because the editors decide that it is the best piece in the issue—the most interesting, the most important, the best written, the most timely. And a wonderful story is utterly useless unless people read it, so it makes sense to package it as attractively as possible. Readers know and recognize this, the argument goes, so as long as there is no blatant attempt at deception, all is well. There is also a circularity to this argument. In effect, those who argue for greater leeway in manipulating covers than in tinkering with news pictures say this: We do it, so readers expect us to do it, so it is OK that we do it.

The question of photo manipulation has become more acute in recent years, not because the practice is new—it is not—but because of changes in the technology that make such alterations virtually undetectable. Photo-illustrations or manipulated images by any other name are as old as photography itself. In the darkroom, photographers have long employed dodging, burning, cropping, and other techniques to bring out the elements in a photograph that the photographer wants to emphasize and to minimize or eliminate altogether those elements that intrude or interfere. Outside the darkroom, artists and illustrators have employed other tools ranging from the airbrush and paint bottles to scissors and paste to do the same.

The standard argument is that today's computer technology makes such manipulation undetectable and therefore more insidious. The intention is a noble one, for journalists' integrity and credibility are, ultimately, all they have to offer.

The fears about the sophistication of modern image-altering technology are grounded in the fear of losing credibility.

However, in important ways, worrying about losing credibility because of changes in technology misses the point. Even with scissors and paste, or a paint brush or an airbrush, image manipulation has been virtually undetectable to the eye of the audience for generations. Red-baiters in the McCarthy era did crudely snip photos apart to make it appear that McCarthy's targets were in league with suspected leftists. But subtler and more successful forms of image manipulation have gone undetected for many, many years.

Back up one step. In making the original print, the darkroom technician can select what part of the negative to print and what parts of the negative to leave out. That is and has been standard practice for a century. Now, back up one more step. At the moment of taking the picture, the photographer has selected lens, camera angle, focal point and a host of other variables in order to emphasize some elements and to make others disappear.

That is not only appropriate journalistic behavior, but is crucial to conveying any meaning at all. There could be a thousand snapshots of a parade—shots of sky, of streets, of bands and floats from all angles, of sidewalk watchers and of frustrated motorists stuck in traffic, of cops leaning on the sawhorse barricades—a jumble of images that add up to . . . nothing. Or there could be a shot or two that capture the essential "paradeness" of the event. A picture is supposed to have meaning. To be anything more than a waste of time and space, it must. Similarly, in written stories, reporters select elements to emphasize and others to play down, and still others to ignore altogether. By definition, not everything can be in the lede and not everything can even go into the story. It is appropriate to the role of journalists, both those with cameras and those with notebooks, that it be so.

It is, then, a false dichotomy to maintain that the raw negative represents reality and digital alteration represents falsehood. The photographer has always selected certain elements to include and others to discard. The editors cropping the pictrure and laying out the pages have done the same. "Old" technology was not responsible for the integrity of images, nor is "new" technology responsible for their corruption. In both eras and with both sets of tools, the responsibility rests with the integrity of the people making the decisions. True, "the camera never lies." Nor does it tell the truth. But photographers can do both.

There remains another fear, one that is, for the most part, still a few years in the future. That is the concern that once cameras loaded with film are replaced with all-digital cameras, there will be no original negative at all. At that point, the critics argue, the possibility for duplicity will be complete. With a film negative, one can always check the final print against the original negative for alterations and tampering. With digital imaging, there will be no original and those who would distort reality for their own nefarious purposes will be able to move pyramids, bring skaters together, and put dead movie stars on the arms of dead presidents at will.

But that argument is predicated on the assumption that it is only the fear of getting caught that prevents that sort of gross distortion today. The truth is that it is preposterous to imagine a million *New York Times* readers trooping down to the paper's photo darkrooms to compare negatives with published prints for unwarranted manipulation. And it is just as unlikely that someone from the "negative police" will make that examination for them. That is not why readers trust the paper now, and those readers will not lose that trust once cameras stop capturing light on a chemical-coated strip of clear plastic. The trust that readers have in one paper and not in another is at once more ephemeral and more durable than that based on direct, personal examination. It is more transitory because readers have never had hard evidence as a reality check for the great bulk of the information journalists provide them. And a visit to the darkroom could not convince them if they did not wish to be convinced because darkrooms are not police evidence rooms. Yet, it is more durable because it does not rely on physical proof but on the paper's history of being trustworthy.

That, at bottom, is the problem with the bogus picture of Harding and Kerrigan. The real lesson from the incident came when Anthony Marro picked up the paper from his front porch and said, "Uh-oh." Writer and editors live with news, with all its nuances, all the time. When Marro approved the use of the composite picture, there had been discussion about whether the use of the infinitive "to meet," to indicate the future tense would sufficiently warn the readers. Then there was the second warning when the caption said they "appear to skate together." What could be clearer than that? And, for good measure, the caption also clearly says "composite photo." But, of course, the editors and writers all knew what the story said. However, the reader, the person who picks the paper up off the steps or who buys it at a newsstand, is not forewarned at all. The reader looks at the picture and says, "Will you look at that! There's that Harding girl skating with the girl who got whacked in the knee." Or some version thereof.

At that point, the damage to the paper's most precious commodity, its credibility, has been done. The reader either reads the caption and realizes the error, or doesn't. Either way, the paper loses, and so does the reader. If the first impression is not corrected, the paper has, unwittingly and perhaps too cleverly by half, misinformed the reader. That is a cardinal sin in the news business. But if the reader, who has to eat breakfast, get the kids off to school, and get to work on time, reads the copy and realizes that the infinitive means future tense, that "composite" means "made up" and "appear to skate" means "not really skating," the paper and the reader still lose. The reader is angry for having been fooled, however briefly, and for being so gullible as to be taken in. And the paper now has a reader who will look at what it publishes hereafter with a new suspicion. Or, maybe, not look at it at all.

Questions to Consider

1. Did *New York Newsday* violate journalistic ethics by running the composite photograph of Harding and Kerrigan? Why or why not?

2. Just how much manipulation of a photograph is permissible in a darkroom or on a computer? Should a photographer remove extraneous people or objects in the middle of the shot (not just through cropping)? Should a photographer make someone look better or worse? How do you draw the line?

3. Are photo-illustrations on cover pages all right, or could they mislead readers? Why or why not? What about on feature pages? What should be the rules for the use of photo-illustrations?

34

The Grisly War Photo: Powerful Information, but What about Taste?

On Monday, October 4, 1993, photo editors and news executives all over the country were faced with a grisly dilemma—whether to publish a ghastly photograph that had just moved over the picture wire. A pair of images from Somalia showed a street mob cheering wildly as the body of a dead U.S. soldier, stripped and trussed up with ropes, was dragged through Mogadishu's dusty streets. In one picture, a person swings a stick at the body as it passes; in the other, a member of the crowd kicks at it.

The photos, taken by the *Toronto Star*'s Paul Watson, carried the warning to editors that the body had not been identified and that the dead man's family might not have been notified.

The images prompted ethical debates all over the country, but no consensus emerged. A group of journalists who happened to be attending an ethics seminar at the Poynter Institute in St. Petersburg, Florida, grappled with the question and split every way imaginable. Some said they would have run the picture on the front page and in color. Others chose black and white, to make the photograph less offensive, but agreed on the front-page placement. Some said they would have run it on an inside page; a few would not have run it at all; some could not decide. Journalists at work that day split in similar ways. A *Minneapolis Star-Tribune* survey of thirty-four major dailies found eleven that had used the picture on the front page. Fifteen used it inside, and eight did not run it at all.

Editors all over the country face this sort of problem almost every day: How graphic is too graphic? At community papers, it comes up when there has been a traffic fatality, and at the big metro dailies, it arises when particularly gruesome images move over the photo wire from Israel, from Bosnia, from Africa or from any of the world's trouble spots. Is there a clear line between providing useful visual information to readers and viewers, even if that information is horrific, and pandering to morbid curiosity, which is forbidden by both decency and the Society of Professional Journalists' Code of Ethics? No. Conscientious people of goodwill can and do disagree over which items should weigh how much in the decision.

Nobody had a tougher call to make than Cole C. Campbell, then the editor of the *Virginian-Pilot*, whose readership draws heavily from military families at Fort Eustis and Norfolk Naval Air Station. The photograph was powerful and compelling, an instant symbol of an American humanitarian mission to a starving African nation gone horribly wrong. Yet, Campbell said in an interview, war pictures in a military town must be handled with special care. "There is a real strong sense that in a military community, we have a different standard to protect the sensibilities of our readership."

Campbell passed the photo around the editors' story conference, the midafternoon meeting held at most newspapers to decide which stories deserve to go on page one, which pictures to use, and so on. (It is a remarkable measure of journalists' continuing concern for ethics that somewhere between eight and two dozen top editors at major papers routinely spend about 10 percent of the workday, often more, deciding the most appropriate use of the precious news hole to best inform their readers, just as television and radio executives meet to allocate their air time. Some discussions concern practical and logistical matters, of course, but the great bulk of story conferences everywhere is taken up with the *should* dimension of journalism. It is hard to think of another major industry whose chief executives spend so much of their time on ethical issues.)

The editors at Campbell's newspaper split nearly evenly over whether to run the picture or not, so Campbell adjourned the story conference out into the newsroom, where the picture could be called up on a pagination computer screen and adjusted so the editors could see how the photo would look on the page in various layouts, croppings, and sizings. "Lots of people gathered around, and we asked each person when they came up what they would do. So we had a whole lot of staff discussion and deliberation on this," Campbell said.

Eventually, it was Campbell's call, and he decided to use the picture, in color, beginning above the fold, with the soldier's body below the fold, accompanied by a story and the headline, "Cheering mob drags body of soldier through streets."

With the story's continuation inside the paper, on what is called the jump page, Campbell offered this note to his readers:

Today's *Virginian-Pilot* includes a photograph of jubilant Somalis dragging the body of a U.S. soldier killed in action Monday. The photograph is difficult to look at. It was difficult for us to publish. We decided to do so only after long discussion involving many voices in our newsroom. There was no unanimity. There was no consensus.

It is painful to publish this photograph in a community in which so many people are connected to the military. More than 125 troops from Fort Eustis are in Somalia, although none of them was among those injured Monday. We can see in this fallen soldier members of our own families. We worry that the indignity imposed by the Somalis is compounded by publication of the photograph.

In the end, this photograph portrays an outrage against a U.S. soldier in a powerful, profound way that words alone cannot convey. In an era of instant, worldwide visual communications, images such as this one shape the reaction of policymakers as well as the public. We could not deny people so closely linked to events so far away the fullest understanding of what is happening and what others are seeing and reacting to.

In an interview after the picture ran, Campbell said, "In the final analysis, this was a question of whether this was a picture that was going to change the course of United States policy, one way or the other, either to intensify our involvement or to limit our involvement. And we decided that it was. Did our readership need to see that? And we decided that it did."

While the *Virginian-Pilot*, like many newspapers, generally does not put pictures of dead bodies on the front page, Campbell said, the picture's news value overrode the usual ban. Campbell saw in that photograph a symbol of an age, an image that transcended the particulars of the moment. Comparable images include the picture taken by an AP photographer, Eddie Adams, of South Vietnamese Brigadier General Nguyen Ngoc Loan executing a Vietcong suspect point blank, or the photograph taken by a Kent State University student, John Filo, of Mary Ann Vecchio kneeling in agony over the body of a student shot on the campus during an antiwar rally in 1971.

So far in this analysis, we have seen that the questions concerning the use of this photograph are fairly straightforward, even if there is no consensus on the answers. That is, we recognize the basic elements to be weighed in making such a decision, although there may be disagreements about how much relative weight each element should have.

The picture has great news value, which is the primary reason to publish it. As a straightforward news photograph, it has important elements of newsworthiness: timeliness, impact, conflict, and human interest. (And for papers like Campbell's, which serve large military areas, it also had a kind of proximity, which increased its news value, but which, at the same, time raised the question of whether it would hit too close to home. Generally, the farther away a gruesome event occurs, the less objectionable pictures or footage of that event will be perceived to be.) The Somalia picture seemed likely to have a serious impact on American foreign policy. Campbell argued that this increased his obligation to show readers something that was likely to cause the Pentagon and the State Department to rethink their policies.

On the other hand, the picture is grisly and extremely distasteful, which is the primary reason not to run it. Different editors put different weights on those two dimensions. Some opted for running it in black and white rather than in color or for playing it inside instead of on the front page in an effort to make it appear less grisly and less startling, thereby tipping the decision toward publishing. Other editors believed that there was no way to tip the balance, and they chose not to publish it at all.

But this is more than just a grisly picture. It involves both a dead body and national humiliation. Some editors make it a policy not to run corpses, period, on the grounds of taste. Others might shy away from this picture on some sort of nationalist grounds. A representative of the greatest military power on earth is being deliberately humiliated by third-world nationals with crude sticks and big grins.

There are other dimensions to this photograph, quite apart from its enormous news value, its grisly image, and, in some eyes, its extremely poor taste. One complex and vexing problem is hinted at in the editor's note written by Campbell: "We worry that the indignity imposed by the Somalis is compounded by publication of the photograph." The people in this photograph, like the people in so many events reported on by print reporters, by still photographers, and by electronic journalists with their microphones and television cameras, did not just happen to behave the way they did spontaneously. Many of the people in this photograph were looking directly at the camera. Much of what they were doing was done at least in part *because* journalists were there to record their actions.

That is a problem for journalists for which there is no fully satisfactory answer. Journalists, especially photographers, are occasionally accused of staging events. When that happens, there are cries of outrage from the journalistic community and from readers and viewers. That is probably as it should be. Yet, at the most basic level, it is undeniable that people behave differently when they know they are being watched, and more so when they know their actions are being recorded for mass distribution. There is a journalistic version of the scientific principle known as the Heisenberg uncertainty principle, which says that the very act of measuring something changes it. In journalism, it may be said that the very act of reporting on events changes them. It is impossible for a journalist to become invisible and thus not affect events at all. If it were possible to blend into the background, would that not raise equally valid questions about reporters using deceptive tactics to do their work?

If, to any degree at all, those Somalis who dragged the body of the serviceman through the streets of Mogadishu were doing so because of the embarrassment and humiliation it would cause, is the journalist aiding and abetting that embarrassment by photographing that event? Media manipulation has always been a serious problem for journalists, particularly the modern public relations industry came of age after World War I, but the problem goes far beyond slick politicians and captains of industry with their high-priced spinmeisters. Nobody in Watson's photograph needed public relations counsel to advise them on how best to humiliate the United States.

In one sense, the job of journalists is to report on real occurrences, not those orchestrated for their eyes, microphones, and cameras. The problem is brilliantly explored by Daniel J. Boorstin, the former Librarian of Congress, in a 1961 book, *The Image*.[1] Yet could anyone truly argue that an event is not newsworthy just because it was set up in whole or in part for the convenience of journalists? Examples abound. Take the arrest of a wanted criminal. The arrest is clearly news. Does it become not news just because the police chief calls a press conference to make the announcement? Or is the picture of the suspect less newsworthy because the suspect, usually called a perpetrator by the police, has been paraded by the authorities for the benefit of photographers and camera crews in a "perp walk"? In

---

[1] It is worth pointing out that the book was written before television became so ubiquitous in American culture; the problems it describes are even more serious today.

the case of the Mogadishu picture, one can argue that it is in such bad taste that it should not have been run, but can anyone argue that it was not news?

Everyone, from politicians to protesters, tries to manipulate reporters all the time, feeding them information that will serve their own interests yet still meet the journalists' standard of newsworthiness. It is tempting to resist being taken in by the manipulators by refusing to photograph or write about anything created or staged for the convenience of reporters. But if the event is legitimate news, it needs to be covered. While it would be irresponsible to swallow whole every line fed to a reporter, it would be just as irresponsible to refuse to report at all on legitimate news that serves some other interest.

The Mogadishu picture raises another question: Who was this soldier, and had his family been notified of his death? Whose son, brother, husband, or boyfriend was he? The dead soldier was not identified, then or later, and many publications have it as one of the most inviolable of newsroom policies to not identify victims until close relatives have been notified. They consider that the news value of the victim's identity is more than offset by the shock and dismay it would cause a reader or viewer to learn first of a family tragedy through as impersonal a medium as a news story. (The rule is far from perfect. Journalists generally agree to wait until a victim's next of kin has been told of the death, but such a standard assumes the universality of a nuclear family, which is not the case. Take a child of divorced parents, for example. Is it appropriate to wait until both parents hear of the child's death through other means before identifying the child in a story, or just until the parent the child was living with has been notified? What about children brought up by other relatives—aunts and uncles, say, or grandparents? What if the child is grown or married? Or has a live-in friend or lover?)

The Pentagon knew which of its soldiers had gone on that mission and who was unaccounted for, so it was able to inform the missing soldiers' next of kin. What the Pengaton could not do for the families was say whose body was being desecrated so grotesquely by the Somalis. The Pentagon called Mary Cleveland of Portsmouth, Virginia, and told her that her stepson, Staff Sergeant William Cleveland, thirty-four, was among the missing, so when she saw the *Virginian-Pilot* the next day, she was spared some of the horror when she thought she recognized the body as that of her stepson. (However, other members of the Cleveland family did not have their shock cushioned by a call from the Pentagon. They saw the picture first.) So the Cleveland family "sat by the phone all day, waiting to hear from the Pentagon," Campbell said. "They didn't hear anything, so the next day they called us and said, 'We think this may be our stepson, but we can't get anything from the Pentagon. Maybe you'll help us.' They actually turned to us for help." Campbell said the paper's military reporters had tried to get identification from the Pentagon, but were not successful.

Campbell stressed that immediately after the picture was published, the Cleveland family saw the paper as a source of information, not as a ghoulish invader of their privacy. "At that stage, there wasn't any anger or hostility on the family's part," Campbell said. However, as days passed and the list of possible soldiers in the picture narrowed—eventually to just five men killed in Somalia—the Cleveland family was "besieged" by reporters, Campbell said. "By the end of the experience, they were very hostile toward the news media," he said. "They decided it was not appropriate for a newspaper to have run this picture."

Sergeant Cleveland's birth mother, Nada Morford, also turned to, not away from, journalists in trying to sort out the horror of the picture.

After Mary Cleveland told the newspaper she thought she recognized the man in the photograph, Morford protested and said it was not, could not be, her son. "I want him to rest in peace," she said then.

But Morford had not yet studied the picture carefully, and the possibility that the photograph was that of her son's body gnawed at her, according to published accounts. She went to the town library to make photocopies of pictures in a *Time* magazine article. Then she asked a reporter for the photograph from Somalia.

She broke down as she described how she pored over the pictures, how she found contours that seemed so familiar, but not enough for her to say with certainty that the soldier in the photograph was her son.

"My son had black eyebrows and eyelashes," Morford said. "He [the soldier in the picture] had light hair, black eyebrows." But then, she said, she noticed that the legs and feet resembled her son's. "I would hate to say this is positively my son and have it be somebody else's," she said. Then, she began to cry, according to published accounts.

Campbell said he conscientiously tries to be sensitive to the individuals and families who might be especially affected by the publication of a story or a picture, but added, "I begin with the strong presumption that we're here to publish the news." Privacy or respect for the grieving might outweigh that obligation to publish, Campbell said, but publishing news "is what the newspaper is all about, to say what are the issues of the day that people need to be aware of."

If the paper knew the identity of a photo subject like the dead soldier, Campbell said, "we would probably contact the family before we published it and tell them that it was our intention to publish it." He also said he would allow the family to see the picture before it appeared in the paper.

The body in the photograph has still not been identified and may never be. The military knows it has to be one of five men who were killed that day in Somalia and whose bodies were temporarily held by the Somalis, but is making no effort to determine for sure which one it was. Several months after the incident, a Pentagon spokesman told reporters, "They were American soldiers. That in itself is jarring enough. You don't need an individual's name to express horror at the treatment of the bodies."

One thing is quite certain. This is not a case of ghoulish editors yielding to tawdry sensationalism to sell more papers. Thousands of readers called and wrote their local newspapers the next day, the vast majority of them to object to the picture's publication, and many canceled their subscriptions in protest. In this instance, the editors who chose to run the picture were printing not what they knew their readers wanted, but what they thought their readers needed to know.

Questions to Consider

1. If you had been the editor of the *Virginian-Pilot*, would you have published the Somalia photo? Why or why not? If you would have published it, in what part of the newspaper would you have published it and in what form?

2. If you had been a television news director, would you have run footage of the body being dragged through the streets of Mogadishu? Does this question raise different issues than the preceding question?

3. Does it actually make a gory picture less offensive to print it in black and white instead of color, to run it inside the paper instead of on the front page, or to run it much smaller than would be customary?

4. What if the picture had been of the body of a police officer being dragged through the streets of a distant U.S. city during a riot—how would that affect your decision about publication, or the use of news footage, if at all? What if the location had been your state capital? What if the location was your town or city? Should the location of an event be a factor in making decisions about taste and propriety? What if the body had been that of a child under each of the circumstances just described?

5. If you were setting policy for a news organization, what would be your policy on running information about fatalities and injuries before family members were notified? Would your policy apply only to family members? Which family members? Would your policy ever allow publication before notification?

6. What do you think of the decision-making process at the *Virginian-Pilot* (which was probably very similar to what took place in newsrooms across the country)? Should the decision have been confined to just the editors in the initial story conference? Did it do any good to get others in the newsroom involved or did it confuse the issue? In the end, Campbell made the decision. Do you think the decision was his to make, or should it have been made through consensus or by a majority vote? If through a vote, who should have voted?

35

Taking Journalism Hostage: Should We Print under Threats?

For seventeen years, a mysterious figure who came to be known as the Unabomber carried on a bizarre reign of terror with package and mail bombs. Beginning in May 1978 on the campus of Northwestern University in Evanston, Illinois, he delivered a series of sixteen bombs, most of them sent through the U.S. mail, to academics, business executives, and other people who were connected to one another, if at all, only by their involvement in science and technology. The FBI began to call the file on the killer the Unabom case because many of the early victims were connected with *uni*versities or *ai*rlines. Over the years, his bombs killed three people and wounded twenty-three more, some seriously. He was thought to have been seen only once, and that was uncertain. A mustachioed man wearing aviator-style sunglasses and a hooded sweatshirt was seen in a parking lot shortly before a bomb went off. Other than that, he was almost a total enigma. He became one of the nation's most sought-after fugitives in one of the Federal Bureau of Investigation's longest-running cases.

In the 1990s, his behavior took on signs of increasing agitation. Shortly after the terrorist attack in Oklahoma City on April 19, 1995, which killed 168 people, the Unabomber killed a timber executive in California. And he issued an airline threat, which he later retracted, as if he feared he was being forgotten.

In April 1995, at the time of the attack on the timber executive, he sent a letter to the *New York Times*, demanding that it, "or some other widely read, nationally distributed periodical," publish a long manifesto of his on modern life and its increasing reliance on technology. The letter specified distribution, royalty rights, and other details worthy of a literary contract and promised that if the manuscript was published "according to our requirements," the bomber would "permanently desist from terrorist activities" directed at people, but left open the possibility of attacks on property. The bomber said that if the manifesto was not published, he would "start building our next bomb."

For three months, editors at the *Times* deliberated the matter, discussing the case with the FBI and with top news executives. In September 1995, the *Times* and the *Washington Post* jointly published the Unabomber's 35,000-word document. It actually appeared only in the *Post* as a stand-alone, eight-page section. The *Times* explained to its readers that limitations on its own presses prevented them from printing it, but the two publications split the $40,000 cost.

As it turned out, publication provided the key clue leading to the subsequent arrest of a brilliant but eccentric hermit named Theodore J. Kaczynski. Kaczynski's brother, David, read the document and thought it chillingly similar to essays written by his brother. Working through an intermediary, he tipped off authorities, telling them of his suspicions. Federal authorities traced Kaczynski to a remote cabin in Montana and arrested him on April 3, 1996. In the cabin, the authorities said, they found bomb-making materials, how-to manuals for making explosives, and many other pieces of incriminating evidence, including an early draft of the manifesto and the manual typewriter that had produced the final copy sent to the *Times*.

As of this writing, Kaczynski has not been convicted of being the Unabomber, but authorities have said that they are positive they arrested the right man. So the newspapers seem to have been vindicated in their decision to publish—there were no more mail bombs and the publication did lead to an arrest.

Yet the matter is by no means clear cut. In hindsight, the decision to publish the manifesto seems to have been sound, but the case is disturbing in several respects. Although these events happened on a grand scale, several principles of the Unabomber case show up in less dramatic form at papers and stations many times a year when questions arise over how much help journalists should give to law-enforcement authorities and even whether they should allow criminals to reach wider audiences by printing or broadcasting what they have to say.

The most compelling arguments against publishing the manifesto really boil down to two, both of them involving the surrender of the cherished and critically important independence of news judgment. The first is whether the news organizations should be seen as yielding to a terrorist's demands. If the Unabomber could make the *Times* and the *Post* print once, he could, theoretically, make them print again. In fact, he said in his demand for publication that he wanted to make periodic updates. And who could say that he could be trusted? Might he not kill again anyway? More broadly, even if the Unabomber proved to be a man of his word and stopped attacking people, when the papers responded to his ultimatum by publishing his screed, they might have been inviting copycat criminals to kill or maim, then issue their own ultimatums. Even if the nation's leading newspapers were willing to be held hostage to an unlimited number of terrorists, some demands would eventually be literally and physically impossible to meet, with potentially disastrous results. In an effort to preserve life, did the papers not, in truth, put many more lives in jeopardy?

The second reason, or set of reasons, cited against publishing deals not with being too accommodating to the bad guys, but being with too accommodating to the good guys, to the federal authorities who advised the newspapers and recommended the manifesto's publication. Jane Kirtley of the Reporters Committee for Freedom of the Press wrote (before, to be fair, Kaczynski was arrested): "News organizations are not, and should never be, perceived to be arms of the government. It has long been an article of faith that journalists will resist efforts by law enforcement to turn them into unpaid investigators by fighting government attempts to subpoena notes, outtakes, or reporters' testimony about criminal activity. While this is often an unpopular position with the public, it is the only position that an independent press can take. The First Amendment will permit no other choice."[1] She cites the publication of the Pentagon Papers by both newspapers as prime examples of news organizations expressly defying governmental judgment about what is good and what is bad for the public to know.

These are strong arguments and may not be dismissed lightly. Arthur O. Sulzberger Jr., the publisher of the *Times*, recognized the difficulty inherent in trusting someone like the Unabomber. On the other hand, he explained on the pages of his newspaper, "you print and he doesn't kill anybody else, that's a pretty good deal. You print it and he continues to kill people, what have you lost? The cost of newsprint?" For Sulzberger, it was an easy equation to solve. The editors discounted the copycat problem, essentially saying that the Unabomber was hardly a crank who had appeared out of nowhere. In fact, since the Unabomber had used a code in communications with the *Times* about earlier attacks, the paper could be fairly sure that the manifesto was really coming from the bomber. The suggestion was that if another killer showed up who had eluded police for seventeen years, maybe the papers would listen to that one, too. Sulzberger noted that the *Times* received threats accompanied by demands to publish some things, or not to publish others, all the time, and responded only by turning the threats and demands over to the authorities.

The second objection also warrants consideration. Yes, journalists cherish their independence—and certainly both the *Post* and the *Times* proved their commitment to independence when both papers defied the government's secrecy rules in printing the Pentagon Papers in the 1970s. But to always refuse to do what the government asks is no more independent than to always accede to the government's wishes. Independence comes from deciding a case on its merits. Both papers determined in the Pentagon Papers case that the government was wrong. In the Unabomber case, they decided it was right.

There is another, even larger, question at work in this case, and that is the question of how much responsibility journalists take or should take for what happens as a result of their stories. The moral arguments made in this book are not fully of the old-school motto, "Publish and be damned! The people have a right to know." Rather, they agree with Cato that there are some truths not worth knowing. Good journalism is hardly a mouthpiece for the government, yet most thoughtful journalists believe that, ultimately, they and their craft stand for something. They tend to believe that reasonable and well-informed people are capable of governing their own lives, that truth is better than falsehood, that compassion is better than

---

[1] Jane Kirtley, "Commentary #1, The End of an Era of Independence," *Journal of Mass Media Ethics*, 10:4 (1995), p. 250.

indifference, and that there are such things as justice and fairness. And they believe that people getting blown up as a result of an editorial decision is not as good an outcome as people not getting blown up. That is not to argue that journalists are morally entitled to slant their stories or to withhold information that may lead to a bad end for some group or another. But the reason they are not so entitled is not because they are indifferent to that bad end. It is because they believe that the integrity of the news product is, in the long run, more important. That is not the same as indifference to outcome.

Questions to Consider

1. Considering the arguments for and against, would you have decided to publish the Unabomber's manifesto? Why or why not?

2. How much of a responsibility do journalists have to keep people from being injured or killed? If a journalist is covering a newsworthy event and sees a chance to help out (e.g., someone setting himself on fire to make a political protest), when should the journalist stop behaving as a journalist and start behaving as a person who wants to prevent harm?

3. Do journalists have a responsibility to help law-enforcement authorities? If journalists made all the information they gathered about criminal activity available to the authorities, how would that affect how they did their jobs as journalists? If journalists refused to cooperate at all with the authorities, what effect would that have?

4. Is it journalists' responsibility to worry about copycat crimes? In this case, copy criminals might kill or injure people just to get something published or broadcast—would that, if it occurred, be the fault of the *Times* and *Post*? Many people are concerned that the coverage of terrorism and suicides can lead to copycat crimes. How should a journalist deal with that issue?

5. Should journalists be in communication with criminals who are still at large? If they are, should they turn over all communications to the authorities?

36

Can We Fix the Problems?
Should We Try?

In this book and in its companion anthology, we have looked at the philosophical and historical underpinnings of journalism ethics and have examined many of the issues journalists spend a lot of time wrestling with. As you have seen, decisive answers to ethical questions in journalism are frequently hard to find; often, the best a journalist can do is to take the path that seems closest to the right thing to do while looking for even better answers down the road.

Why do journalists fret about these issues? Because they are trying to fulfill their responsibilities in a representative democracy, trying to give the sovereign people the information they need to govern themselves in a way that is as fair and impartial as possible,and, even beyond that, because they want to do their part in making the world a better place—not to fix all the problems, certainly, but to warn of the dangers, to "report the drifting castaway whom the ship can save," in the words of Joseph Pulitzer, words that open this book. If journalists dig up and present the crucial information, will their readers, listeners, and viewers fulfill their responsibilities and take the necessary steps to right wrongs and make society function as well as it can? If they do not, does that rob journalism of its meaning?

These are questions that Robert E. Sullivan, news manager for the Americas at Worldwide Television News, a television news service, has thought about in his more than thirty years in the field. He spent many of those years as a foreign correspondent, covering the war and in Vietnam and unrest in South America. In the following, which concludes this book, Sullivan, focusing primarily on coverage of foreign affairs, presents the answers that work for him, and may work for you.

CAN JOURNALISM SOLVE THE PROBLEMS?[*]

The short question for journalists is: "If we show it (write it, tell it), will it get fixed?" And the short answer is: no.

---

[*] Written for this volume by Robert E. Sullivan

If every evil or shortcoming that we know of could be fixed by making people aware of it—through the media—then there wouldn't be much evil left on earth. That's because the evil we know of, at least for most of the writers and readers of books like this one, is evil we have read about, seen on TV, or heard on radio.

It can be hard to direct people's attention to wrongs around the world, even if there is powerful television footage. I'd venture that it is fairly well known that even the most dramatic reportage will have an uphill battle getting an audience if a country's (or town's or city's, etc.) direct interests are not involved. It may be hard to point to action taken to right wrongs that is a direct consequence of media coverage alone.

In cases where the United States has taken action to right a wrong after media coverage, the action can usually be linked to a direct American interest, not just to the coverage. The United States jumped in to help Kuwait in the Persian Gulf War in 1991, but—besides reporting about babies being snatched from incubators (allegedly) by Iraqis—Kuwait had oil. Television didn't stop the Vietnam War, not without a movement of scores of thousands of different types of people to convince even more people that the war was not in America's interests. The reporters brought that inclination with them from America, not the other way around. Americans witnessed the slaughter in Rwanda, but despite horrific, graphic pictures of bodies, the United States didn't move any troops until it became a refugee problem, that is, a problem to be solved with money but not American blood. Americans witnessed the situation in Bosnia: Remember years of pictures of little children's severed feet scattered across playgrounds and ski slopes? Funerals for people killed in indiscriminate mortar attacks, then funerals for the funeral-goers, themselves blown up by more indiscriminate mortar attacks? Remember the ribs on the men in the concentration camps? Remember the weekly civilian massacres? America did nothing until it was perceived that doing nothing would weaken NATO and the country's strategic position.

But that's the short, if realistic, answer. And it is wrong.

Because if it is right, why are good men and women in journalism in the first place? It would be a peculiar kind of man-made hell if reporters spent their entire lives writing, reporting, or showing things that did not accomplish anything and never will. That would make them all followers of Sisyphus. Perhaps they should all get out and leave the field to people who are genuinely concerned about which celebrity is bedding which other celebrity. That kind of reporting sells more ads, anyway.

Clearly the situation in Bosnia would have been entirely different if absolutely no one other than the combatants themselves knew anything at all about it. (There are, in fact, anywhere between two and five civil wars going on at any given time in Burma and very few people know much about them, and very few people are doing very much about them.)

And, obviously, muckraking and investigative reporting have, for centuries, exposed evils that were then at least addressed, if not corrected. Jacob Riis writing about the slums in New York comes to mind, as does Lincoln Steffens's work on government corruption and Edward R. Murrow's "Harvest of Shame" television documentary about migrant workers. In each example, government hearings were called and legislation was passed.

So if the answer is not "no" and clearly not "yes," what is the answer? The answer is: the question is wrong. The question should be: "How can we do our jobs in such a way that our reports will have impact?"

After thirty years in the business, I have come to notice a few attributes of really effective reporters. They:

- Know their subject.
- Know their medium.
- Care.

Knowing the subject is essential. At Worldwide Television News, we have a policy on hiring sports staffers. They don't have to have a minute's experience in television, but they do have to have a passion for sports. We'll teach them the medium. Nothing is easier to spot on a sports page than a newswriter who was called in to replace a sick sportswriter. A crusading journalist who wants to write a series about the downtrodden Kurds, for instance, had better know enough to get it right, especially if his medium has outlets in Turkey. Someone who wants to document anti-Catholic discrimination in Northern Ireland had better know enough to prove it. There is another side to most issues, even those that most of your friends agree are beyond arguing. Remember all the statistics about how much it costs the government to care for all the nasty people who smoke those nasty cigarettes—our tax dollars keeping them in the cancer wards? A recent report in the *New York Times* showed precisely the opposite. It appears, the *Times* said, that smokers save society money overall because most of them don't make it to the cancer wards. They die. Get it right.

To be effective, you must know your medium. Styles of communications change, but before they do, they're usually very strict. From the iambic verse of Greek tragedy through the careful meters of each age of poetry, and until and including the free verse of the modern ages, writers had to master the skills of their times. Take a ruler to a really good thriller. You can measure the sentences getting shorter as the action heats up. That's no accident. People study how to do that. I have silently tapped my feet to the rhythm of the voice of an Irish storyteller. It is like music, and it keeps its beat, its meter, even if the storyteller changes the story. Shakespeare didn't dash out any line, no matter how brilliant the thought, in any old manner; a method had to be used, a technique or technology appropriate for the time. Herman Melville and James Fenimore Cooper's paragraphs and sentence structure are, for many, difficult to follow now. But they weren't when they were written. That's because the authors knew very well indeed the appropriate technique of the time, or they created new styles for which the audience was ripe. And they studied their crafts' techniques.

Now, as then, reporters have to know what works. If they came back from the dead, Jacob Riis and Upton Sinclair would have to learn (not necessarily mimic, but know) just exactly how *USA Today* writes a story, and they'd not fail to note the new Macparagraphs that open the book in *Newsweek* and even the *Christian*

Science Monitor. They would have to learn what to use and what doesn't make sense for their stories. But first, they'd have to get to know the audience and what it can handle.

In television, it appears, as of this writing, that MTV-style television is taking the lead. The style consists of what seems incredible to older eyes: changing shots by flipping from one to the other and back, plus a deliberately rocky, shaky camera, coming in from deliberately strange angles. Teenagers with remotes can decide in a single instant what they are *not* going to watch; often, they make that decision because of the video style (which may indicate the content, but the result is the same). I have already seen MTV-style reporting from Bosnia on a major network. ABC's Roone Arledge was credited with drawing huge new audiences into the sports events he produced, including the Olympics. He did it because he knew, and creatively changed, the potential of television. They moved him to news, and his impact is being felt.

Producers and reporters must either be aware of, or take the lead in, the trends of the technology in their fields. Trends aren't trends until someone follows them—usually the young, the audience of the future.

But it is just as important to care about what you're doing. The best reporters I know care about their subjects, and it is reflected in their reports. I am not a fan of advocacy journalism because it is limiting and sometimes blinding. I prefer the old-fashioned attempt to at least try for the elusive impartiality. But that doesn't mean you don't care. If you care deeply about an issue, it will show in your effort, and if you attempt to be impartial, it will be a better report. I also agree with Murray Kempton, who recently passed on one of his guiding principles: look for the victim. In most major pieces of news, even "good" news, there will be a victim. (Why is GNP growth always good? Why did the nation do "better" one year than another? Do we say growth is good because this country needs more factories in the countryside, or, in the long run, a lot more people?)

I particularly liked a television report from southern Lebanon recently. I found out later that the producer actually lives in southern Lebanon, as opposed to most of his colleagues, who live in the much more comfortable environment of Israel. The producer knew and cared about the people he was covering, and it showed in the story. A colleague of mine somehow became interested in the problems of the Papuans, residents of a country he had never visited. He came to believe that they were being unfairly treated in the United Nations. He started doing research, and the more he studied, the more concerned he became. He would write a series on Papua that not only was good journalism, but also was able to convince the totally uninterested (including me) to read it.

I once dashed off four quick paragraphs on an unimportant event that somehow got under my skin—a reunion of German and British pilots to toast each other's bravery. My editor said those four paragraphs were the best paragraphs I had ever written. "You must have been really pissed off," he said. I was.

Even if you follow the above Robert's Rules, the world doesn't fall at your feet. Two decades after Murrow, NBC did a follow-up of "Harvest of Shame." The reporter stood in the same field where Murrow had filmed his closing and reported that things hadn't become much better. A decade later, yet another network did yet another report on migrant workers and didn't find much improvement. The answer might be that the American public wants cheap orange juice and orange soda.

Slums may be better, but now there are the homeless. Sinclair, I dare say, could find a tad of corruption in modern government. The best reporting may never change strongly held opinions. Warren Zemmermann, formerly the U.S. ambassador to Yugoslavia, recently told the *American Journalism Review*, "It wouldn't have mattered if television was going 24 hours around the clock with Serb atrocities. [President George] Bush wasn't going to get in." On the other hand, apartheid is gone in South Africa, the Vietnam War *is* over (and they are capitalists), and women are getting a fairer shake. Tammany Hall is dead. In most cities, one can deal with honest bureaucrats. And, although sweatshops are now in most cities, the beneficiaries of their cheap labor—outed once again by the media—are at least embarrassed and have expressed some interest in doing something about it.

Bibliography

American Society of Newspaper Editors. *Thinking Big about Small Newspapers*. Reston, Va: Small Newspaper Committee of the American Society of Newspaper Editors, 1993.

Bacon, Francis. *Novum Organum* [microform], edited by Joseph Devey. New York: P. F. Collier, 1901.

Bagdikian, Ben H. "Lords of the Global Village." *Nation,* June 12, 1989.

Beittel, K. *Zen and the Art of Pottery*. New York: Weatherhill, 1992.

Bennett, James Gordon. "To the public—enlargement of the *Herald*." *New York Herald*, January 1, 1836.

Bok, Sissela. *Lying: Moral Choice in Public and Private Life*. New York: Pantheon, 1978.

Boorstin, Daniel J. *The Image: A Guide to Pseudo-Events in America.* New York: Atheneum, 1961.

Breed, Warren. "Social Control in the Newsroom." *Social Forces* 33, no. 4 (1955).

Charity, Arthur. *Doing Public Journalism*. New York: Guilford, 1995.

Commission on Freedom of the Press. *A Free and Responsible Press*. Chicago: University of Chicago Press, 1947.

Facts about Newspapers. Reston, Va.: Newspaper Association of America, 1994.

Frankena, William K. *Ethics*. 2d ed. Englewood Cliffs, N.J.: Prentice Hall, 1972.

Greeley, Horace. "A great journalist dead." *New York Tribune*, June 3, 1872.

Hobbes, Thomas. *The Leviathan*. London: G. Routledge, 1907.

Klaidman, Stephen, and Tom L. Beauchamp. *The Virtuous Journalist.* New York: Oxford University Press, 1987.

Lauterer, Jock. *Community Journalism: The Personal Approach.* Ames, Iowa: Iowa State University Press, 1995.

Lewis, Anthony. *Make No Law: The Sullivan Case and the First Amendment*. New York: Random House, 1991.

Liebling, A. J. *The Press*. New York: Ballentine, 1961.

Lippmann, Walter. *Public Opinion*. New York: Macmillan, 1922.

Locke, John. *On Civil Government: The Second Treatise*. 1691.

Marx, Karl. *Capital: A Critique of Political Economy*. Vol. 1. Translated by Ben Fowkes. New York: Vintage Books, 1981.

Merrill, John C. *The Imperative of Freedom*. New York: Hastings House, 1974.

Mill, John Stuart. *Utilitarianism*. New ed. with selections from Auguste Comte and positivism. Edited by H. B. Acton. London: Dent, 1972.

Milton, John. *Aeropagitica: A Speech of Mr. John Milton for the Liberty of Unlicensed Printing to the Parliament of England*. Edited by Isabel Rivers. Cambridge, Eng.: Deighton, Bell, 1973.

Niebuhr, H. Richard. *The Responsible Self.* New York: HarperCollins, 1963.

Pingree, Suzanne, and Robert Hawkins. "News Definitions and Their Effects on Women." In *Women and the News*, edited by Laurily Keir Epstein. New York: Hastings House, 1978.

Plato. *The Republic.* Translated by Robin Waterfield. Oxford: Oxford University Press, 1993.

Pulitzer, Joseph. "The great issue." *St. Louis Post and Dispatch*, January 10, 1879.

Rosen, Jay. *Getting the Connections Right: Public Journalism and What It Means to the Press*. New York: Twentieth Century Fund, 1995.

Sinclair, Upton. *The Brass Check*. Pasadena, Cal.: The author, 1920.

Smith, Adam. *An Inquiry into the Nature and Causes of the Wealth of Nations*. 6th ed. Edited by Edwin Cannan. London: Methuen, 1961.

Stepp, Carl Sessions. "Public Journalism: Balancing the Scales." *American Journalism Review,* May 1996.

Stiff, C. *Untitled*. Abstract accepted for presentation to the Huck Boyd National Center for Community Media and National Newspaper Association Symposium on Community Journalism, Nashville, Tenn., March 20, 1996.

Thames, R. "Public Journalism: Some Questions and Answers." Handout accompanying session on public journalism at the ASNE annual convention, Washington, D.C., April 16, 1996.

Thomson, John. *An Enquiry, Concerning the Liberty, and Licentiousness of the Press and the Uncontroulable Nature of the Human Mind*. New York: Johnson and Stryker, 1801.

Trenchard, John, and Thomas Gordon. *The Third Collection of Political Letters in the* London Journal. N.p., 1720.

Warren, Samuel, and Louis Brandeis. "The right to privacy." *Harvard Law Review* 4, no.5 (1890).

Wilson, James Q. *The Moral Sense*. New York: Free Press, 1993.

Winship, Thomas. "Jim Batten and Civic Journalism." *Editor & Publisher*, April 1995.

Wortman, Tunis. *A Treatise Concerning Political Enquiry and the Liberty of the Press*. New York: n.p., 1801.

Index

About the Author

STEVEN R. KNOWLTON is Associate Professor of Journalism at Hofstra University. He has been a reporter, editor, photographer, and newspaper owner for more than 30 years. He is coeditor of *The Journalist's Moral Compass: Basic Principles* (Praeger, 1994).